D0078293

THE WRATH OF ATHENA

PUBLISHED FOR THE CENTER FOR
HELLENIC STUDIES

Jenny Strauss Clay

THE WRATH OF
ATHENA

Gods and Men in
the *Odyssey*

PRINCETON UNIVERSITY PRESS
PRINCETON, NEW JERSEY

Copyright © 1983 by Princeton University Press

Published by Princeton University Press, 41 William Street, Princeton,
New Jersey 08540

In the United Kingdom: Princeton University Press, Guildford, Surrey

Library of Congress Cataloging in Publication Data will be found on the last
printed page of this book

ISBN 0-691-06574-8

Publication of this book has been aided by the Whitney Darrow
Publication Reserve Fund of Princeton University Press

This book has been composed in Linotron Sabon

Clothbound editions of Princeton University Press books are printed on acid-
free paper, and binding materials are chosen for strength and durability.

Printed in the United States of America by Princeton University Press,
Princeton, New Jersey

IN MEMORY
OF MY FATHER
LEO STRAUSS

CONTENTS

ACKNOWLEDGMENTS

To undertake a book on the *Odyssey* demands not only a kind of mad courage, but also the sane encouragement of friends. In these I have been thrice and four times blest. A few words here cannot suffice to convey my abiding gratitude.

Thanks are due first to Bernard Knox and the Center for Hellenic Studies for providing a shining haven during 1978-1979, when this study first took shape. That year, in an atmosphere of serenity with none but self-imposed pressures, was all an aspiring scholar could hope to experience. On many occasions thereafter, the Director and the Staff of the Center graciously permitted me to make use of the library to complete my research. Professor Michael Putnam of Brown University and Senior Fellow of the Center provided crucial help at a crucial moment. The Committee on Small Grants of the University of Virginia aided the completion of this project.

Diskin Clay witnessed the first beginnings of this work many years ago and patiently urged me to continue and to test my fledgling wings. He has my heartfelt thanks. I also had the great good fortune to read the *Odyssey* with Joseph A. Russo, over frothy cups of cappuccino. Gregory Nagy, with his boundless enthusiasm for all things Homeric, read bits and pieces of the manuscript at various times—and must have wondered what I was up to.

Joanna Hitchcock, Executive Editor, and Marilyn Campbell of Princeton University Press deserve thanks for tactfully shepherding the manuscript to publication. The Introduction's epigraph from " Ὁ Στράτις Θαλασσινὸς ἀνάμεσα στοὺς Ἀγαπάνθους" is published with the kind permission of Mrs. Maro Seferiades.

I owe the greatest debt of gratitude to Werner J. Dannhauser. His flair for sense and style saved me from countless infelicities and obscurities. (Those that remain are due to my pigheadedness.) But, more than that, his probing questions forced me to come to a deeper and clearer understanding of what I was about, and his steadfast support gave me the courage to elaborate what I had learned.

My students allowed me to try out and sharpen my ideas. Through their insights and questions, they frequently obliged me to rethink and revise my thoughts. Moreover, they proved to me that scholarship, learning, and teaching are inseparable.

My daughter Andreia deserves a good word. True to her name, she courageously and good-humoredly put up with her mother's frequent grouchiness and obsessive distraction during the writing of this book. My mother taught me the first things, without which foundation nothing of value can be built.

Finally, this book is dedicated to the memory of my father. He would not have wanted me to say much here; and others can write of him more eloquently and wisely. Although I was never his student, he taught me by his example what a life of study can be, and he set my feet on the path of the Journey.

ABBREVIATIONS

AJP	*American Journal of Philology*
Ameis-Hentze	K. F. Ameis and C. Hentze, eds., *Homers Odyssee*, revised by P. Cauer, 2 vols. in 4 (Leipzig, 1908-1920)
Chantraine	P. Chantraine, *Dictionnaire étymologique de la langue grecque* (Paris, 1968-1977)
CJ	*Classical Journal*
CP	*Classical Philology*
CQ	*Classical Quarterly*
DK	H. Diehls and W. Kranz, *Die Fragmente der Vorsokratiker*, 7th ed. (Berlin, 1954)
Eustathius	*Eustathii Commentarii ad Homeri Iliadem et Odysseam pertinentes ad fidem exempli Romani editi* (Leipzig, 1825-1829) M. H. van der Valk, ed., *Eustathii Archiepiscopi Thessalonicensis Commentarii ad Homeri Iliadem pertinentes ad fidem codicis Laurentiani editi* (Leiden, 1971-)
Fr. Gr. H.	F. Jacoby, *Die Fragmente der griechischen Historiker* (Berlin and Leiden, 1923-1958)
Frisk	H. Frisk, *Griechisches etymologisches Wörterbuch* (Heidelberg, 1960-1972)
GRBS	*Greek, Roman and Byzantine Studies*
HSCP	*Harvard Studies in Classical Philology*
JHS	*Journal of Hellenic Studies*
L.-P.	E. Lobel and D. Page, eds., *Poetarum Lesbiorum Fragmenta* (Oxford, 1955)
LSJ	H. G. Liddell, R. Scott, and H. S. Jones, *A Greek-English Lexicon* (Oxford, 1968)

MH	*Museum Helveticum*
RE	G. Wissowa et al., eds., *Paulys Realencyclopädie der classischen Altertumswissenschaft* (Stuttgart, 1894-)
REG	*Revue des Études Grecques*
RM	*Rheinisches Museum*
Roscher	W. H. Roscher, *Ausführliches Lexikon der griechischen und römischen Mythologie* (Leipzig, 1884-1937)
Scholia (*Iliad*)	H. Erbse, ed., *Scholia graeca in Homeri Iliadem*, 5 vols. (Berlin, 1969-1977)
Scholia (*Odyssey*)	W. Dindorf, ed., *Scholia graeca in Homeri Odysseam*, 2 vols. (Oxford, 1855)
SMEA	*Studi micenei ed egeo-anatolici*
TAPA	*Transactions and Proceedings of the American Philological Association*
WS	*Wiener Studien*

THE WRATH OF ATHENA

INTRODUCTION

Τὸ πρῶτο πράγμα ποὺ ἔκανε ὁ θεὸς εἶναι ἡ ἀγάπη
ἔπειτα ἔρχεται τὸ αἷμα
κι' ἡ δίψα γιὰ τὸ αἷμα
ποὺ τὴν κεντρίζει
τὸ σπέρμα τοῦ κορμιοῦ καθὼς τ' ἁλάτι.
Τὸ πρῶτο πράγμα ποὺ ἔκανε ὁ θεὸς εἶναι τὸ μα-
κρινὸ ταξίδι. . . .

—George Seferis

For those who study the *Odyssey* over a long period, this poem becomes their book. We each live it in our own fashion; to study the poem of Return means to make our own return. Those who are bold enough to write on the *Odyssey* experience in turn the terrors and temptations of a marvelous journey. To escape them, one must remain constantly alert and cling to the one sure point of departure and final goal: the text of the *Odyssey* itself with all its charm, toughness, and wisdom.

One of the obstacles to this undertaking has been an excessive preoccupation with questions regarding the genesis and composition of the Homeric epics. To be sure, the Homeric Question is coeval with modern classical philology. Readers may well be disappointed to discover that I have not begun by staking out a position on this venerable question, and they may attribute my reticence to cowardice or lack of polemical zest. The truth, however, is that I consider the problem of composition secondary to the problem of interpretation, although I am not so naive as to ignore the fact that the latter has implications for the former. My prejudices concerning the Homeric Question will become apparent soon enough.

Still, perhaps a few words are in order here. The history of the Homeric Question could well be written by focusing on the way scholars have dealt with contradictions within the

Homeric texts. During the 19th and into the 20th century, the so-called Analysts held the field. Given their assumption that no one man could have composed the Homeric epics, they resolved all problems of internal inconsistencies by resorting to theories of multiple authorship. An older poem or poems was expanded or reworked by a subsequent poet or poets whose intentions, talents, and outlook differed substantially from the original composition. Under such circumstances, consistency or even comprehensibility could not be expected. The tracking of the *Ur-Homer, Redaktor, Bearbeiter,* and a host of other unlikely characters became the philologists' national pastime. Unfortunately, no two scholars could agree on the distribution of these roles. But to be fair, the Analysts, through the care and sustained attention they brought to the examination of the Homeric poems, were the first to pinpoint genuine difficulties. Their solutions, however, were crude; wherever the Analyst found a knot, he was more likely to cut it out than to unravel it patiently.

The views of the Analysts were countered by the Unitarians, who rightly insisted on the integrity of the poems. Yet their arguments were largely negative: if one removes the presumed later additions, the remainder becomes even more incoherent and incomprehensible and finally collapses into total chaos. Unity of authorship must therefore be postulated. Those discrepancies which could not be ignored or glossed over had to be due not to several poets but to the varied sources upon which one author drew. Let me cite one such Unitarian:

> The new conceptions are brought into prominence wherever practical. . . . But the stories retain their traditional motivation—without a thought for the contradiction. While one can distinguish the traditional from the new, one cannot separate the new conceptions. For they are not later additions to an older poem, but rather they demonstrate a new manner of telling an old story.[1]

---

[1] K. Rüter, *Odysseeinterpretationen* ed. K. Matthiessen, Hypomnemata 19 (Göttingen, 1969), p. 82.

The Unitarian position has been strengthened by the Oral Hypothesis, for it presupposes a long oral tradition behind the Homeric poems during which varied traditions were incorporated into the monumental epics. The problem of internal contradictions, however, abides. To the Neo-unitarians now correspond the Neo-analysts, who attempt to identify and separate into strata the various traditions and sources of the Homeric poems: *Sage*, folktales, hymn poetry, etc. Appeal to the "tradition" now replaces multiple authorship. A recent example:

> There is, in fact, good reason to believe that one poet could incorporate discordant ideas into a single poem. He was, after all, working within a tradition which preserved masses of older material. . . . These different views doubtless came into being at different times; in this respect the analysts have always been right. But these different times were probably anterior to the Homeric poems.[2]

So we have really not made much progress in solving problems of internal inconsequences and incongruities. All these views have a common foundation: discrepancies in the Homeric epics arise from the historical evolution of the poems. Internal contradictions can be explained by the incorporation of diverse materials at diverse periods without an attempt to bring about a synthesis.

None of this would be very serious if the contradictions were minor ones which we could easily overlook. But in the case of the *Odyssey*, they are not minor: the character of the hero is full of ambiguities and inconsistencies, and the poem seems to lack coherence in its moral and religious outlook. Some, of course, argue that such consistency cannot and should not be expected, given the circumstances of the poem's composition. The poet is capable of constructing only one scene at a time with a view to its immediate effect on his audience. He does not worry about its suitability to the adjoining epi-

---

[2] B. Fenik, *Studies in the Odyssey*, Hermes Einzel. 30 (Wiesbaden, 1974), pp. 218-219, 221.

sodes nor about its relevance to the whole. If his hearers are momentarily moved or delighted, that is enough for him.

We have, then, come to an impasse, one well described by Adam Parry:

> Freed from the shadow of Multiple Authorship, the critic now finds his way darkened by the all-embracing Tradition and by the alleged rules of oral style. If he now tries to present an interpretation of the *Iliad* or the *Odyssey* involving the relation between one passage and another, he will have to fear the objection that the oral poet plans no such coherent structures, and that the occurrence of the passages in question is due to the fortuitous operation of the Tradition.[3]

And, yet, interpretation of necessity means to make connections and to detect interrelations. "Only connect" applies to the critic as well as to the poet. I have taken as my guiding principle the venerable axiom: one must interpret Homer from Homer—Ὅμηρον ἐξ Ὁμήρου σαφηνίζειν.

We must set forth again and make our way back to the poem, remaining open to the possibility that its ambiguities and apparent inconsistencies may be meaningful. But this can only be accomplished if we refuse to gloss over them or fail to take them seriously. The *Odyssey*, like its hero, is multifaceted, diverse, and varied; but multiplicity need not mean incoherence. Our experience of the world is similarly contradictory, but that does not imply that it has no meaning. We are continually aware that the way things ought to be is often not the way things are. Life, in fact, is polymorphic, Protean; yet we still try to tie it down to yield its truth. And the *Odyssey* has been called "a fair mirror of human life."[4]

The present study does not pretend to be exhaustive, but it does embody an argument or, at least, the red thread of a coherent theme. It begins, naturally enough, from an exami-

---

[3] A. Parry's Introduction to Milman Parry's *The Making of Homeric Verse* (Oxford, 1971), p. liv.

[4] καλὸν ἀνθρωπίνου βίου κάτοπτρον, Alcidamas, cited by Aristotle, *Rhetoric* III. 3. 3, 1406b.

nation of the proem, which raises questions concerning the poet's relation to the Muses, the ambiguous character of his hero, and the choice of Homer's point of departure. These questions, in turn, have a common denominator: the relationship between the divine and the human in the *Odyssey*. Subsequent chapters attempt to deal with those relationships from various perspectives.

The *Odyssey* celebrates the virtues of intelligence, versatility, and patience. The task of interpretation demands the same qualities, and it is these we must bring to the study of the poem. Others must judge the extent to which I have succeeded. But it hardly matters much; I have learned many things on the way.

The text of the Homeric poems used throughout is the Oxford edition of T. W. Allen. Books of the *Iliad* are referred to in Roman numerals; those of the *Odyssey*, by Arabic numbers. All translations, unless otherwise indicated, are my own. Work on this manuscript was completed in August of 1981. I have been unable to integrate research published subsequently.

CHAPTER I

THE BEGINNING OF
THE *ODYSSEY*

τὸ μὲν οὖν ἀναγκαιότατον ἔργον τοῦ προοιμίου καὶ
ἴδιον τοῦτο, δηλῶσαι τί ἐστι τὸ τέλος οὗ ἕνεκα ὁ
λόγος.
(Aristotle, *Rhetoric* 3. 1415a22)

Mousa

The *Odyssey* begins with Homer's calling on the Muse, asking
her to tell the story of Odysseus' return after the destruction
of Troy. For us, this invocation may seem a mere old-fashioned convention, slightly irritating, something we rather wish
were not there at all. But a proper understanding of the Muse
forms the foundation both of Homeric poetics and theology.
Moreover, we must keep in mind that the poet attributes all
of his poem except the prologue (lines 1-10) to the Muse. Any
serious study of Homer thus does well to begin with a consideration of the nature of the Muse and the problem of invocation.

Formally, an invocation is a subspecies of prayer, which
can be defined as a respectful verbal communication between
men and gods. Like the priest, the poet calls on the Muse not
simply for himself, but on behalf of a larger community, his
listeners. But unlike most other Greek prayers, neither sacrifice
nor the promise of future gifts accompanies the poetic invocation, nor does it contain a reminder of past benefits, either
given or received—all of which constitute standard elements
of ordinary prayer.[1] These omissions suggest more than an
unusual degree of intimacy between the poet and his Muse.

[1] Consider, for example, the prayers of Odysseus and Diomedes at *Il.* X.
278-294. Cf. W. Burkert, *Griechische Religion* (Stuttgart, 1977), p. 128;
K. von Fritz, "Greek Prayer," *Review of Religion* 10 (1945-46): 18-23; and
s. v. "Gebet," *Reallexikon für Antike und Christentum* (1972), 8:1139-1141.

The prayer of invocation involves nothing extraneous to itself. Without reference to past or future favors, invocation becomes, in a sense, pure prayer in which the medium of words is sufficient unto itself. The purity of prayer is echoed in the purity of the response. For the Muse is asked—and consents—to sing or tell a story rather than to grant success or prosperity of either a specific or general character. The poem the Muses inspire fully demonstrates their power and graciousness. The invocation and the response of the Muse, the song that follows, complete the act of communication between man and god, an act that exists purely and exclusively within the sphere of language.[2]

The poet mediates between Olympus and his audience. In calling on the Muse and transmitting her song, the poet presents himself as a mere instrument, a vehicle of the goddess, submerging his own voice to the song of the Muse. Yet such self-effacement is merely apparent; it contains no tinge of modesty, but rather masks the highest of claims. The Muses' mouthpiece cannot be challenged precisely because both invocation and song remain completely enclosed within the sphere of words. The efficacy of his invocation vouches for the authenticity of his song. Without his lyre, the poet is totally helpless; with it, he is loved by the gods and honored by men.

With the perfect reticence praised by Aristotle,[3] Homer never speaks about the Muses in his own name, unlike Hesiod, who

---

[2] The unchallengeable autonomy of the song of the Muses is conveyed by their cryptic statement to Hesiod (*Theog.* 27-28) that they can tell lies similar to true things as well as speak the truth when they wish. Cf. the discussion of P. Pucci, *Hesiod and the Language of Poetry* (Baltimore, 1977), pp. 1-44. I cannot, however agree with Pucci, p. 1, that "Hesiod . . . is convinced that such a dangerous *logos* is administered by the Muses to other poets, not to himself." For studies of poetry and the Muses in the Epic, see W. Marg, *Homer über die Dichtung*, Orbis Antiquus 11 (Münster, 1957); W. F. Otto, *Die Musen* (Darmstadt, 1961); H. Maehler, *Die Auffassung des Dichterberufs im frühen Griechentum*, Hypomnemata 5 (Göttingen, 1963), pp. 9-34; E. Barmeyer, *Die Musen* (Munich, 1968); J.-P. Vernant, *Mythe et pensée chez les Grecs* (Paris, 1965), pp. 51-94; and M. Detienne, *Les maîtres de vérité dans la Grèce archaïque* (Paris, 1967), pp. 9-27.

[3] *Poetics* 24. 1460a5-7.

in the *Theogony* describes his encounter with them on Helicon. But the *Odyssey* does include the famous description of Demodocus, blind poet of the Phaeacians, which offers a dramatic presentation of their role. The poet sings at the feasts of men, just as the Muses and Apollo entertain the Olympians at their feasts (*Il*. I. 603-604). Phemius, the bard in Odysseus' palace, claims that he sings for both gods and men (*Od*. 22. 346). In complimenting Demodocus, Odysseus praises the combination of feast and song (9. 3-11).[4] Demodocus is first introduced as follows:

τὸν πέρι Μοῦσ᾽ ἐφίλησε, δίδου δ᾽ ἀγαθόν τε κακόν τε·
ὀφθαλμῶν μὲν ἄμερσε, δίδου δ᾽ ἡδεῖαν ἀοιδήν,

Him the Muse loved exceedingly, but she gave him
    good and evil;
for she deprived him of his eyes, but granted him
    sweet song.

(8. 63-64)

Demodocus receives the gift of singing from the Muse, but the *kakon*, the blindness of the poet, is a concomitant of that gift. The portrait of Demodocus is surely the source of the very ancient tradition of Homer's own blindness.[5] We will never be able to ascertain whether the composer of the *Odyssey* was in fact blind or not. But the conception of the blind bard conforms closely to the wider Greek tradition of the blindness of visionaries. The poet's blindness finds a parallel in the blindness of the most famous seer of Greek myth, Teiresias.[6] The singer's knowledge of the world no longer derives

---

[4] Song and dance accompany the suitors' carousing in Ithaca (1. 152-155), the wedding feast at Sparta (4. 17-18), as well as the pretended wedding after the slaughter of the suitors (23. 133-136). Curiously, there is no singing in old-fashioned, slightly austere Pylos.

[5] Cf. the *Hymn to Apollo* 172.

[6] Another blind seer: Phineas. On the similarity of poet and prophet, compare Vernant (1965), p. 53: "Aède et devin ont en commun un même don de 'voyance,' privilège qu'ils ont dû payer au prix de leurs yeux. Aveugles à la lumière, ils voient l'invisible . . . les réalités qui échappent au regard humain . . . ce qui a eu lieu autrefois, ce qui n'est pas encore." Blindness can also be

from his sight, as does that of other men, but from the Muse. Hence his vision is turned not outward toward the world around him but inward toward events of the past. The knowledge received from the Muses could be called derivative, indirect, aural rather than visual, in fact, hearsay—yet the poet lays claim to its superiority. For the poet sees what others are unable to see. In a passage which refers to both the Muses and Homer, Pindar says: "Blind are the wits of the man who seeks the steep path of wisdom without the Muses" (*Paean* 7b. 13-15). The basis for the poet's claim to superior knowledge rests on the difference between divine and mortal knowledge. That claim, in turn, creates a paradox demanding exploration: that the poet is able to see more by hearing more.

This paradox becomes especially striking in view of the fact that the Greeks thought hearing immeasurably inferior to seeing, since the latter sense yielded incomparably more certain knowledge. The equation between seeing and knowing, well known to all students of Hellenic thought, can be summed up in the Greek verb οἶδα, which means "I have seen," hence, "I know." Eumaeus' remark to Telemachus offers a neat example of this equation:

ἄλλο δέ τοι τό γε οἶδα· τὸ γὰρ ἴδον ὀφθαλμοῖσιν.

And I know another thing, for I saw it with my eyes.

(16. 470)

Eumaeus then proceeds to tell how he saw (ἰδόμην) a ship coming into the harbor and *thought* it was the suitors, but he does not *know* it for sure (οὐδέ τι οἶδα, 16. 472-475). The verbs εἰδέναι, ἱστορεῖν, and γιγνώσκειν all involve knowledge gained through eyewitness or direct observation.[7] Thus the third line of the *Odyssey* states that

---

the characteristic punishment of the Muses for lying or hybristic poets: Thamyris, for challenging the Muses at singing (*Il.* II. 594-600), and Stesichorus, for telling lies about Helen (Plato *Phaedrus* 243a-b). Cf. Barmeyer (1968), pp. 104-107.

[7] Cf. B. Snell, *Die Ausdrücke für den Begriff des Wissens in der vorplatonischen Philosophie*, Philologische Untersuchungen 29 (Berlin, 1924), pp. 20ff.

πολλῶν δ᾽ ἀνθρώπων ἴδεν ἄστεα καὶ νόον ἔγνω,

He saw the cities of many men and knew their mind.

This kind of cognition, as opposed to knowledge through hearing, was considered by the Greeks to be the highest possible form of knowledge.[8] Several passages in the *Odyssey* exemplify the superiority of seeing to hearing. In response to Telemachus' question concerning the whereabouts of his father—"if perhaps you have seen him with your own eyes, or have heard the tale from another" (3. 93-94)—Nestor, like Eumaeus, says that he "knows nothing" (οὐδέ τι οἶδα) about the fate of the other Greeks. Yet he is quite willing to tell Telemachus what he has *heard* (3. 184-187). In Book 4, Nestor's son, while gently reproving Menelaus for his overindulgence in lamentation, remarks that he too lost a brother, by no means the worst of the Greeks, in the Trojan War. Menelaus must know this for a fact (μέλλεις δὲ σὺ ἴδμεναι) but he himself "never met nor laid eyes on him" (οὐδὲ ἴδον). "They *say*, however, that he surpassed others in swift running and fighting" (4. 200-202). Finally, Telemachus' quest for news of his father culminates in Menelaus' account of Proteus' eyewitness report which begins: τὸν ἴδον, "I saw him" (4. 556).

Knowledge through sight, *eidenai*, is, of course, common to both gods and men, but divine *eidenai* surpasses that of mortals in its scope. The gods possess extraordinary keenness of vision and the ability to see from afar. These qualities are the special attributes of the celestial divinities, wide-gazing (εὐρύοπα) Zeus and Helios, "who sees and hears all" (ὃς πάντ᾽ ἐφορᾷ καὶ πάντ᾽ ἐπακούει).[9] Zeus owes his preemi-

---

[8] Consider, for example, Heraclitus Fr. 101a *DK*; Herodotus II. 99.1; and especially the beginning of Aristotle's *Metaphysics*. For modern discussions, see Snell (1924), p. 26; J. Bechert, *Die Diathesen von ἰδεῖν und ὁρᾶν bei Homer*, Münchener Studien zur Sprachwissenschaft 6 (Munich, 1964), pp. 21-22; and D. Bremer, *Licht und Dunkel in der frühgriechischen Dichtung*, Archiv für Begriffsgeschichte Suppl. 1 (Bonn, 1976):45-51.

[9] Cf. R. Pettazzoni, *The All-Knowing God*, trans., H. J. Rose (London, 1956), pp. 5-12.

nence among the gods not only to his superior strength and age, but also to his superior *eidenai* (πλείονα ἤδη *Il* XIII. 355). The far-ranging and penetrating gaze of Zeus observes the doings of men from the mountain tops. To control the battle between the Greeks and the Trojans, Zeus takes up his position on Ida in order to look down upon the battlefield (*Il.* VIII. 51-52). Helios, who oversees and overhears all, also has exceptional sharpness of vision, and it is he who spies out the adulterous pair, Ares and Aphrodite (8. 302). As a result, both Helios and Zeus are frequently invoked as ἵστωρες, or συνίστωρες, that is, eyewitnesses in oaths.[10]

All the major Homeric divinities share this ability to see from afar, to the extent that the Olympians are all to a greater or lesser degree celestial (Οὐρανίωνες). For instance, on his return from the Aethiopians, Poseidon catches sight of Odysseus on his raft from far off (τηλόθεν, 5. 282-283).The Olympians' *eidenai* depends in part on their superhuman mobility, on their ability to be present as eyewitnesses to any action or event if they so chose. Though confined to one locale, even lesser divinities possess *eidenai*. The Sirens, those deadly Muses, tempt Odysseus with their global knowledge:

ἴδμεν γάρ τοι πάνθ' ὅσ' ἐνὶ Τροίῃ εὐρείῃ
Ἀργεῖοι Τρῶές τε θεῶν ἰότητι μόγησαν·
ἴδμεν δ' ὅσσα γένηται ἐπὶ χθονὶ πουλυβοτείρῃ.

For we know all that in wide Troy
the Argives and the Trojans suffered by the will of the
gods;
and we know all that comes to pass on the rich earth.
(12. 189-191)

They have already provided striking proof of their claim by their immediate recognition of Odysseus and their florid address to him (12. 184).[11] Circe's special knowledge reveals

[10] See, for example, *Il*. III. 276-280 and X. 329-331. Cf. Snell (1924), pp. 60-61; and R. Hirzel, *Der Eid* (Leipzig, 1902), pp. 23-24, 214.
[11] On the diction of the Sirens' song, see P. Pucci, "The Song of the Sirens," *Arethusa* 12 (1979):121-32.

itself in her detailed account of the route Odysseus must take
to return home (12. 37ff.). Her remarkable grasp of geography
and the clarity and precision of her descriptions may perhaps
be linked to her being the daughter of Helios, who, as we
have previously noted, has extraordinary powers of vision.
In the preceding examples, divine *eidenai* shows itself to be
relatively or quantitatively superior to that of mortals. To be
sure, the gods can see farther than men, but, like men, their
gaze can be averted or their attention diverted, as when even
great Zeus succumbs to the charms of Hera and is distracted
from the battlefield (*Il.* XIV. 352ff.). In their ability to recognize each other, however, the gods demonstrate their absolute superiority over mortals. Thus Calypso immediately
recognizes Hermes when he arrives on remote Ogygia:

οὐ γάρ τ᾽ ἀγνῶτες θεοὶ ἀλλήλοισι πέλονται
ἀθάνατοι, οὐδ᾽ εἴ τις ἀπόπροθι δώματα ναίει.

For the immortal gods are not unknown to each other,
not even if one lives far off.

(5. 79-80)

On rare occasions, a god can render himself invisible to another god, but only with the aid of unusual devices. The *Iliad*
mentions two such devices. One is the helmet of Hades or the
cap of invisibility[12] Athena dons as she sets out against Ares,
"so that mighty Ares would not see her"(V. 845). The other
is the golden cloud Zeus spreads about himself and Hera after
assuring his wife that neither god nor man will be able to
observe their lovemaking: "Not even Helios, who has the
power to look upon even the brightest light, may look through
and observe us" (XIV. 344-345). The extraordinary measures
required to hide from other gods demonstrate the general
validity of the rule—that the gods are not unknown to one
another.
    When dealing with mortals, the gods generally disguise

[12] For a discussion of this helmet, which he believes to be properly the
helmet of invisibility (ἀ-ιδος*), see J. Roeger, ΑΙΔΟΣ ΚΥΝΕΗ (Graz, 1924).

themselves or choose to remain invisible.[13] Men may not recognize a divinity unless the latter is willing. In a rare rhetorical question, Odysseus asks:

τίς ἂν θεὸν οὐκ ἐθέλοντα
ὀφθαλμοῖσιν ἴδοιτ᾽ ἢ ἔνθ᾽ ἢ ἔνθα κιόντα;

Who can behold with his eyes
a god against his will, as he moves here and there?
(10. 573-574)

The *Iliad* explains this curious limitation of human vision. The eyes of mortals are veiled by a dark mist which prevents them from distinguishing clearly between gods and men; Athena instructs Diomedes:

ἀχλὺν δ᾽ αὖ τοι ἀπ᾽ ὀφθαλμῶν ἕλον, ἣ πρὶν ἐπῆεν,
ὄφρ᾽ εὖ γιγνώσκῃς ἠμὲν θεὸν ἠδὲ καὶ ἄνδρα.

I have taken from your eyes the mist which before was
upon them,
so that you may well recognize god and man.
(V. 127-128)

An ancient commentator on this passage correctly defines this mist as "blindness."[14] As a result of such blindness, men continually mistake gods for men and men for gods. For example, the suitors fail to realize that the figure of "Mentes" or "Mentor" conceals the goddess Athena. But Noemon, who had previously lent Telemachus his ship as well as seen "Mentor" embarking and now enjoys the benefits of hindsight, suspects something:

ἐν δ᾽ ἀρχὸν ἐγὼ βαίνοντ᾽ ἐνόησα
Μέντορα, ἠὲ θεόν, τῷ δ᾽ αὐτῷ πάντα ἐῴκει.
ἀλλὰ τὸ θαυμάζω· ἴδον ἐνθάδε Μέντορα δῖον
χθιζὸν ὑπηοῖον. τότε δ᾽ ἔμβη νηὶ Πύλονδε.

---

[13] See J. S. Clay, "Demas and Audê: The Nature of Divine Transformation in Homer," *Hermes* 102 (1974):129-36.
[14] Schol. A at V. 127.

I saw Mentor boarding as leader
—or a god; he resembled him in every way.
But I marvel at it, for I saw godlike Mentor here
yesterday, but then he boarded the ship for Pylos.
(4. 653-656)

When Odysseus claims to be unsure whether the Phaeacian
princess Nausicaa is a mortal woman or a goddess (6. 149ff.),
he may well be attempting to win her with flattery;[15] but he
can only succeed because of the commonplace possibility of
mistaking gods and mortals. Shortly thereafter, indeed, the
sudden appearance of Odysseus at the hearth of Alcinoos
provokes astonishment and invites a similar uncertainty (7.
199). Telemachus can only be persuaded with difficulty that
the suddenly rejuvenated Odysseus before him is his own father
rather than some god (16. 178ff.). Finally, one of the suitors,
while trying to restrain Antinoos' bullying of Odysseus in
beggar's garb, warns Antinoos that the stranger before them
may turn out to be a god:

Ἀντίνο᾽, οὐ μὲν κάλ᾽ ἔβαλες δύστηνον ἀλήτην,
οὐλόμεν᾽, εἰ δή πού τις ἐπουράνιος θεός ἐστι.
καί τε θεοὶ ξείνοισιν ἐοικότες ἀλλοδαποῖσι,
παντοῖοι τελέθοντες, ἐπιστρωφῶσι πόληας,
ἀνθρώπων ὕβριν τε καὶ εὐνομίην ἐφορῶντες.

Antinoos, you did no fine thing in striking the poor
    beggar,
and you will be cursed, if somehow in fact he is some
    god from heaven.
For the gods, disguised as strangers from foreign parts,
in all shapes and sizes, visit cities,
watching over both the violence and orderliness of men.
(17. 483-487)

Examples abound, then, to show that the gulf between divine
and mortal *eidenai* reveals itself most clearly in men's inability

---

[15] Cf. W. B. Stanford, ed., *The Odyssey of Homer*, 2nd rev. ed. (London,
1965), at 6. 149, who comments on the "masterly tact" of this speech.

to see or recognize the gods. Hence men cannot have sure knowledge of them.

On the general blindness of mankind concerning the gods, Homer would agree with his great critic, Xenophanes: καὶ τὸ μὲν οὖν σαφὲς οὔτις ἀνὴρ ἴδεν οὐδέ τις ἔσται / εἰδὼς ἀμφὶ θεῶν . . . (Fr. 34 *DK*).[16] The knowledge of the poet, the gift of the Muses, is not subject to this limitation; the case of Demodocus from whom we began proves as much.

Before the assembled Phaeacians, Demodocus recounts two episodes from the heroic tradition of the Trojan War: "The Quarrel of Odysseus and Achilles" and "The Stratagem of the Wooden Horse." The memory of these events in which he actively participated brings tears to the eyes of Odysseus, whose identity has not been revealed to his hosts.[17] At one point, he compliments the bard on the excellence of his performance:

Δημόδοκ᾽, ἔξοχα δή σε βροτῶν αἰνίζομ᾽ ἁπάντων·
ἢ σέ γε Μοῦσ᾽ ἐδίδαξε, Διὸς πάϊς, ἢ σέ γ᾽
  Ἀπόλλων.
λίην γὰρ κατὰ κόσμον Ἀχαιῶν οἶτον ἀείδεις,
ὅσσ᾽ ἔρξαν τ᾽ ἔπαθόν τε καὶ ὅσσ᾽ ἐμόγησαν
  Ἀχαιοί,
ὥς τέ που ἢ αὐτὸς παρεὼν ἢ ἄλλου ἀκούσας.

Demodocus, I consider you outstanding among all men;
indeed, either the Muse, child of Zeus, instructed you, or
  Apollo.
For all in due order you sing the fate of the Greeks,
what they did and endured and suffered,
as if you yourself were present, or heard it from another.
                                        (8. 487-491)

[16] G. S. Kirk and D. S. Raven, *The Presocratic Philosophers* (Cambridge, 1957), p. 179, translate: "No man knows, or ever will know, the truth about the gods. . . ." But their rendering does not succeed in conveying the notion inherent in the Greek that to have knowledge concerning the gods means to have seen them clearly.

[17] For the contrast and parallelism of *penthos*, 'grief,' and *kleos*, 'fame,' see G. Nagy, *Comparative Studies in Greek and Indic Meter* (Cambridge, Mass., 1974), pp. 255-61.

Odysseus' words here resemble the appeal to the Muses before the great Catalogue of Ships in the *Iliad*, when the poet prepares to list the names and numbers of all the Greek forces that fought before Troy:

Ἔσπετε νῦν μοι, Μοῦσαι Ὀλύμπια δώματ᾽
ἔχουσαι—
ὑμεῖς γὰρ θεαί ἐστε, πάρεστέ τε, ἴστέ τε πάντα,
ἡμεῖς δὲ κλέος οἶον ἀκούομεν οὐδέ τι ἴδμεν.

Tell me now, Muses, who have your homes on
Olympus—
for you are goddesses, are present, and know all things;
but we hear only rumor, nor have sure knowledge of
anything.

(II. 484-486)

Compared to the divine knowledge of the Muses, mortals possess mere *kleos*, aural rather than visual, based on vague hearsay. The Muses, on the other hand, know the truth about every event because they have seen it; they can recount past events accurately in every detail because they were there.[18] The precision of the Muses' knowledge depends on their omnipresence. In describing the activities of men, it differs from the accounts of ordinary mortals in clarity as well as exactitude. The half-remembered tales of men of the past are re-created in vivid and minute detail by the poet whom the Muse endows with the gift of divine *eidenai*. Or, to preserve the meaningful ambiguity of the Greek, the agency of the Muses transforms κλέος οἶον, "mere rumor," into κλέος ἄφθιτον, "imperishable fame."[19]

But the *klea andron*, the famous deeds of the heroes, constitute only one facet of the Muses' power. As Olympians, the Muses possess the ability, common to the gods, to know and

---

[18] Cf. W. Luther, *Wahrheit und Lüge im ältesten Griechentum* (Leipzig, 1935), p. 86; and B. Snell, *Die Entdeckung des Geistes*, 4th ed. (Göttingen, 1975), pp. 127-8.

[19] Cf. Nagy (1974), pp. 244-52. On *kleos* in archaic Greek poetry, see M. Greindl, ΚΛΕΟΣ ΚΥΔΟΣ ΕΥΧΟΣ ΤΙΜΗ ΦΑΤΙΣ ΔΟΞΑ (Langerich, 1938), pp. 5-29.

recognize the gods. What distinguishes the Muses from other divinities is that they convey this superhuman knowledge to the poets. Through the Muses, their disciples the poets differ radically from ordinary mortals in their knowledge of the gods. Between the two narratives drawn from the traditions of the Trojan War, Demodocus sings a very different kind of song, "The Lay of Ares and Aphrodite," describing in somewhat ribald fashion the intimate lives of the Olympians.[20] The doings of the gods, both on Olympus and in their relations with men, are as important a part of the Muses' domain as the *klea andron*. And this aspect, too, of their knowledge they share with the poets. According to Penelope, the poets sing ἔργ' ἀνδρῶν τε θεῶν τε, "the deeds of gods and men" (1. 338).[21] Hesiod, too, declares the task of the singer to be twofold:

αὐτὰρ ἀοιδὸς
Μουσάων θεράπων κλεῖα προτέρων ἀνθρώπων
ὑμνήσει μάκαράς τε θεοὺς οἳ Ὄλυμπον ἔχουσιν.

But the singer,
servant of the Muses, hymns the famous deeds of men
of the past
and the blessed gods who live on Olympus.
(*Theog.* 99-101)

Hesiod's lengthy prologue to the Muses in the *Theogony* (lines 1-114), recounting his nocturnal meeting with them on Helicon, is necessitated by the subject matter of the poem that follows. For the origins of the gods are a theme beyond normal human ken;[22] and the Muses themselves must guarantee the accuracy of the poet's account. The *Works and Days*, on the other hand, dealing as they do with the nature of human life, require no such lengthy guarantee or introduction.

---

[20] On the relevance of the song to the *Odyssey* as a whole, see W. Burkert, "Das Lied von Ares und Aphrodite," *RM* 103 (1960):130-44.

[21] Cf. the *Hymn to Apollo* 189-193, where the Muses are said to "hymn the immortal gifts of the gods and the sufferings of men."

[22] Similarly, Pindar *Paean* 6. 50ff., asks how strife arose among the gods, but then comments that such matters cannot be known for certain by men, although the Muses know them.

According to some scholars, the double character of the Epic arose from the linking of what were originally two separate *genres*: hymn poetry or songs in praise of the gods, and *Sage*, accounts of the exploits of the heroes.[23] This view of the genesis of the Epic poses problems, not the least of which is that the heroes almost by definition are those in whom the gods take an active interest, whether for good or ill. But, no matter the origins, what matters to us is that Homer displays a conscious awareness of the double function of the Muses and exploits the twofold character of his poetry. This becomes apparent in the fact that Homer presents a distinction in the *Odyssey* between his own narrative, whose words are inspired by the Muse, and the speeches of his characters.

The poet's awareness of the privileged character of his utterance explains the important observation of Jørgensen that Odysseus and the other characters in the poem rarely refer to a divinity by name, but usually employ a vague generic term like "a god," "some god," "the gods," "Zeus," or "a *daimon*."[24] The characters' ignorance compels them to use such general terms for divinity, whereas the poet knows precisely which of the gods is involved and calls him by name.

The most striking indication of Homer's exact knowledge of divinity and the imprecision of others' occurs in the many doublets where the same incident is related once by the poet and once again by one of his characters.[25] Such repetitions sometimes occur after the intervention of several books. For instance, when Odysseus, after being battered by the storm, finally arrives on Scheria and makes himself a bed of leaves, Homer tells us that Athena poured sleep over him (5. 491).

[23] See W. Kullmann, *Das Wirken der Götter in der Ilias* (Berlin, 1956), pp. 10-41. For a Dumézilian view of this duality in archaic poetry based on the warrior and priestly functions of Mycenean society, see Detienne (1967), pp. 16ff. But Detienne splits Homer from Hesiod too sharply. For Homeric epic, while not theogonic, is surely theological; that is, it offers a *logos* concerning the gods.

[24] "Das Auftreten der Götter in den Büchern ι-μ der Odyssee," *Hermes* 39 (1904):357-82. For exceptions, see E. Hedèn, *Homerische Götterstudien* (Uppsala, 1912), pp. 19-20; and G. M. Calhoun, "The Divine Entourage in Homer," *AJP* 61 (1940): 269-73.

[25] Cf. Jørgensen (1904), pp. 366-67.

Later, however, when Odysseus describes his landing to Alcinoos, he knows only that "a god" gave him sleep (7. 286).
Even more impressive are those cases when only a few lines
separate the version of the poet from that of a character.
For example, in Book 5. 282-296, Poseidon stirs up a mighty
storm against Odysseus. Eight lines later (5. 304), the hero
places the blame for the storm on "Zeus." The poet knows—
as do we—who is really responsible. Subsequently, Odysseus
does learn the truth from Leucothea, a *goddess*, that Poseidon
caused the storm (5. 339-341); and he makes use of this god-
given knowledge later when he prays to Athena on Scheria
(6. 326). Similarly, in the last book (24. 367), Athena beautifies Odysseus' old father Laertes as he comes from his bath,
but Odysseus can only surmise that "some one of the gods"
has suddenly glorified his aged parent (24. 373). More examples could easily be cited: the distinction between what the
poet knows and the clouded perceptions of his characters is
applied consistently throughout the poem. Homer thereby reveals his constant awareness of the disparity between divine
and human knowledge and of the gift the Muses have be-
stowed upon him. Moreover, he insists on keeping before us,
his audience, the extraordinary character of the vision the
Muses grant him.

The importance of Jørgensen's observation for Homeric
poetics has gone largely unrecognized. Jørgensen himself was
satisfied to label it "ein episches Stilmittel." That, however,
simply begs the question, for this "Epic device" clashes with
another and far more pervasive one; it requires the poet to
forgo formulaic repetition when recounting the same incident
twice and the characteristic economy of the Epic style.[26] Nor
is it sufficient to recognize that, in the Homeric poems, the

---

[26] The distinction between the diction of the poet and that of his characters
has been almost totally ignored by Homerists, although the subject is well
worth examining. I have come across only P. Krarup, "Verwendung von
Abstracta in der direkten Rede bei Homer," *Classica et Mediaevalia* 10 (1948):1-
17. Both D. Lohmann, *Die Komposition der Reden in der Ilias* (Berlin, 1970)
and J. Lactacz, "Zur Forschungsarbeit an den direkten Reden bei Homer,"
Gräzer Beiträge 3 (1975):395-422, ignore the question.

characters may offer a realistic representation of the contemporary beliefs of the poet's society by their indefinite references to the gods.[27] One may well admit historical verisimilitude—that men thought and spoke about the gods in the way Homer depicts them—but one cannot deny the *poetic* purpose. The poet is at constant pains to keep his audience aware of his superior knowledge concerning the gods. As Else puts it, "the differences in usage" between the poet and his characters

> arise not from differing opinions as to the basic assumption, but from different kinds and degrees of knowledge in the speaker. The gods know each other and each other's names and activities and have no occasion for the indefinite θεός or θεῶν τις except when talking to men. Neither does the poet, whose knowledge is accredited as coming from the gods. Both the gods and the poet, then, are correctly polytheistic in their language.[28]

Like Demodocus, Homer can describe the activities of both gods and men in all their fullness. A mortal without the special gift of divine knowledge may know the latter, albeit imperfectly, but not the former. An eloquent example occurs at the beginning of the *Iliad*. As an ordinary mortal, the poet asks: "Who of the gods brought the two of them [Achilles and Agamemnon] into battling strife?" Then, with the inspiration of the Muse, he provides the answer: "the son of Leto and Zeus."[29]

A telling confirmation of this rule occurs in the longest

---

[27] Hedèn (1912), pp. 25-27, maintains incorrectly that the speeches of Homer's characters reflect a more abstract, hence later and more enlightened, conception of the gods. E. Ehnmark, *The Idea of God in Homer* (Uppsala, 1935), pp. 64-73, agrees that the speeches "give a psychologically correct description of the way men think and talk" (65), but rightly observes that the vague terms used by men are due to their ignorance rather than to their enlightenment. M. Nilsson, *Geschichte der griechischen Religion*, 3rd ed., (Munich, 1955), 1:368, n. 2, remains aware of the poetic purpose as well as the historical relevance of this Homeric usage.

[28] G. F. Else, "God and Gods in Early Greek Thought," *TAPA* 80 (1949):28.

[29] Compare the eighth line of the *Aeneid*: "Musa, mihi causas memora, quo numine laeso . . . ."

speech in the *Odyssey*, which takes up Books 9 through 12: Odysseus' narration of his wanderings. When Odysseus interrupts his story, a hush of wonder and amazement falls over his Phaeacian audience at Alcinoos' palace. Urging his guest to continue, the king compares Odysseus to a poet or bard (*aoidos*, 11. 368). But wrongly. Odysseus has indeed succeeded in charming his hearers, but he has been talking about himself and describing adventures in which he played the leading role. Moreover, Odysseus speaks not only from the perspective of his own actions and experiences, but also with the benefit of hindsight.[30] Nevertheless, unlike the poet's narrative, that of Odysseus is singularly free of references to divine activities. Throughout, he employs those general terms for the gods which are characteristic of human speech. The hero, however eloquent, cannot rival the bard.

The only important exception confirms the poet's tacit insistence that Odysseus is not an *aoidos* and cannot know what the poet knows.[31] In Book 12 (376-388) Odysseus gives an account of a conversation between Zeus and Helios—in clear violation of the Epic rule. Helios demands revenge for the eating of his cattle, and Zeus agrees to destroy Odysseus' companions. Immediately thereafter come two lines in which Odysseus divulges the source of his information:

Ταῦτα δ' ἐγὼν ἤκουσα Καλυψοῦς ἠϋκόμοιο·
ἡ δ' ἔφη Ἑρμείαο διακτόρου αὐτὴ ἀκοῦσαι.

---

[30] Cf. the observations of W. Suerbaum, "Die Ich-Erzählungen des Odysseus," *Poetica* 2 (1968):150-77, on the narrative technique of Books 9-12.

[31] The intervention of Hermes in 10. 277-307 is not, as Jørgensen (1904), pp. 373-75, claims, a true exception. Hermes' appearance as a youth resembles the description of the god in *Il.* XXIV. 347-348, when he accompanies Priam to Achilles' tent. Priam has no inkling of who his escort may be, but after they arrive at Achilles' camp and Hermes has identified himself, he adds: "I shall go back, nor shall I enter the sight of Achilles; for it would be a shameful thing for an immortal god thus to show his love of mortals openly" (462-464). Hermes' words suggest that Achilles could recognize him. Some people, one may conclude, are better at recognizing the gods than others; "for the gods do not appear openly to all" (16. 161). Odysseus has rather special talents in this sphere. Consider 22. 210, where Odysseus suspects Athena's presence under the guise of "Mentor."

These things I heard from lovely-haired Calypso,
and she said she heard them from Hermes, the guide.
(12. 389-390)

Critics have heaped abuse on these lines and have found them
extremely awkward, since we are never told that Hermes mentioned the incident to Calypso, nor that Calypso informed
Odysseus.[32] The verses may very well be awkward, but they
are also essential. Homer is not nodding; rather he demonstrates that, no matter how talented a storyteller Odysseus
may be, he remains unable to describe Olympian scenes without divine intermediaries. It is precisely the awkwardness of
Odysseus' necessary aside that draws our attention to the gulf
between ordinary mortal knowledge of the gods and the extraordinary knowledge the poet possesses through his privileged relation to the Muses.

Through the inspiration of the Muses, the gaze of the poet
encompasses what happens on earth; he also witnesses what
goes on in Olympus. The words and deeds of the gods are no
strangers to him. As a result, the poet is constantly a theo-
logian, literally, a *theologos*—and an ironist. At each moment,
he knows which god is intervening in human affairs—something the mortal characters can only guess—and he is aware
at all times what the gods are thinking and planning as well
as what their motives are. The poet's conception of his own
role through his relation to the Muses must necessarily shape
the way we approach and interpret the *Odyssey*. In other
words, we must take his claim seriously.

Andra Polytropon

Let us begin again, returning to the proem and turning from
the poet to the central character of his poem. The first word
of the *Odyssey* announces its subject, *andra*, 'the man,' just

[32] For a summary of the old controversy, see P. Cauer, *Grundfragen der
Homerkritik*, 3rd ed., (Leipzig, 1923), pp. 639ff. Dio Chrysostom XI. 20-21
praises these verses since they correctly handle the problem of how mortals
can have knowledge of divine conversations.

as the subject of the *Iliad* announces itself to be *menis*, 'the
wrath.' Both epics further define the theme word with an
epithet (πολύτροπον, οὐλομένην) and a relative clause (ὃς
μάλα πολλὰ πλάγχθη ..., ἣ μυρί᾽ Ἀχαιοῖς ἄλγε᾽ ...).[33]
This striking formal symmetry invites a closer comparison of
the two proems, for in a sense, the *Iliad* is the canon against
which the *Odyssey* measures itself. The complex relationship
between the two epics as a whole cannot be explored here,
but a comparison of their opening lines illuminates some telling features of the *Odyssey*.

Andra, the man, the subject of the *Odyssey*, is described—
one might even say circumscribed—in the invocation, but,
most remarkably, Odysseus' name is not mentioned. In fact,
it is withheld until line 21. Consider the contrast to the opening of the *Iliad*: "Sing, goddess, the wrath of Achilles, the son
of Peleus." The principal hero is named at once: Achilles, the
son of Peleus. His patronymic, his ancestral lineage, go far in
defining his heroic greatness;[34] and his very birth from the
union of a mortal and the goddess Thetis already implies his
tragic fate as well as his famous choice between a short and
glorious life and a long and obscure one.[35] In the *Odyssey*,
however, the hero as he is first introduced is anonymous. He
is in no way defined by his patronymic. To call him the son
of Laertes, that shadowy figure, is not to characterize him.[36]
He is far better characterized by the multiplicity of his ex-

[33] For comparisons of the openings of the two epics, see S. E. Bassett, "The
Proems of the Iliad and the Odyssey," *AJP* 44 (1923): 339-48; B. A. van
Groningen, "The Proems of the Iliad and Odyssey," *Med. Ned. Ak. Afd.
Letterk.* 9, 8 (1946):279-92; and Rüter (1969), pp. 28-34.

[34] Cf. S. Benardete, "Achilles and the Iliad," *Hermes* 91 (1963):12.

[35] R. Shannon, *The Arms of Achilles*, Mnemosyne Suppl. 36 (Leiden, 1975),
p. 70, considers Achilles' ash spear, the only equipment of the hero not later
replaced by divine armor, to symbolize Achilles' mortality. Its regular epithet
is "Pelian" and refers to Achilles' mortal father Peleus.

[36] Cf. Benardete's (1963) discussion (pp. 12-14) of the difference between
Achilles and Odysseus. Benardete cites Ovid *Metamorphoses* 13. 140-141,
where Odysseus says of himself: "nam genus et proavus et quae non fecimus
ipsi / vix ea nostra voco" ("For lineage and ancestor and whatever I did not
accomplish myself, those I scarcely call my own."). Cf. also Apuleius *De deo
Socratis* 24.

perience—"He saw the cities of many men and learned their minds"—and his sufferings—"Many were the woes he suffered in his heart on the sea"—and his intelligence. The absence of the name of the hero has not gone unnoticed by commentators ancient and modern. Eustathius, for example, remarks that "the poet keeps silent concerning the name of Odysseus from the beginning, signaling him out by solemn and praiseworthy epithets . . . [thereby] he has revealed Odysseus par excellence."[37] One can argue that the description of Odysseus in the proem identifies the *andra* beyond any doubt and renders the name superfluous.[38] That may be true enough, but it still does not completely account for its curious and striking omission.

The suppression of the hero's name is but the first and most obvious of Homer's silences. Others of equal importance will occur elsewhere in the text, and it may be useful to recall the judgment of the Scholiast that Homer "considered not only what he said, but also what he did not say."[39] But what is more, the absence of Odysseus' name characterizes not only the proem; for throughout a good part of his adventures, the hero is nameless. In the cave of Polyphemus, he owes his escape to the adoption of the guileful pseudonym Outis, "No-One." In Phaeacia, the queen demands point-blank to know the identity of the mysterious stranger who has suddenly appeared at her hearth, wearing clothes from the palace (7. 238). The question remains unanswered for two books during which Odysseus maintains his anonymity.[40] Later, Alcinoos asks again

---

[37] Eustathius 1381. 20-25: Σημείωσαι δὲ ὅτι σιωπᾷ τὸ τοῦ Ὀδυσσέως ἐξ ἀρχῆς ὄνομα ὁ ποιητὴς, ἐξαίρων αὐτὸν σεμνοῖς ἐπιθέτοις καὶ ἐγκωμίοις . . . τὸν Ὀδυσσέα ἐδήλωσε κατ' ἐξοχήν.

[38] As does Rüter (1969), pp. 34-37.

[39] Scholia bT at *Il.* I. 449: οὐ γὰρ μόνον, τί εἴπῃ, ἀλλὰ καὶ τί μὴ εἴπῃ, ἐφρόντισεν. Compare Schol. H.Q.R. at 4. 52, who add: καὶ οὐχ ἧττον ἐξ ὧν κατορθοῖ ἐν οἷς λέγει σοφὸς εὑρίσκεται ἢ ἐν οἷς ἀποσιωπᾷ καὶ οὐ λέγει. Cf. D. N. Maronitis, Ἀναζήτηση καὶ Νόστος τοῦ Ὀδυσσέα (Athens, 1973), p. 74 and n. 5, who is correct in recognizing that the poet's silence here is intentional and connected with the poet's recasting of the traditional figure of Odysseus. Cf. below pp. 68ff.

[40] For a recent discussion with bibliography of this Homeric problem and the theme of the "nameless stranger," see Fenik (1974), pp. 5-60.

for the name of his guest and bids him "not to hide it with guileful thoughts" (8. 548). Finally, the king observes:

οὐ μὲν γάρ τις πάμπαν ἀνώνυμός ἐστ᾽ ἀνθρώπων,
οὐ κακὸς οὐδὲ μὲν ἐσθλός, ἐπὴν τὰ πρῶτα γένηται,
ἀλλ᾽ ἐπὶ πᾶσι τίθενται, ἐπεί κε τέκωσι, τοκῆες.

No man is completely nameless among men,[41]
be he base or noble, when first he is born,
but all receive names from their parents when first they
   bring them forth.

(8. 552-554)

Moreover, on Ithaca Odysseus studiously keeps his identity hidden while concocting his sundry Cretan tales.

Fully as central to the plot of the *Odyssey* as the suppression of Odysseus' name is its revelation. Aristotle correctly calls the *Odyssey* "recognition throughout" (*Poetics* 24. 1459b15). Thus, the hero's sufferings at the hands of Poseidon after the blinding of the Cyclops depend on his boastful announcement of his true name, which allows Polyphemus to pronounce the curse and the god to carry it out. So too, part of the magical temptation of the Sirens lies in their immediate and flattering recognition of the wandering hero's identity (12. 184). In other situations, however, the nameless Odysseus must continually prove himself to be Odysseus through his actions and through his wits. Circe, for example, recognizes him only after he shows himself immune to her magic (10. 330). When, at long last, Odysseus proudly declares himself to the Phaeacians— "I am Odysseus, son of Laertes, who am famous among all men for my tricks (*doloi*) and my fame reaches heaven" (9. 19-20)—he knows full well that the reputation he claims has preceded his announcement. After all, Demodocus had previously recounted two incidents from Odysseus' illustrious career, one about the *dolos* of the wooden horse (8. 499ff.), and the other concerning the quarrel between Odysseus and

---

[41] Note the poet's (not Alcinoos') allusion to the Outis story here.

Achilles, who there are called the "best of the Achaeans" (8. 78).[42]

The omission of the hero's name from the prologue cannot, then, be regarded as merely accidental. It points to an important thematic component of the *Odyssey*. The name itself deserves further discussion, but one best left for a later chapter.

Though the *Odyssey* does not begin by giving the name of its hero, it does begin at once to describe the protagonist. The first epithet applied to the nameless man who will be the subject of the poem is *polytropos*, 'of many turns,' 'of varied turnings.' Milman Parry singles out *polytropos* as his first example of the "particularized epithet" and remarks that "Homer's audience . . . realized straightway that the poet had special reasons for putting it into his song."[43] But such an immediate realization was probably accompanied by a sense of puzzlement on the part of that audience. For while we might reasonably expect the first adjective which describes the hero to single out and illuminate his most characteristic quality, this particular epithet is both rare and its meaning obscure. "Of many turns": is one meant to think of turnings in space, and is the allusion therefore primarily to Odysseus' wanderings? Or are these mental turns which refer in some way to the hero's mental dexterity? The ancients preferred the latter explanation which is borne out by the application of the epithet to the trickster god Hermes in the *Hymn to Hermes* (lines 13, 439). Plato, for example, contrasts the character of Achilles as "truthful and simple" (ἀληθής τε καὶ ἁπλοῦς) to that of Odysseus, "polytropic and lying" (πολύτροπός τε καὶ ψευδής).[44] Yet many modern scholars have insisted on

---

[42] On this scene, see G. Nagy, *The Best of the Achaeans* (Baltimore, 1979), pp. 15ff. and below, pp. 97ff.

[43] *The Making of Homeric Verse*, ed. A. Parry (Oxford, 1971), p. 154.

[44] *Hippias Minor* 365b. Consider also Scholia H.M.Q.R. at 1.1. Compare among the moderns van Groningen (1946), p. 293; Rüter (1969), p. 36; and especially Maronitis (1973), pp. 81-85, for the most perceptive discussion of the term.

the sense "much wandering."⁴⁵ Among translators, Pope gives
"The man for wisdom's various arts renown'd"; Lawrence
offers "the various-minded man." Lattimore's rendering retains the ambiguity of the Greek with "of many ways," while
Fitzgerald, perhaps a bit verbosely, tries to bring out both
meanings with "skilled in all ways of contending / the wan-
derer."

The *Iliad* provides no help in establishing the sense of *polytropos*; the word never occurs. In fact, it appears only one
more time in the *Odyssey* itself, that is, at the moment when
Circe's magic has failed to transform Odysseus into a pig, and
he has proved himself immune to her spells. She then asks
who he is; no other man could have withstood her potions,

σοὶ δέ τις ἐν στήθεσσιν ἀκήλητος νόος ἐστίν.
ἦ σύ γ᾽ Ὀδυσσεύς ἐσσι πολύτροπος, ὅν τέ μοι αἰεὶ
φάσκεν ἐλεύσεσθαι χρυσόρραπις ἀργειφόντης,
ἐκ Τροίης ἀνιόντα θοῇ σὺν νηῒ μελαίνῃ.

But there is some uncharmable mind in your heart.
You must indeed be Odysseus *polytropos*, whom always
Hermes of the golden staff used to tell me would come,
returning from Troy with a swift black ship.
                                    (10. 329-332)

Here too *polytropos* constitutes the one identifying epithet of
Odysseus, whereby Circe singles him out from all others.⁴⁶
Yet here again the sense of the word remains opaque. If *polytropos* is linked closely to the preceding line, it must refer
to some quality of mind. The explicit mention of Hermes in
line 331 and the god's important role throughout the entire
sequence is suggestive. After all, his gift of *moly* and his advice

⁴⁵ See, for example, T. Kakrides, "Die Bedeutung von πολύτροπος in der
Odyssee," *Glotta* 11 (1921):288-91; W. J. Woodhouse, *The Composition of
Homer's Odyssey* (Oxford, 1930), p. 24; and W. B. Stanford (1965) in his
commentary at 1.1.

⁴⁶ Parry, (1971), pp. 156-57, points out that an exact metrical equivalent
for Ὀδυσσεύς . . . πολύτροπος at 10.330 exists within the Homeric corpus: Ὀδυσεύς . . . διίφιλος (*Il.* X. 527), but that in the *Odyssey* passage,
"Homer did not make use of the epithet which would have come immediately
to his mind had he not been thinking of the action of the moment."

have saved Odysseus from Circe's enchantments; and he is the same god who is twice called *polytropos* in the *Hymn to Hermes*.[47] But if *polytropos* is to be taken with what follows, it would refer to the hero's return from Troy and his travels.

The Circe passage, then, maintains the initial obscurity of *polytropos*, and its ambiguity closely parallels that of the proem. There, the lines following describe a man who was driven many places, saw the cities of men and learned their minds, and suffered many woes in the sea. "Many," *polla*, occurs three times in these initial lines, and its stem is, of course, the same as the first half of *polytropos*. The first descriptive clause that portrays the hero as "driven," πλάγχθη, brings out a passive sense of *polytropos*, but this is counterbalanced by line 4's active verbs of cognition, "saw," "learned," ἴδεν, ἔγνω. The proem deepens rather than resolves the ambiguity of *polytropos*; it emphasizes not only the multiplicity of Odysseus' wanderings and sufferings, but also the multiplicity of his mind.

In other words, *polytropos* most appropriately sums up and captures the two major aspects of the protagonist. The merest glance at some of Odysseus' other epithets which recur throughout the poem confirms this point. A striking number share the *poly*- prefix,[48] and they fall into two distinct groups. One refers to the hero's agile mind, the other, to his multiple sufferings. Odysseus is called *polytlemon*, *polytlas*, 'much enduring'; *polyplanktos*, 'much wandering'; *polypenthes*, 'of many sorrows'; *polykedes* and *polystonos*, 'of many woes.' Compared to these, *polytropos* is both less specific and less emotionally charged.

Another group of *poly*- epithets describes Odysseus' mental versatility: *polymetis*, *polyphron*, 'many-minded,' similar to *poikilophron*, 'of varied mind'; *polymechanos*, 'of many devices'; and *polykerdes*, 'of much cunning.' All these adjectives refer to the quality of Odysseus' mind. It is characterized not so much by wisdom, or even by intelligence as such, but by the multiplicity of mind, by mental dexterity, by what the

---

[47] Cf. Maronitis (1973), p. 83.
[48] For a complete list, see W. B. Stanford, "Homer's Use of Personal πολυ-Compounds," *CP* 45 (1950):108-110.

Greeks called *metis*.[49] The subject of Odysseus' *metis* will be explored at greater length in the next chapter, but the range of the word's meanings can be grasped in a preliminary way by noting the divinities with whom Odysseus shares some of these epithets. Hephaestus, the divine craftsman and technician, is both *polyphron* and *polymetis* (*Il.* XXI. 355, 367; *Od.* 8. 297, 327); Athena, Odysseus' patroness, receives the epithet *polymetis* in the second line of the *Hymn to Athena*, while in Homer she is twice called *polyboulos*, "of many plans" (*Il.* V. 260; *Od.* 16. 282). *Polytropos* itself, as we have seen, as well as *polymetis*, are used of the master thief and trickster, Hermes, with whom Odysseus has special connections (*Hymn to Hermes* 13, 439, 319). Finally, the substantive, *polymechanie*, describes the trickery of Circe and is equivalent to *dolos*, 'trick or ruse' (23. 321).[50] It is worthwhile to note that only the active *poly-* compounds are common to Odysseus and the gods. Rüter comments aptly that the ability to know and to act belongs also to the gods, but that Odysseus embodies, in addition, the specifically human ability to suffer and experience.[51]

From these examples, it is clear that these terms for mental agility have a wide range of meaning encompassing technical skill, cleverness, craftiness, and duplicity. Many of these epithets have the same edge to them that 'clever' often has: when someone is called clever, it frequently means that he is too clever. *Polytropos*, by contrast, remains morally neutral and ambiguous precisely because of its opaqueness and semantic obscurity.[52] The intellectual qualities (*metis*) that *polytropos* designates are in themselves profoundly ambiguous. They are, to be sure, admirable, but they are also a source of uneasiness

---

[49] For an illuminating discussion of *metis*, see M. Detienne and J.-P. Vernant, *Les ruses de l'intelligence: la mètis des Grecs* (Paris, 1974). While not treating the *Odyssey* directly, this work is fundamental to an understanding of the character of Odysseus.

[50] Cf. *Hymn to Hermes* 319.

[51] Rüter (1969), p. 36. Like Odysseus, Eris, "Strife," is once called *polystonos* (*Il.* XI. 73), but there the sense is active: "causing many woes."

[52] Maronitis (1973), p. 83 correctly stresses this important point. But the Scholia on *polytropos* already felt obliged to defend Odysseus against the distasteful implications of the epithet.

and suspicion. In their study of *metis* Detienne and Vernant emphasize the tension characterizing *metis*:

> Depending on the context, it can arouse contrary reactions. At times, one will consider it to be the result of a deception in which the rules of the game have not been respected. On other occasions, it will excite all the greater admiration through the effect of surprise, since the weaker has, contrary to all expectation, found within himself enough resources to put the stronger at his mercy. In certain of its aspects, *metis* stands on the side of disloyal deception, perfidious lying, and treachery, the despicable weapons of women and cowards. But in other aspects, *metis* appears more precious than force; it is in some sense the absolute weapon, the only one which has the power to assure victory and domination over others, no matter what the circumstances and conditions of the struggle.[53]

Because of the hostile or suspicious reactions it provokes, *metis* tends to hide or disguise itself.[54] Such dissimulation is apparent in Homer's choice of *polytropos*, whose meaning remains polyvalent. Subsequently, in later literature, the figure of Odysseus appears both as the wise philosopher and the archvillain.[55] In the Homeric character, however, the multiple possibilities of this polyvalent character are held in a wonderful state of balance—summed up in that first epithet, *polytropos*.[56]

[53] Detienne-Vernant (1974), pp. 19-20. Compare *Il.* VII. 142-144, where a certain Lycourgus kills the club-bearing Areïthoos: "Lycourgus killed him by stealth (*dolos*), and not at all by force, / on a narrow path, where his iron club did not protect him from destruction." On the other hand, before his duel with Ajax, Hector proudly disdains such ruses: "Great as you are, I would not want to strike you / secretly lurking, but rather openly. . . ." (VII. 242-243).

[54] Cf. Detienne-Vernant (1974), pp. 29-31. The authors give as one of their examples Odysseus' conscious assumption of the appearance of gaucherie before addressing the Trojan assembly (*Il.* III. 216-224).

[55] See W. B. Stanford, *The Ulysses Theme*, 2nd ed. (Oxford, 1963) for an account of the later literary fortunes of Odysseus.

[56] Cf. Stanford (1963), p. 80.

The first four lines of the poem, then, programmatically announce the multiplicity that is Odysseus, both as active agent and as passive sufferer. They point as well to the multiple facets of the hero's outstanding characteristic, his mind—both in its positive or admirable aspect of intelligence, and in its negative undertones of trickery and deceit.

Homeros Philodysseus: THE POET'S BIAS

We have but begun to explore some of the implications of the proem to the *Odyssey*. In fact, we have only touched upon the first four verses, drawing attention to the relation between the poet and his Muse and the manner in which the hero is introduced. At the risk of seeming like a dog worrying his favorite bone, I must reiterate a fact of capital importance: the poet pronounces the first ten lines of the *Odyssey*; the rest of the poem belongs properly to the Muse—or, at least, the poet transformed by the inspiration of the Muse. These introductory lines are the only ones that can be ascribed to the poet *in propria persona*. In this light, the second half of the prologue (lines 6-9) demands renewed scrutiny, for here, speaking in his own voice, Homer reveals his partisanship for his hero.

Of the ten-line proem, it is striking that four verses deal exclusively with Odysseus' companions, with Odysseus' efforts on their behalf, and with their ultimate destruction:

ἀλλ᾽ οὐδ᾽ ὣς ἑτάρους ἐρρύσατο, ἱέμενός περ·
αὐτῶν γὰρ σφετέρῃσιν ἀτασθαλίῃσιν ὄλοντο,
νήπιοι, οἳ κατὰ βοῦς Ὑπερίονος Ἠελίοιο
ἤσθιον· αὐτὰρ ὁ τοῖσιν ἀφείλετο νόστιμον ἦμαρ.

But he could not save his companions, even though he
   tried;
for they were destroyed by their own recklessness,
poor fools, who devoured the cattle of the Sun;
but he deprived them of their day of return.

(1. 6-9)

Such emphasis on Odysseus' men creates an obvious lopsidedness in the proem. The loss of Odysseus' companions is unquestionably important, but it scarcely seems to be the most critical of his adventures;[57] and it is hard to see why this particular incident should be developed at such great length here in the invocation. What one expects, instead, is, in some sense, a programmatic statement for the entire *Odyssey*. Appeals to Homer's primitive mentality do not quite convince.[58] Our not unreasonable expectations of coherence are curiously thwarted.

Before I put forth my own suggestions as to how this problematic passage should be understood, it is necessary to examine and, finally, to dispose of the generally accepted interpretation of these lines. Later I will take up the bigger issue of the moral and ethical dimensions of the *Odyssey* which form its presuppositions. Here, I will merely consider the question insofar as it bears upon our understanding of the proem.

In his opening speech to the divine assembly in Book 1, Zeus complains that men blame the gods for their misery. He rebuts that charge by noting that men also bring troubles on themselves through their own recklessness:

οἱ δὲ καὶ αὐτοὶ
σφῇσιν ἀτασθαλίῃσιν ὑπὲρ μόρον ἄλγε᾽ ἔχουσιν.

They also on their own
by their own recklessness have griefs beyond what is
fated.

(1. 33-34)

---

[57] Rüter (1969), p. 50, calls the lines indispensable because of the need to explain Odysseus' complete isolation at the beginning of the poem. He fails to explain, however, why this could not have been accomplished in a word or two, with Homer reserving a fuller explanation for a later place in the poem.

[58] Van Groningen (1946), p. 286, goes a desperate route when he calls lines 6-9 "a by-path which he [the poet] certainly did not mean to tread" and explains them by "the casual nature of the association of his thoughts. . . . The result is that an element of very little interest in the whole finds a place here."

The word *atasthaliai* (which, I would warn, must not be translated as 'sin' or even 'sin against the gods'; 'blind recklessness'
or 'reckless mistakes' provide better renderings) occurs both
in Zeus' speech and in line 7. The common view imports not
only the sense but the context of line 34 into the proem.[59] In
Zeus' mouth, *atasthaliai* unquestionably refer to those crimes
for which men alone are responsible. That, of course, is the
point of his entire speech whose purpose is to absolve the gods
of a role in the sufferings of mankind. But can it be correct
or permissible to transfer the larger context of *atasthaliai* here
into the earlier passage? In the very opening lines of the poem,
does the poet really want to stress the point that the companions of Odysseus perished deservedly, that they lost their
lives through their own responsibility and *not* through the
fault of the gods? Such an interpretation seems far-fetched
and is a priori unlikely; nor, in fact, is it borne out by the
account of the destruction of Odysseus' men later in the *Odyssey* (see below p. 230).

We need a more satisfactory explanation, one that takes
into account the integrity of the proem—whose subject is the
aner polytropos—and gives the verbal parallel to Zeus' speech
its due. A glance at a few other passages involving similar
constructions with *atasthaliai* provides precisely that. The closest
parallel to the seventh line of the *Odyssey* comes from *Il.* IV.
409 where, responding to Agamemnon's rebuke of Diomedes,
Sthenelos claims that both Diomedes and he are better men
than their fathers. That is because, trusting in the gods, they
succeeded in storming Thebes with a smaller force, while their
fathers not only failed but lost their lives in the attempt through
their "reckless stupidity" (Lattimore's translation): κεῖνοι δὲ
σφετέρῃσιν ἀτασθαλίῃσιν ὄλοντο.[60] The weight of the

[59] Consider, for example, Rüter (1969), p. 78: "V. 34 klingt so stark an
V. 7 an, dass wir sicher sein können, die Worte des Zeus von den Leiden der
Menschen auch auf die Gefährten beziehen zu dürfen."

[60] It appears from this passage that *Od.* 1. 7 is a formulaic line, and one
should be leery of making too much of its unique significance.

passage lies not in the opposition between destruction brought about by the gods and that which has a purely human cause, but rather in the contrast between "us" and "them"—our success versus their failure. According to Sthenelos, "our" fathers' faults led to their destruction; "we" are superior because we are free of those faults. The same point can be gleaned from another passage. Shortly before his final ordeal with Achilles, Hector realizes that his folly has brought destruction upon his own people: ὤλεσα λαὸν ἀτασθαλίῃσιν ἐμῇσιν (XXII. 104). No sins against the gods are at issue. With the possessive, "my" recklessness, Hector assumes the blame for the destruction of his own people and at the same time absolves the Trojans of any fault. Finally, in the *Odyssey* itself, Eurylochus places the sole blame on Odysseus for the loss of men in the Cyclops' cave: τούτου γὰρ καὶ κεῖνοι ἀτασθαλίῃσιν ὄλοντο (10. 437). In each of these examples, similar constructions of *atasthaliai* with possessive adjectives or pronouns serve to make a similar point: to place the blame for a destructive act on one party while absolving another.

With these passages in mind, we may return to the beginning of the *Odyssey*. A straightforward interpretation of the parallel expressions in lines 34 and 7 of the *Odyssey* must note that in both places *atasthaliai* with its possessives involve antitheses: gods and mortals in the one case; Odysseus and his men in the other. Zeus tries to exculpate the gods from human misery; Homer in the proem exculpates Odysseus from the destruction of his companions.[61] Zeus asserts the gods' innocence; the poet asserts the innocence of his hero.

---

[61] Cf. Maronitis (1973), p. 95: "Lines 7-9 must not be understood as a programmatic criticism of the behavior of the companions, but rather as a kind of indirect and sorrowful defense of Odysseus for the loss of his companions." Maronitis underlines the importance of these verses for the characterization of Odysseus. But I would place the emphasis not, as he does, on *Odysseus philhetairos* but rather on *Homeros philodysseus*. See also M. H. van der Valk, *Textual Criticism of the Odyssey* (Leiden, 1949), p. 243, on Zeus' speech: "For here even the god tries to exculpate himself from moral responsibility by accusing the other party." Consider also A. Heubeck, *Der Odyssee-Dichter und die Ilias* (Erlangen, 1954), p. 86, n. 121: "Auch in der

The invocation of the *Odyssey* demonstrates the poet's desire to relieve Odysseus of any blame for the death of his own men. Once again, the contrast with the beginning of the *Iliad* is strikingly instructive. There, the wrath of Achilles is blamed for the destruction of countless *Greeks*, and is also, it may be noted, described in four lines. What is shocking about the *menis* of Achilles is not that it should lead to the deaths of many Trojans—which, of course, it does—but that its consequences backfire upon those who should naturally be his friends.[62] But in the one place where he can speak in his own name, the poet of the *Odyssey* defends and proclaims the innocence of his hero. Eustathius was right to call Homer *philodysseus*.[63] Less obviously, the poet completely suppresses a major cause of Odysseus' troubles; the proem is silent about the blinding of Polyphemus, which is only revealed some sixty lines later. From the outset, then, Homer reveals a desire to present Odysseus in a favorable light. Such bias may entail the suppression or playing down of certain unsavory incidents; it may also require the rearrangement of the poet's traditional material in order to bring out the more positive aspects of Odysseus' character. Subsequent analysis will demonstrate how the bias of the poet affects the structure of the *Odyssey* and the characterization of its hero.

To speak of Homer's partisanship may appear to contradict what was noted earlier concerning the delicate balance between positive and negative qualities the poet maintains in his portrait of Odysseus. The contradiction, however, is only apparent and leads to an important conclusion: only the poet's bias for Odysseus allows him to keep all those ambiguous and paradoxical aspects of his hero in a state of balanced tension.

... Formulierung des Prooimions, die auf das Thrinakia-Abenteuer vorausweist, liegt der Akzent weniger auf der Selbstschuld als auf der Tatsache, dass Odysseus nicht an dem Untergang der Gefährten schuldig war."

[62] Rüter (1969), pp. 31-32, sees the announcement of many sufferings in the proems of both the *Iliad* and the *Odyssey* as a "Grundthema der frühgriechischen Epik."

[63] 1878. 47.

The Beginning of the *Odyssey*

τῶν ἁμόθεν γε, θεά, θύγατερ Διός, εἰπὲ καὶ ἡμῖν.

Of these things, from some point at least, goddess,
   daughter of Zeus, tell us too.

Having studied the proem, we must at long last venture to begin the *Odyssey* as a whole, taking our bearings from a simple observation. The *Odyssey* recounts the Return of Odysseus and begins, as Horace says all epics should, in the middle of things—or rather, toward the end of the hero's adventures. Such a beginning requires the story to move backward and forward in time and space (even excluding the secondary strand of the Telemachy which occupies Books 1 to 4) and entails the lengthy first-person account of Books 9 to 12. According to some critics, the poet's presumed desire to have the hero narrate some of his adventures adequately accounts for the point of departure of our *Odyssey*. For example, the venerable Kirchhoff claims that "the apparently arbitrary choice of the starting point is determined by the poetic motive, whereby the greatest part of the adventures is presented in the form of an inserted narrative from the mouth of the hero himself, and this arbitrary choice finds in that circumstance alone its sufficient justification."[64] I must confess that I very rarely find a "poetic motive" a "sufficient justification" for anything; rather, such an explanation usually covers an insufficient understanding. In fact, we could easily imagine an *Odyssey* that still retains a first-person narrative but that starts elsewhere. For example, Odysseus could well have told his troubles to Circe or, in the manner of Scheherazade, to Calypso, during his long and uneventful years with her. The complex narrative texture of the poem and the compression of its action have elicited admiration since Aristotle.[65] But

[64] A. Kirchhoff, *Die homerische Odyssee*, 2nd ed. (Berlin, 1879), p. 165; cf. pp. 275-76. An earlier version of this section appeared in *AJP* 97 (1976):313-26.

[65] Cf. *Poetics* 8. 1451a22ff.; 23. 1459a30ff. E. Belzner, *Homerische Probleme* (Leipzig, 1912), 2:234, speaks of "eine meisterliche Konzentration des ganzen Epos und zugleich eine hochwillkommene Abwechslung im Stil der

such appreciation of the artistry of the *Odyssey* remains inadequate. Kitto correctly insists that the form of the *Odyssey* has some relevance to its meaning:

> It is traditional to say that the structure of the poem is one of the surest signs of the poet's genius. The raw material of which it is composed is abundant and diverse, far flung both in time and space, yet it is organised by Homer into a plot of the utmost clarity and simplicity, so that the action occupies only thirty-seven days. Is this not a masterstroke? Certainly—but let us not suppose that when we say this we are saying anything of great importance. The plot is an example of poiesis on the grand scale, and poiesis has to do with more than literary skill: it has something to do with mind and thought.[66]

Our admiration must not be allowed to obscure a crucial question: why does the *Odyssey* begin where it does?

The invocation itself compels us to reflect on this question. Once again, a comparison with the beginning of the *Iliad* highlights the peculiarities of the opening of the *Odyssey*. The subject of the *Iliad* is the Wrath of Achilles and its consequences. The Muse is given the theme and instructed precisely where to begin: the quarrel between Achilles and Agamemnon and its cause. Finally, the poet of the *Iliad* asks which god instigated the chain of events leading up to the quarrel. The *Odyssey* poses no such question. There, the poet indicates his theme:

Ἄνδρα μοι ἔννεπε, Μοῦσα, πολύτροπον, ὃς μάλα πολλὰ
πλάγχθη, ἐπεὶ Τροίης ἱερὸν πτολίεθρον ἔπερσε

---

epischen Erzählung und dazu ein erwünschter Ruhepunkt in der Mitte des Ganzen." Similarly, Bassett (1923), p. 341: "the constructive masterstroke of the poem is the concentration of the action into a period of approximately forty days."

[66] H.D.F. Kitto, *Poiesis* (Berkeley, 1966), p. 117. Kitto's whole discussion, pp. 116-52, is well worth reading.

> Tell me, Muse, of the man of many turns, who
> was driven far and wide, after he sacked the sacred
> citadel of Troy . . .

That subject is Odysseus' wanderings after the fall of Troy; in other words, it is the Return or *nostos* of Odysseus.[67] Now the *nostos* of Odysseus begins at Troy,[68] but the *Odyssey* begins elsewhere. Homer leaves the choice of the starting point to the Muse: "Of these things, from some point at least, tell us too." This final invocation of the Muse as "goddess, daughter of Zeus" is both solemn and august,[69] and lends weight to the importance of the impending choice. It seems fair to ask why the Muse, thus invoked, chooses this particular moment to begin the story, and it is worth our while to recover the significance of this particular beginning.

The story itself begins with a depiction of Odysseus' situation. He is described both in time and in space: the time is after the return of the other surviving heroes; the place is Calypso's island (1. 11-21). These lines, then, present the Muse's choice of the starting point.[70] At the beginning of his poem, the hero languishes in a state of complete isolation and immobility. The action, properly speaking, of the *Odyssey* begins

[67] Poems recounting the Returns of the heroes from Troy, called *Nostoi*, were known in antiquity. Only late summaries and sparse fragments have come down to us. But the existence of such traditions is already well attested from the tales of Nestor and Menelaus in Books 3 and 4 of the *Odyssey*.

[68] As does his account to the Phaeacians (9. 39) and to his wife (beginning with the first adventure of the Cicones) (23. 310).

[69] W. F. Bakker, *The Greek Imperative* (Amsterdam, 1966), pp. 11ff., points out that the Muses are usually addressed in the present imperative in Greek (cf. ἔννεπε in the first line). While Bakker does not discuss εἰπέ in *Od.* 1. 10, his study suggests that the aorist stem was generally held to be more suitable to prayer than to invocation. Cf. K. Lehrs, "Das Proömium der Odyssee," *RM* 19 (1864):305.

[70] Cf. Woodhouse (1930), p. 28; Rüter (1969), pp. 42ff.; and Bassett (1923), p. 343: "vss. 11-19a, not paralleled in the *Iliad*, are made necessary by ἁμόθεν (vs. 10), which needs a clearer demarcation." Both Rüter and Bassett view the proem as extending to line 21 and hence fail to take seriously enough the distinction between the first ten lines and the rest of the poem and, hence, the importance of the Muse.

on Olympus with the first divine council. A precondition to that action appears to be the absence of Poseidon, who is off feasting among the Aethiopians (1. 22-26). The immobility of Odysseus can only be altered by divine action. Its source is Athena. Not suprisingly, it is the impetus of Athena which puts Odysseus into motion, for Athena is Odysseus' special patron. The bond between them arises from the similarities of their natures; as the goddess herself puts it in Book 13:

. . . εἰδότες ἄμφω
κέρδε᾽, ἐπεὶ σὺ μέν ἐσσι βροτῶν ὄχ᾽ ἄριστος
    ἁπάντων
βουλῇ καὶ μύθοισιν, ἐγὼ δ᾽ ἐν πᾶσι θεοῖσι
μήτι τε κλέομαι καὶ κέρδεσιν.

                            . . . we both know
tricks, since you are by far the best among all men
in counsel and tales, but I among all the gods
have renown for wit (*metis*) and tricks.
                            (13. 296-299)

In Book 3 Nestor speaks to Telemachus about the wondrous character of this relationship and hopes that Telemachus will enjoy similar protection from the goddess:[71]

εἰ γάρ σ᾽ ὣς ἐθέλοι φιλέειν γλαυκῶπις Ἀθήνη
ὡς τότ᾽ Ὀδυσσῆος περικήδετο κυδαλίμοιο
δήμῳ ἔνι Τρώων, ὅθι πάσχομεν ἄλγε᾽ Ἀχαιοί—
οὐ γάρ πω ἴδον ὧδε θεοὺς ἀναφανδὰ φιλεῦντας
ὡς κείνῳ ἀναφανδὰ παρίστατο Παλλὰς Ἀθήνη.

Would that grey-eyed Athena should care to love you
as once she cherished mighty Odysseus
in the land of the Trojans, where we Achaeans suffered
    woes—

---

[71] For Athena's relationship to Telemachus, compare that of Diomedes and Athena in the *Iliad*. There, too, the goddess extends her protection from father to son.

for I never saw the gods showing such open affection
as Pallas Athena stood by him for all to see.

(3. 218-222)

At Troy, Athena constantly stood by Odysseus, loving and
supporting him. In the action of the *Odyssey*, from the time
Odysseus leaves Calypso's isle to the final truce in Ithaca,
Athena likewise aids her favorite, both directly (after his arrival on Ithaca) and indirectly (among the Phaeacians). But
between Odysseus' departure from Troy and the moment at
which the poem opens, Athena is absent.

Among critics, the absence of the goddess has not gone
unnoticed, but none of their explanations, which range from
appeals to "artistic and technical requirements"[72] to some
kind of symbolic interpretation, carries much conviction. One
scholar, for example, suggests that "The nature of the material
[its fairy-tale character] made it inconvenient to introduce the
goddess in a majority of the episodes, and she could not be
popping in and out like a jack-in-the-box. Consequently it
seemed better to leave her out entirely in this portion of the
poem."[73] Another is content to ascribe Athena's absence to
the "poet's manner," whatever that may be, and adds: "The
adventures are more thrilling than if Odysseus were under the
constant protection of Athena. . . ."[74] Possibly, but not necessarily. The presence of the gods does not in and of itself
remove suspense, as can easily be recognized by comparing
Book 5 of the *Iliad*, where Athena dominates the action, to
the subsequent books where no gods are present.[75] Furthermore, one may well question whether the desire to thrill the
audience plays a dominant role in the adventure tales. A very
different approach relates Odysseus' wanderings to a dark
chthonic world where Athena, who belongs to the clear Olym-

[72] Calhoun, (1940), p. 275.

[73] Calhoun (1940), pp. 274-75.

[74] S. Bassett, "Athena and the Adventures of Odysseus," *CJ* 13 (1918):528.

[75] Cf. S. Benardete, "The *Aristeia* of Diomedes and the Plot of the Iliad," *ΑΓΩΝ* 2 (1968):17ff.

pian sphere, can find no place: "In Ithaca and Troy he [Odysseus] stands in closest relation to his goddess. . . . But as soon as he embarks, leaving the coast of Troy, the chthonic world embraces him."[76] This view raises more problems than it solves, since the Homeric epics themselves suggest no clear distinction between the chthonic and the Olympian. Finally, an allegorizing tendency is evident in some explanations. For instance: "Athena, as the goddess of wisdom, stands for Odysseus' total σοφία, and it is appropriate that she does not appear while he is in the process of acquiring the various separate parts of his knowledge."[77]

If these interpretations leave us dissatisfied, we have no choice but to return to the text in the hope of discovering a more convincing explanation. One must begin from Athena's own explanation for her absence in Book 13 where, for the first time since Troy, she again appears to Odysseus face to face. There, she claims she did not wish to quarrel with her uncle Poseidon, who was angered by Odysseus' treatment of Polyphemus (13. 341-343; cf. 6. 329-331). Many critics gullibly swallow the goddess' alibi,[78] but her excuse is at best partial. In fact, Odysseus, the man of many wiles, seems well aware of its inadequacy, for he has just told the goddess:

τοῦτο δ᾽ ἐγὼν εὖ οἶδ᾽, ὅτι μοι πάρος ἠπίη ἦσθα,
ἧος ἐνὶ Τροίῃ πολεμίζομεν υἷες Ἀχαιῶν.

---

[76] P. Philippson, "Die vorhomerische und die homerische Gestalt des Odysseus," *MH* 4 (1947):15.

[77] A. Amory, "Omens and Dreams in the Odyssey" (Ph.D. diss., Harvard University, 1957), p. 86. Amory is followed recently by D. Wender, *The Last Scenes of the Odyssey*, Mnemosyne Suppl. 52 (Leiden, 1978), p. 30; and J. H. Finley, *Homer's Odyssey* (Cambridge Mass., 1978), p. 31. Similarly, already C. F. Nägelsbach, *Die homerische Theologie* (Nuremberg, 1840), pp. 51-52.

[78] See, for instance, H. Erbse, *Beiträge zum Verständnis der Odyssee* (Berlin, 1972), p. 158; G. B. Bona, *Studi sull' Odissea* (Turin, 1966), pp. 48-49; and U. Hölscher, *Untersuchungen zur Form der Odyssee*, Hermes Einzel. 6 (Berlin, 1939), p. 83, who surely oversimplifies: "Poseidon tritt ab, Athena tritt auf: das ist für die Odyssee bezeichnend, die den Streit der Götter nicht mehr erträgt." Cf. also R. Lattimore's Introduction to *The Odyssey of Homer* (New York, 1965), p. 11.

αὐτὰρ ἐπεὶ Πριάμοιο πόλιν διεπέρσαμεν αἰπήν,
βῆμεν δ᾽ ἐν νήεσσι, θεὸς δ᾽ ἐκέδασσεν Ἀχαιούς,
οὐ σέ γ᾽ ἔπειτα ἴδον, κούρη Διός, οὐδ᾽ ἐνόησα
νηὸς ἐμῆς ἐπιβᾶσαν, ὅπως τί μοι ἄλγος ἀλάλκοις . . .
πρίν γ᾽ ὅτε Φαιήκων ἀνδρῶν ἐν πίονι δήμῳ
θάρσυνάς τε ἔπεσσι καὶ ἐς πόλιν ἤγαγες αὐτή.

This I know full well, that formerly you were kind to me
when we sons of the Achaeans fought at Troy.
But when we sacked the steep city of Priam,
and boarded our ships, and a god scattered the Achaeans,
I never saw you thereafter, daughter of Zeus, nor noticed
you boarding my ship, so that you might ward off from
  me some disaster . . .
until the time in the fertile land of the Phaeacians
you encouraged me with words and yourself led me into
  the city.

(13. 314-319; 322-323)

Odysseus, it appears, knows the precise extent and duration of the goddess' absence; in addition, he alludes to his recognition of Athena disguised as a small girl on Scheria (7. 19ff.).[79] The goddess' alibi covers only the period *after* the blinding of the Cyclops and gives no account of her whereabouts during the preceding period, from the time Odysseus left Troy up to the Polyphemus incident. The resultant inconsistency has been succinctly put: "Athena's absence in the tale of wandering is not exactly coincident with the wrath of Poseidon; the goddess fails to aid Odysseus in his adventures prior to the blinding of Polyphemus, when she would not have offended Poseidon by so doing. . . ."[80] Upon reflection, then, it turns out that "Athena's reply is, it must be confessed, of the feeblest, and is in fact false."[81]

This conclusion finds confirmation in an examination of Odysseus' narration of his adventures in Books 9-12. There,

[79] For a detailed discussion of this passage, see pp. 201f. below.

[80] Calhoun (1940), pp. 268-69. Cf. J. A. Scott, "The First Book of the Odyssey," *TAPA* 67 (1936):5.

[81] Woodhouse (1930), p. 38.

we find that Athena is mentioned only three times, and each time, the reference is significant. Her name occurs twice in the Nekyia, Odysseus' visit with the dead. First, she is named as the judge in the famous contest between Ajax and Odysseus over the arms of the slain Achilles, that is, at a time when she was still well-disposed to Odysseus—for her favorite won the contest (11. 547). Athena comes up again as one of Heracles' escorts (along with Hermes) in that hero's descent into Hades (11. 626). That passage suggests a contrast between the divine aid enjoyed by Heracles and its absence in Odysseus' own journey to the Shades. The sole other occurrence of Athena's name comes at a crucial point in Odysseus' story. In the cave of Polyphemus Odysseus plots his escape and vengeance for the men who perished:

> αὐτὰρ ἐγὼ λιπόμην κακὰ βυσσοδομεύων,
> εἴ πως τισαίμην, δοίη δέ μοι εὖχος ᾿Αθήνη.

> But I was left brooding evil thoughts,
> if somehow I might pay him back, and Athena might
>   grant me glory.

> (9. 316-317)

What makes this passage so crucial is that here, immediately *before* the crime that provokes Poseidon's wrath, Athena does not intervene on behalf of the hero. Odysseus' invocation of the goddess at this critical moment highlights her absence prior to the Cyclops adventure and reveals the feebleness of her later excuse for not aiding Odysseus. Perhaps the goddess herself has reason to be evasive and to hide her motive for not supporting Odysseus during his wanderings.

The *Odyssey* itself unambiguously states why Athena refrained from helping the hero. *The goddess was angry.* The references to the *Wrath of Athena* have been collected and discussed by others,[82] but they bear reexamination; taken together, they present an ensemble wherein the theme of the goddess' anger progressively unfolds and is firmly established

---

[82] See especially Woodhouse (1930), pp. 35-39; and J. Irmscher, *Götterzorn bei Homer* (Leipzig, 1950), pp. 69-71.

in the early books of the *Odyssey*. In the first book, the suitors are listening to Phemius' rendition of the Return of the Achaeans:

ὁ δ᾽ Ἀχαιῶν νόστον ἄειδε
λυγρόν, ὃν ἐκ Τροίης ἐπετείλατο Παλλὰς Ἀθήνη.

He sang the return of the Achaeans,
the baneful one, from Troy, which Pallas Athena
inflicted upon them.

(1. 326-27)

Thus it was Athena who made the homecoming of the Greeks baneful. Some further details are supplied by Nestor in the third book, when he recounts the events after the fall of Troy:

αὐτὰρ ἐπεὶ Πριάμοιο πόλιν διεπέρσαμεν αἰπήν,
βῆμεν δ᾽ ἐν νήεσσι, θεὸς δ᾽ ἐκέδασσεν Ἀχαιούς,
καὶ τότε δὴ Ζεὺς λυγρὸν ἐνὶ φρεσὶ μήδετο νόστον
Ἀργείοις, ἐπεὶ οὔ τι νοήμονες οὐδὲ δίκαιοι
πάντες ἔσαν· τῶ σφεων πολέες κακὸν οἶτον ἐπέσπον
μήνιος ἐξ ὀλοῆς γλαυκώπιδος ὀβριμοπάτρης.

But when we had sacked the steep city of Priam,
we boarded our ships, and a god scattered the Achaeans,
even then Zeus planned in his heart a baneful return
for the Argives, since not all were conscientious
or just; hence many of them found an evil fate
from the dread wrath of the grey-eyed daughter of the
    mighty father.

(3. 130-135)

Here we learn that Zeus too was involved in the misfortunes of the Greeks. That should not surprise us if we consider some parallel episodes in the *Odyssey*. The angry Helios asks Zeus' requital for the loss of his cattle (12. 377-383), and Zeus himself carries out the required punishment. So too, Zeus sanctions Poseidon's wrath against Odysseus and his men after the blinding of Polyphemus (9. 553-554).

Nestor continues by relating how, during the drunken assembly that followed the sack of Troy, Menelaus counselled

an immediate return home, but Agamemnon decided to stay
at Troy in an attempt to propitiate the angry goddess:

βούλετο γὰϱ ᾑα
λαὸν ἐϱυκακέειν, ῥέξαι θ' ἱεϱὰς ἑκατόμβας,
ὡς τὸν 'Αθηναίης δεινὸν χόλον ἐξακέσαιτο,
νήπιος, οὐδὲ τὸ ᾔδη, ὃ οὐ πείσεσθαι ἔμελλεν·
οὐ γάϱ τ' αἶψα θεῶν τϱέπεται νόος αἰὲν ἐόντων.

For indeed, he wished
to hold the people there and to sacrifice sacred
    hecatombs,
in order to appease the dreadful anger of Athena—
fool, he did not know that he was not to persuade her;
for the mind of the eternal gods is not quickly turned.
(3. 143-147)

The army then split between the two quarreling leaders, and
Odysseus went with Menelaus to Tenedos. There, a second
division arose when Odysseus decided to rejoin Agamemnon
who was still at Troy.[83] At that moment, with a premonition
of evil to come, Nestor fled and managed to return safely to
Pylos.

Nestor's account of Odysseus' vacillating actions have a
mysterious and intriguing ring to them. Presumably, Odysseus' decision to return to Agamemnon was the only occasion
on which Nestor and Odysseus ever disagreed: only a few
lines earlier, Nestor described the complete unanimity existing
between himself and Odysseus at Troy:

οὔτε ποτ' εἰν ἀγοϱῇ δίχα βάζομεν οὔτ' ἐνὶ βουλῇ,
ἀλλ' ἕνα θυμὸν ἔχοντε νόῳ καὶ ἐπίφϱονι βουλῇ
φϱαζόμεθ' 'Αϱγείοισιν ὅπως ὄχ' ἄϱιστα γένοιτο.

Never did we speak on different sides in the
assembly or council, but with one mind and careful
    planning,
we considered how things might be best for the Argives.
(3. 127-129)

---

[83] For a possible allusion to this incident, see Aeschylus *Agamemnon* 841,
where Agamemnon praises Odysseus' loyalty.

Odysseus himself, when he begins the narrative of his adventures, tells us nothing more than that he left Troy. *Iliothen*, "from Ilium," he begins his tale (9. 39). One can only suspect that Odysseus' delayed return to Troy suggests his awareness of Athena's anger as well as a belated attempt to propitiate the goddess and to avoid the impending consequences of her wrath.

To this wrath there are further references in Book 4 when Menelaus relates the fate of Locrian Ajax (4. 499-511). The latter was also the object of Athena's hatred, yet he might indeed have escaped death. But at the very moment of safety, his impious boasting caused his destruction by Poseidon. The sequence of wraths—first Athena, then Poseidon—in the Ajax story provides an intriguing parallel to Odysseus' fate, though the outcome there is different. So far, these references suggest a general wrath of Athena against the whole Greek army on its return from Troy. In the fifth book, however, just before Odysseus' first appearance in the *Odyssey*, the god Hermes, in the course of conveying the instructions of Olympus to Calypso to allow the hero to return home, makes explicit the relation of Odysseus' misfortunes to Athena's anger. He states:

. . . τοι ἄνδρα παρεῖναι ὀϊζυρώτατον ἄλλων,
τῶν ἀνδρῶν οἳ ἄστυ πέρι Πριάμοιο μάχοντο
εἰνάετες, δεκάτῳ δὲ πόλιν πέρσαντες ἔβησαν
οἴκαδ᾽· ἀτὰρ ἐν νόστῳ Ἀθηναίην ἀλίτοντο,
ἥ σφιν ἐπῶρσ᾽ ἄνεμόν τε κακὸν καὶ κύματα μακρά.
ἔνθ᾽ ἄλλοι μὲν πάντες ἀπέφθιθεν ἐσθλοὶ ἑταῖροι,
τὸν δ᾽ ἄρα δεῦρ᾽ ἄνεμός τε φέρων καὶ κῦμα πέλασσε.

. . . you have with you a man most miserable
of all those who fought around the city of Priam
for nine years, and in the tenth they sacked the city
and embarked for home; but during their return, they
   sinned against Athena,
and she raised against them an evil wind and high waves.
Then all his other noble companions perished,
but him the wind and the wave carried and brought here.
                                                      (5. 105-111)

An ancient commentator on these lines notes: "these verses are odd and at variance with the story."[84] Modern scholars question the soundness of the text although there are no solid grounds for doing so.[85] I know of only one critic who tries to defend the lines on the basis of Hermes' motivation *ek prosopou*, but unsuccessfully: "The god despises the mortal (cf. l. 105), only relates his adventures superficially and inaccurately and does not omit adding maliciously that the same Athene who has now sent him on this unpleasant voyage [to Calypso's] . . . formerly caused the shipwreck herself."[86] This interpretation attributes motives to Hermes for which there is no evidence in the text. We may admit that these verses are indeed as odd as the Scholiast claims, but they are not at odds with the plot. After all, up to this moment, the net of allusions to the wrath of Athena has encircled Odysseus ever more tightly. Now, at last, this remarkable passage explicitly implicates Athena in Odysseus' troubles, from his departure from Ilium, including the loss of his companions, and continuing up to his arrival on Ogygia. The placement of these lines— immediately before Odysseus' first entrance in the *Odyssey*— could not be more emphatic or significant. The goddess who, from now on, will protect and support the hero has not always been so favorably disposed. Her present benevolence must be understood as a change from an earlier hostility.

Some scholars acknowledge the existence of a Wrath of Athena, but they generally view it as a mere narrative device to explain the goddess' absence and Odysseus' troubles prior to Polyphemus' curse. They consider the wrath a matter of secondary importance, awkwardly handled, and, all in all, rather a blemish. Woodhouse, for example, concludes his discussion of the anger of Athena with a sigh of resignation: "In

[84] Scholium PQ at 5. 105.

[85] For textual questions concerning these lines, see Clay (1976), p. 322, n. 23.

[86] Van der Valk (1949), pp. 228-29. G. Dimock, "Punishment in the Odyssey," *Yale Review* n.s. 60 (1971):204-214, while discussing the earlier references to Athena's anger, ignores this passage. Hence, he mistakenly concludes: "There is no evidence whatever that Athena was ever angry at him [Odysseus] specifically" (210).

the great banquet of Homer one must take the thick with the thin."[87]

I consider the Wrath of Athena to be neither a flaw nor a feeble device. Rather, I understand it to be a key to the structure of the entire *Odyssey* and to provide the answer to the question: why does the *Odyssey* begin where it does? In the opening scene of the poem, Athena intervenes on behalf of Odysseus. In all that follows, she aids him constantly. In all events from Odysseus' departure from Troy, by contrast, she had helped him not at all.[88] The beginning of the *Odyssey* signals the end of Athena's anger.[89]

This interpretation admittedly is open to an obvious objection; it more or less ignores the explicit motivation for the *Odyssey*'s beginning: the temporary absence of Poseidon. His absence is a precondition for the gods' decision to allow Odysseus to make his way home. The anger of Poseidon will continue to affect Odysseus' journey until he finally reaches Ithaca. It will influence Athena to help Odysseus only in indirect and hidden ways until he is home. Yet Poseidon's absence in Book 1 is only a necessary but not sufficient condition for putting Odysseus into motion. Zeus may remember Aegisthus and his fate, but it is Athena who must draw his attention to Odysseus. In Book 5 when Poseidon catches sight of Odysseus on his flimsy raft, he immediately realizes that the gods no longer oppose the hero:

[87] Woodhouse (1930), p. 39. Cf. Irmscher (1950), p. 71, n. 1.

[88] Cf. Scott (1936), pp. 5-6: "It is a remarkable fact and the key to the *Odyssey* that Athena does nothing for Odysseus during all the long years of his wanderings which were prior to the first book, and that she is not absent from a single book which describes events later in time than that book." This elegant formulation points to the pivotal character of the moment the *Odyssey* begins. But Scott totally ignores the role of Athena's anger and places all responsibility for the goddess' intervention upon Zeus.

[89] The other wraths of divinities against mortals in the *Odyssey* offer interesting parallels. For these wraths each involve something quite rare in the poem: a divine scene containing a conversation between the injured god and Zeus (12. 377-387; 13. 125-158). Cf. Fenik (1974), p. 209. The pattern of these divine scenes suggests that the opening *concilium deorum* of the *Odyssey* has a similar function.

Ὢ πόποι, ἦ μάλα δὴ μετεβούλευσαν θεοὶ ἄλλως
ἀμφ᾽ Ὀδυσῆϊ ἐμεῖο μετ᾽ Αἰθιόπεσσιν ἐόντος

Alas, indeed the gods have changed their minds
concerning Odysseus, while I was among the
Aethiopians.

(5. 286-287)

Athena's proddings produce the divine assembly's change of
heart in respect to Odysseus.

The anger of Athena against Odysseus is only alluded to
sparingly in the poem, and its precise cause is not immediately
apparent. The claim of its crucial importance for an understanding of the Odyssey clearly requires further justification.
A larger and at times circuitous investigation must be undertaken, one that keeps in mind two crucial questions. 1) Why
was the goddess angry at Odysseus? 2) Why did Athena stop
being angry? Only convincing answers to these questions can
ultimately validate the thematic importance we have ascribed
to the Wrath of Athena. They in turn demand an overall
examination of the relations between gods and men in the
Odyssey—and especially between Athena and Odysseus–and
of the lines of demarcation separating mortals from immortals
and of the common interests uniting them. For the present, it
must suffice to recognize that a study of Athena's anger returns
us to the prologue of the Odyssey and confirms what we there
observed to be the partisanship of the poet for his hero. Even
as he absolves Odysseus of blame for the destruction of his
companions, even as he passes in silence over the cause of
Poseidon's anger, so too does the poet play down the degree
of Odysseus' involvement in Athena's wrath.

The complexity of the Odyssey is in large part due to the
shattering of a simple chronological and spatial framework.
The impetus for this innovation may have arisen from profound thematic considerations as much as from a desire to
experiment with complex narrative techniques. To put it simply, if Homer had begun the story of Odysseus' nostos from
its natural starting point, from Troy, he would have had to
begin from the anger of Athena against his hero—"Who among

the gods?" (Τίς τ' ἄρ . . . θεῶν) as the *Iliad* has it.⁹⁰ Perhaps others had done so.⁹¹ But the decision to present a favorable account of his hero—what I have called the poet's bias—entailed the further decision to minimize Odysseus' involvement in Athena's wrath. That, in turn, demanded a radical restructuring of the story of Odysseus, one that takes as its point of departure the end of Athena's anger. A series of intelligible decisions thus results in the distinctive shape of our *Odyssey*.

⁹⁰ It may well have been traditional in the epic to begin from a divine agent. Outside of the beginning of the *Iliad*, we have two pieces of evidence from the *Odyssey* itself. In Book 1 Phemius sings of the baneful homecoming of the Greeks from Troy, "which Pallas Athena set upon them" (327). When Demodocus begins his song of the Wooden Horse, we are told: ὁ δ' ὁρμηθεὶς θεοῦ ἄρχετο (8. 499). The Greek is ambiguous; it could mean "stirred by the god, i.e., the Muse, he began" or "stirred, he began from the god, i.e., Athena." See Stanford's (1965) note at 8. 449.

⁹¹ There can be no doubt that traditions about Odysseus were in existence before our *Odyssey*. The last line of the proem as good as states this: "Of these things, from some point at least, tell us too." The significance of the beginning of the *Odyssey* would not have been lost on an audience well-acquainted with tales of the *nostos* of Odysseus.

CHAPTER II

ODYSSEUS

κερδαλέος κ' εἴη καὶ ἐπίκλοπος ὅς σε παρέλθοι
ἐν πάντεσσι δόλοισι . . .

He would have to be a sly one and a thievish rogue, who
    could surpass you
in all your wiles . . .
        (13. 291-292)

Our preliminary study of the proem has raised more questions
than it has answered. The poet's awareness of his privileged
position as mediator between gods and men, the purposeful
structuring of his narrative, and the portrayal of his enigmatic
hero—these are some of the strands that emanate from the
proem, and these are the red threads we must follow through
the labyrinth of the poem. At its center is Odysseus, the man
of many wiles, whose most characteristic trait is "the fundamental ambiguity of his essential qualities."[1] We must exercise patience and dexterity to track and perhaps to capture
this elusive figure. For *metis* does not yield to frontal assault
but escapes from our grasp like the ghosts of Hades or the
varied shapes of Proteus. Comprehension of the multiplicity
of Odysseus demands a multiple and sometimes indirect approach. His name and origins, certain objects with which he
is closely associated, and his relation to other heroes provide
varied perspectives on this most complex and intriguing figure
of Greek literature.

THE NAME OF ODYSSEUS

Language, modern linguists assure us, is an arbitrary system
of signs. The Greeks were not so sure. The debate between
those who maintain that language is purely conventional and

[1] Stanford (1963), p. 79.

their opponents who believe that language is "by nature" has a long history which cannot be traced here.[2] But most early etymological speculation presupposes that a name and the thing denominated are closely related, i.e., that a name, correctly understood, indicates the nature of the thing named. The fact that many Greek proper names have transparent meanings (e.g., Aristodemus 'Best-of-the-people,' Telemachus 'Far-fighter,' and Patroclus 'Glory-of-the-father') lends powerful support to such a view. The more opaque names and epithets of the most mysterious of beings, the gods, and the famous heroes of the past tease the ingenuity of the Greeks from the earliest times. When Sappho ponders the meaning of Hesperus, the evening star (104a L.-P.), or when Aeschylus has the Chorus of the *Agamemnon* pause to reflect on the name of Helen (689-690), or when, in the same play, Cassandra recognizes the source of her destruction in the name of Apollo (1080ff.), they are not indulging in mere punning or wordplay. Rather, they manifest a time-honored conviction that a proper understanding of a name will reveal the hidden nature of what the name designates. Such a name is called an *onoma eponumon*, a name that corresponds appropriately to the person or object designated. Homer and Hesiod offer numerous examples of this kind of etymological thinking,[3] and it is not surprising that Homer should allow himself to speculate about the meaning of the name of Odysseus.

Our attention has already been drawn to that name indirectly through its omission in the proem, which introduced an anonymous hero whose polytropic character is revealed in his passive ability to endure great suffering and in his active role as the man of *metis*.[4] The same double perspective is retained at the end of the poem. After Odysseus and Penelope

---

[2] The most important ancient discussion is, of course, Plato's *Cratylus*.

[3] See E. Risch, "Namensdeutungen und Worterklärungen bei den ältesten griechischen Dichtern," in *Eumusia: Festgabe für E. Howald* (Zurich, 1947), pp. 72-91.

[4] Cf. D. Frame, *The Myth of Return in Early Greek Epic* (New Haven, 1978), concerning the connection between "mind" and "returning home" which Frame detects in the verbal root *nes-*.

are finally reunited and have taken their pleasure in lovemaking, they each tell their stories. Odysseus' summary of his long travels and adventures—of his Odyssey—is introduced as follows:

αὐτὰρ ὁ διογενὴς Ὀδυσεὺς ὅσα κήδε᾽ ἔθηκεν
ἀνθρώποις ὅσα τ᾽ αὐτὸς ὀϊζύσας⁵ ἐμόγησε,
πάντ᾽ ἔλεγ᾽.

But Zeus-born Odysseus told her all—all the troubles he set
upon men, and all that he himself had suffered in misery.
(23. 306-308)

Troubles inflicted and troubles endured—these are the two-fold aspects of the hero. The name itself, Odysseus, embraces both and is profoundly ambiguous in its significance.

Odysseus' naming is recounted within the framework of the famous recognition scene. The old nurse Eurycleia washes the feet of her master, who is still disguised as a beggar (19. 361ff.). As she touches the old scar which identifies the stranger as Odysseus, its history is told in a leisurely fashion—how, as a youth, Odysseus visited his maternal grandfather Autolycus and took part in a hunt for a boar on the slopes of Parnassus. The boar attacked and wounded Odysseus who then succeeded in killing the beast. The sons of Autolycus healed the wound, which left the identifying scar, and then sent the young hero home with splendid gifts. The parents rejoiced at the safe and triumphant return of their son, who recounted his adventures with the boar. At this point, the narrative returns to the main story: Eurycleia touches the old scar, recognizes it, and drops the foot of Odysseus into the washbasin with a great splash. Eurycleia's joy at the return of her absent master differs from the parents' simple joy of long ago which accompanied the return of their young son (χαῖρον νοστήσαντι 19. 463); hers is mixed with pain (χάρμα

⁵ Note the homophony between *oïdzysas*, 'having suffered woe,' and the name of Odysseus. Cf. 4. 152, 3. 95 = 4. 325, 4. 832, 5. 105, 11. 167.

καὶ ἄλγος 19.471). The old woman's eyes fill with tears and she gasps, "Indeed, you are Odysseus, dear child" (19. 474). Framed within the tale of the boar's hunt and Odysseus' scar—in the manner of Chinese boxes—is the story of Odysseus' naming by his grandfather Autolycus. At first, its connection to the narrative of the scar seems tangential, if not gratuitous. The only apparent link is that the hunt was undertaken in the company of Autolycus and his sons. At any rate, we get a brief description of Autolycus and an account of his earlier visit on the occasion of Odysseus' birth. At that time, Autolycus invited his grandson to visit him when he had grown up, promising to give him many gifts. And so, years later, Odysseus came to Parnassus and earned his scar. What first appear to be purely associative and somewhat rambling digressions turn out to be an exemplary model of the characteristic Homeric technique of ring-composition, in which narrative material is arranged in the general form *A B C B A*.[6] If ring-composition accounts for the formal structure of this digression, it does not in itself throw light on the organic interconnections of the passage on the level of content. To be sure, the story of how Odysseus acquired his scar follows quite reasonably upon Eurycleia's recognition of the scar, but Odysseus' acquisition of his name appears at first to be unrelated to the overall narrative frame.

In a well-known essay, Erich Auerbach begins his study of the Western tradition of the literary representation of reality

[6] W.A.A. van Otterlo, "Untersuchungen über Begriff, Anwendung, und Entstehung der griechischen Ringkomposition," *Med. Ned. Akad. Wetensch. Afd. Letter.* n.s. 7, 3 (1944):133, defines this structure as follows: "das an den Anfang gestellte Thema eines bestimmten Abschnitts wird nach einer längeren oder kürzeren sich darauf beziehenden Ausführung am Schluss wiederholt, so dass der ganze Abschnitt durch Sätze gleichen Inhalts und mehr oder weniger ähnlichen Wortlauts umrahmt und so zu einem einheitlichen, sich klar vom Kontext abhebenden Gebilde geschlossen wird." Van Otterlo, pp. 146-47, considers our passage "ein Musterbeispiel für unsere Kompositionsweise." For a schematic outline of the episode, see J. H. Gaisser, "A Structural Analysis of the Digressions in the Iliad and the Odyssey," *HSCP* 73 (1969):20-21.

by comparing the Homeric epic with Biblical narrative.[7] With admirable sensitivity, he contrasts the clarity, fullness, and plasticity of the epic with the inward and elliptical style of Biblical storytelling. For all his merits, Auerbach is rather unfortunate in choosing the passage involving Odysseus' scar to exemplify the epic style as "externalized, uniformly illuminated phenomena . . . in a perpetual foreground."[8] He claims that "When the young Euryclea (vv. 401ff.) sets the infant Odysseus on his grandfather Autolycus' lap after the banquet, the aged Euryclea . . . has entirely vanished from the stage and from the reader's mind."[9] Auerbach seems to forget that only Eurycleia, who was Odysseus' nurse and present at his naming, could pronounce the words

ἦ μάλ' Ὀδυσσεύς ἐσσι, φίλον τέκος . . .

You indeed are Odysseus, dear child . . .
(19. 474)

The formula in this line has occurred only twice before in the *Odyssey*. At the moment Circe recognizes Odysseus as *polytropos*, she exclaims:

ἦ σύ γ' Ὀδυσσεύς ἐσσι πολύτροπος . . .

You indeed are *polytropos* Odysseus . . .
(10. 330)

The formula is to be found once more, when Telemachus *denies* that the strange beggar suddenly beautified by Athena can be his father:

οὐ σύ γ' Ὀδυσσεύς ἐσσι πατὴρ ἐμός . . .

You indeed cannot be Odysseus, my father . . .
(16. 194)

---

[7] "Odysseus' Scar" in *Mimesis*, trans. W. R. Trask (Princeton, 1953), pp. 3-23.

[8] Auerbach (1953), p. 11.

[9] Auerbach (1953), p. 5. For a critique of Auerbach along different lines, see A. Köhnken, "Die Narbe des Odysseus," *Antike und Abendland* 22 (1976):101-114.

Yet Odysseus is indeed Telemachus' father, despite such denials; to Circe, he is the man of many turnings; but only for Eurycleia, present at his birth and childhood adventures, does he remain "dear child." Background illuminates foreground. The naming scene belongs within the context of the description of the scar. The name—and the story behind it—identifies Odysseus fully as much as his scar.[10] Odysseus' maternal grandfather, Autolycus, whose name suggests something like Lone Wolf, comes to Ithaca to name the infant. Eurycleia places the child on Autolycus' lap and urges him to choose a name for his grandson. Tactfully, she suggests "Polyaretus" or Much-Prayed-for.[11] But Autolycus has other ideas:

γαμβρὸς ἐμὸς θυγάτηρ τε, τίθεσθ' ὄνομ' ὄττι κεν εἴπω·
πολλοῖσιν γὰρ ἐγώ γε ὀδυσσάμενος τόδ' ἱκάνω,
ἀνδράσιν ἠδὲ γυναιξὶν ἀνὰ χθόνα
πουλυβότειραν·
τῷ δ' Ὀδυσεὺς ὄνομ' ἔστω ἐπώνυμον.

My son-in-law and daughter, give the name I say:
for I come here a curse (*odyssamenos*) to many
men and women all over the much-nurturing earth;
therefore let his name appropriately be Odysseus.
(19. 406-409)

Autolycus derives the name Odysseus from the verb *odysasthai*, which means 'to have hostile feelings or enmity toward

[10] See N. Austin, "The Function of Digressions in the *Iliad*," *GRBS* 7 (1966): 310: "The digression on Odysseus' scar . . . is not really on the scar at all. The scar is but the vehicle for the explication of the real subject, which is the name and identity of Odysseus." There may well be a subtle wordplay connecting name and scar. The Greek word for scar is *oulē*, and some of the variants of Odysseus' name (not attested in Homer but perhaps early) are Olysseus, Olytteus, from which we get the Latin Ulixes, Ulyxes. For a list of these variant spellings and their sources, see E. Wüst, "Odysseus," *RE* 17, 2 (1937), 1906-909.

[11] Cf. Eustathius 1871. 15-17. At 6. 280, Nausicaa flatters Odysseus by suggesting that the townspeople, observing the stranger in her company, might think him a "god much-prayed-for" (πολυάρητος θεός).

someone.'[12] The word embraces a range of meanings, including 'to be angry,' 'to hate someone,' 'to vex,' 'to trouble,' 'to offend.' A few translators have attempted to bring the play on words over into English. Fitzgerald translates: "odium and distrust I've won. Odysseus / should be his given name;"[13] Lattimore renders it as follows: "since I have come to this place distasteful to many . . . so let him be given / the name Odysseus, that is distasteful." Giving up on the pun, I have translated *odyssamenos* as 'a curse' to bring out the fact that the name Autolycus chooses is the very opposite of the one the nurse proposes. Eumaeus, the faithful swineherd, seems to allude to the ill-omened character of his absent master's name when he speaks of him to the disguised beggar:[14]

[12] Compare the two-line fragment from a lost play of Sophocles (Fr. 965 Pearson = 965 Radt): ὀρθῶς δ᾽ Ὀδυσσεύς εἰμ᾽ ἐπώνυμος κακῶν· / πολλοὶ γὰρ ὠδύσαντο δυσμενεῖς ἐμοί.

J.H.H. Schmidt, *Synonymik der griechischen Sprache* (Leipzig, 1879), 3:570, tries to distinguish *odysasthai* from its near synonyms and to illuminate the relation between feeling anger and hatred. However, he pays too little attention to its context. W. B. Stanford, "The Homeric Etymology of the Name Odysseus," *CP* 47 (1952):209, suggests that "its meaning was probably wide enough to imply either anger or hatred." The most thorough discussion of Homeric etymologizing and punning on Odysseus' name can be found in L. Rank, *Etymologiseering en verwandte Verschijnselen bij Homerus* (Assen, 1951), pp. 51-63. See also Risch (1947), pp. 85-86. For the practice of naming children after a characteristic of a parent or ancestor, see M. Sulzberger, "ONOMA EΠΩΝΥΜΟΝ: Les noms propres chez Homère," *REG* 39 (1926):381-447. See also the discussion of Maronitis (1973), pp. 152ff. and the quirky but stimulating essay of G. Dimock, "The Name of Odysseus," in *Homer: A Collection of Critical Essays*, ed. G. Steiner and R. Fagles (Englewood Cliffs, N.J., 1962), pp. 106-121. Dimock connects *odysasthai* with *odynē*, 'pain,' and translates the verb as "to cause pain and to be willing to do so" (107) and renders Odysseus as "Trouble." Homer certainly toys with the similarity in sound of *odynē* and Odysseus, as he does with *oïdzysas* and *odyromai*, 'to lament.' On the latter, see Rank (1951), pp. 51-52.

[13] Cf. Stanford's attempt in his commentary (1965, p. 332): "Since with the *odium* of many . . . let his name with significance be *Odysseus*."

[14] Cf. F. Adami, "Zu P. Linde, Homerische Selbsterläuterungen," *Glotta* 18 (1930):111; and especially, H. Sedlmayer, "Lexikalisches und Exegetisches zu Homer," *Zeitschrift f. Oesterr. Gymn.* 61 (1910):294 (cited by Rank [1951], p. 63, n. 116), who renders Eumaeus' words as follows: "Haszmann hiesz mein Herr, ich schäme mich, es zu sagen, denn er liebte mich, sein richtigerer Name ist Liebermann."

τὸν μὲν ἐγών, ὦ ξεῖνε, καὶ οὐ παρεόντ᾽ ὀνομάζειν
αἰδέομαι· πέρι γάρ μ᾽ ἐφίλει καὶ κήδετο θυμῷ·
ἀλλά μιν ἠθεῖον καλέω καὶ νόσφιν ἐόντα.

Stranger, I am ashamed to name him in his absence.
For he loved me greatly and cared for me in his heart;
instead, I shall call him "dear friend" even if he is far
away.

(14. 145-147)

This interpretation of Odysseus' name is borne out indirectly by the fictitious name and lineage Odysseus concocts
when he introduces himself to his aged father in the last book
of the *Odyssey*. There, he calls himself Eperitus, son of Apheidon, grandson of Polypemon (24. 305-306). As we might
expect, all these names are significant and reveal something
about Odysseus' character. Pape-Benseler gives "Strife" as the
meaning of Eperitus, but offers no explanation.[15] It seems to
derive from ἐπήρεια, 'insulting treatment,' 'abuse,' and is
possibly related to ἀρειή, 'menace,' 'threat,' and Sanskrit
irasya, 'hostility,' cf. Latin *ira*, 'anger.'[16] Homer may also have
incorrectly connected it with ἐπαράομαι, 'to curse.' In any
case, the name Odysseus manufactures for himself corresponds closely to the meaning of his true name. Apheidon
clearly means 'Unsparing' and should, I suggest, not be connected with thrift but with ruthlessness, a quality not altogether foreign to Odysseus' character. We may remember Eu-
rymachus' plea at the beginning of the slaughter of the suitors:
"Spare your people" (σὺ δὲ φείδεο λαῶν 22.54). Mercilessly,
Odysseus rejects his entreaty. Finally, Polypemon, 'Much-pain,'
has the same double sense which conforms to all we have
observed of Odysseus; it can mean both 'Suffering-much-pain'
and 'Causing-much-pain.'

[15] *Griechische Eigennamen*, 2 vols. (Braunschweig, 1911) 1:364. The name
is not attested in F. Bechtel, *Die historischen Personennamen des Griechischen
bis zur Kaiserzeit* (Halle, 1917). That is not surprising, given its unpleasant
connotations. Eustathius 1962. 9-20, perhaps garbling an older tradition,
derives Eperitus from ἐρίζω, 'to quarrel,' or ἐπίρρητος, 'infamous.'
[16] See H. Frisk, *Griechisches etymologisches Wörterbuch* (Heidelberg, 1960),
1:135, 535.

The name of Odysseus is similarly double and my rendering, 'curse,' solves the problem of whether Autolycus' *odyssamenos* should be taken as active or passive—'angry at many' or 'incurring the anger of many.'[17] In Greek, the verb is in the middle voice, that is, something between active and passive, which, as Benveniste defines it, is "an act in which the subject is affected by the process and is himself situated within the process."[18] This double and reciprocal sense of incurring and dealing out enmity[19] perfectly suits the trickster Autolycus, of whom we have just learned:

> . . . ὃς ἀνθρώπους ἐκέκαστο
> κλεπτοσύνῃ θ᾽ ὅρκῳ τε. θεὸς δέ οἱ αὐτὸς ἔδωκεν
> Ἑρμείας. . . .

> . . . he surpassed all men
> in thievery and equivocation; and a god gave him this talent,
> Hermes. . . .

(19. 395-397)

'Curse,' as I have translated *odyssamenos*, also has the advantage of having religious overtones. Such a connotation is singularly fitting, since elsewhere in Homer *odysasthai* is used exclusively to designate divine displeasure or wrath. The verb occurs four times in the *Iliad*, and its subject is always Zeus or "the gods."[20] The most illuminating passage involving *odysasthai* appears in Book 6 within the context of the famous encounter between Diomedes and Glaucus on the battlefield, which ends with their discovery of ancient ties of hospitality

[17] The question already vexed the ancients, as the Scholium V at 19. 407 testifies. For it glosses *odyssamenos* as μισηθείς· ἢ ὀργὴν ἀγαγών· ἢ βλάψας, 'hated or provoking anger or causing injury.' Stanford (1952), pp. 209-213, traces scholarly opinion on this matter. His own view—that Homer maintains a delicate balance between the active and passive sense—comes very close to my own. Cf. Rank (1951), pp. 56ff.

[18] *Problèmes de linguistique générale*, 2 vols. (Paris, 1966), 1:168-75.

[19] Cf. W. W. Merry, ed., *Homer: Odyssey*, 2 vols. (Oxford, 1901), on 19. 406.

[20] VI. 138; VIII. 37 = VIII. 468; XVIII. 292.

between their families. The weight of mortality hangs over the meeting.[21] Only a short time before, Diomedes had wounded both Ares and Aphrodite with Athena's help, but now he seems unsure whether his new adversary is a god or a mortal. If he should be a god, Diomedes refuses to fight with him. As an example of the dangers consequent to fighting with the gods, Diomedes then recounts the story of Lycourgus who had the temerity to attack Dionysus:

τῷ μὲν ἔπειτ᾽ ὀδύσαντο θεοὶ ῥεῖα ζώοντες,
καί μιν τυφλὸν ἔθηκε Κρόνου πάϊς· οὐδ᾽ ἄρ᾽ ἔτι δὴν
ἦν, ἐπεὶ ἀθανάτοισιν ἀπήχθετο πᾶσι θεοῖσιν.

Thereafter, the gods who live easy were angered at him,
and the son of Cronus made him blind, nor did he
live long, since he was hated by the immortal gods.
(VI. 138-140)

Therefore, Diomedes concludes, "I would not want to battle with the immortal gods" (VI. 141). The enmity of the gods is aroused by Lycourgus' "contending with the celestial gods" θεοῖσιν ἐπουρανίοισιν ἔριζεν (VI. 131); his punishment is blindness and premature death.

In the *Odyssey* we find—with the sole exception of the Autolycus passage—that *odysasthai* is consistently limited to the denotation of divine enmity and, more precisely, to the anger of the gods against Odysseus. It occurs in a prominent place of the poem's first scene. Speaking of Odysseus, Athena accuses Zeus: "Why are you so wroth with him?" (τί νύ οἱ τόσον ὠδύσαο, Ζεῦ; 1 .62). The goddess employs a form of the same word Autolycus used in naming his grandchild. But here Odysseus is represented, not as one who provokes anger in his fellow men, but as one who undeservedly suffers the wrath of the gods.[22]

Similar plays on Odysseus' name occur three more times in the poem. First, in Book 5 the sea nymph Leucothea takes

[21] Cf. Benardete, (1968), pp. 17-18. On the diction of the Lycourgus-episode, see G. A. Privitera, *Dioniso in Omero* (Rome, 1970), pp. 53-74.

[22] Cf. Maronitis (1973), pp. 152-56.

pity on the storm-tossed hero struggling on his raft: "Poor wretch," she says, "why does Poseidon rage (ὠδύσατ᾽) at you so terribly, so that he sows many evils for you?" (5. 339-340). Shortly thereafter, when the storm has subsided and land is in sight, Odysseus still fears further mishaps at sea; he says to himself, "I know how much the famous earth-shaker is angered (ὀδώδυσται) at me" (5. 423). Finally, in Ithaca, during the first interview between Odysseus and Penelope, the disguised hero announces not only that Odysseus still lives, but also that he is on his way home with many treasures. But, he tells Penelope, the hero's companions have all perished: "for Zeus and Helios were angry (ὀδύσαντο) with him" (19. 275-276).

The name of Odysseus, then, reveals itself to have not one but two senses. It refers both to the active Autolycan troublemaker and to the passive victim of divine wrath. As the Man of Wrath, Odysseus both causes trouble and vexation and is much vexed by the hostility of the gods. These two aspects of Odysseus as victim and victimizer coexist side by side and correspond to the same doubleness we have already observed in his identifying epithet, *polytropos*. The doubleness of Odysseus pervades the *Odyssey*.

Yet the *Odyssey* does not exist in a void; it often seems to take its cues from the *Iliad*. It is striking that the two-fold meaning of Odysseus' name has a parallel in the name of the hero of the *Iliad*. In a stimulating study of this problem, G. Nagy derives the name of Achilles from ἄχος-λαός, 'the man who has grief for and of the people,' and shows how the plot of the *Iliad* embodies the meaning of the hero's name.[23] The proem announces the wrath of Achilles which brings "countless woes on the Achaeans," and, in the first book, the Greeks' grief at the plague sent by Apollo leads to Achilles' intervention and the quarrel with Agamemnon. In turn, the *achos*, grief, that the hero suffers on account of his wounded honor brings grief to his people when he withdraws from battle.

[23] Nagy (1979) pp. 69-83, first published as "The Name of Achilles," *Studies in Greek, Italic, and Indo-European Linguistics Offered to Leonard R. Palmer* (Innsbruck, 1976), pp. 209-237.

That grief is momentarily relieved when Achilles sends his friend Patroclus into battle, but the outcome, Patroclus' death, means unceasing grief for Achilles himself. Finally, the lamentation over Patroclus prefigures the grief of the Greeks over Achilles, soon to follow. The plot of the *Iliad* can, then, be meaningfully summarized in that Achilles, the man of sorrow, both suffers grief and inflicts it on his people. According to Nagy's analysis, Achilles' name ends up having a double sense. That name offers a suggestive counterpart to the twofold meaning of the name of Odysseus. It is possible that—like Achilles in his story—the name of Odysseus sums up and defines the plot of his poem. We have already observed that the *Odyssey* begins with the cessation of Athena's wrath. The story of Odysseus, the Man of Wrath, must be understood in terms of his both provoking and incurring wrath.

A further striking and at first puzzling symmetry between the *Iliad* and the *Odyssey* demands attention. With the unique exception of the Autolycus passage, the Epic, as we have seen, restricts the subject of the verb *odysasthai* to the gods. Other words for wrath and anger are shared by both gods and men.[24] The *noun* which corresponds to *odysasthai* and whose usage in Homer is similarly limited to divine agents is *menis*.[25] Divine *menis* is provoked by the breach of certain fundamental rules of human society: there are, for example, sacrifice to the gods (V. 178, cf. I. 75); hospitality toward strangers and the proper behavior of guests (XIII. 624, 2. 66, 14. 283); and due burial of the dead (XXII. 358, 11. 73). In addition, *menis* is the

---

[24] Cf. Irmscher (1950), pp. 5ff.; H. Frisk, "ΜΗΝΙΣ: Zur Geschichte eines Begriffes," *Eranos* 44 (1946):28-40; and the important correctives of P. Considine, "Some Homeric Terms for Anger," *Acta Classica* 9 (1966):15-25. For a possible etymology of *menis*, see E. Schwyzer, "Drei griechische Wörter," *RM* 80 (1931):213-217. The most thorough discussion of the semantics of *menis* is C. Watkins's "À propos de ΜΗΝΙΣ," *Bull. de la Société de Ling. de Paris* 72 (1977):187-209.

[25] The verb derived from *menis*, μηνίω, is, on the other hand, not limited to the gods. Cf. Considine (1966), p. 17, and the remark of Nagy (1976), p. 211, n. 21: "In studying the semantic range of forms in formulaic diction, it is methodologically important to distinguish derived forms from basic forms, since the two will not have the same range of applications."

reaction of the gods to conduct which is superhuman or which tends to erase the distinctions between gods and men. Both Patroclus and Diomedes arouse the *menis* of Apollo at the moment they are characterized as δαίμονι ἶσος "equal to a *daimon*" (XVI. 705, V. 438). In the latter passage Apollo makes explicit the reason for his intervention and warns Diomedes:

φράζεο, Τυδεΐδη, καὶ χάζεο, μηδὲ θεοῖσιν
ἶσ᾽ ἔθελε φρονέειν, ἐπεὶ οὔ ποτε φῦλον ὁμοῖον
ἀθανάτων τε θεῶν χαμαὶ ἐρχομένων τ᾽ ἀνθρώπων.

Take thought, son of Tydeus, and withdraw, nor desire to have
a mind equal to the gods, since never alike is the race
of the immortal gods and of men who walk on the ground.

(V. 440-442)

In the *Hymn to Aphrodite*, the goddess warns the mortal Anchises to respect the *menis* of Zeus, who will strike him down with the thunderbolt if ever Anchises reveal that Aphrodite lay with him and bore his child, Aeneas (281-290). With the same words (5. 146), Hermes warns Calypso to send off Odysseus rather than to keep him as her consort and make him immortal. In every case, *menis* arises from an attempt to blur or overstep the lines of demarcation separating gods from men.

Elsewhere applied only to the gods, *menis* is used of only one mortal agent, the wrath of Achilles, the subject of the *Iliad*. Defined in superhuman terms, Achilles' wrath makes him more than human. Achilles ascends to an almost divine stature by mimicking and making his own the anger that belongs properly to the gods alone. When the raging Achilles attacks Troy, a simile makes this explicit:

ὡς δ᾽ ὅτε καπνὸς ἰὼν εἰς οὐρανὸν εὐρὺν ἵκηται
ἄστεος αἰθομένοιο, θεῶν δέ ἑ μῆνις ἀνῆκε,
πᾶσι δ᾽ ἔθηκε πόνον, πολλοῖσι δὲ κήδε᾽ ἐφῆκεν,
ὡς Ἀχιλεὺς Τρώεσσι πόνον καὶ κήδε᾽ ἔθηκεν.

As when smoke ascends and comes to wide heaven
of a city in flames, and the wrath of the gods has ignited
  it,
and it sets toil on all and woe on many;
so did Achilles set toil and woe on the Trojans.
                              (XXI. 522-525)

In the last book of the *Iliad*, the return of Hector's corpse
presents Achilles' return to mortality and his acceptance of
the rules that govern human society. In his last moments, the
dying Hector had begged Achilles to give back his body for
burial, and his plea had ended with a threat: "lest I become
a cause of divine wrath against you" (XXII. 358; cf. the words
of Elpenor to Odysseus 11. 73). By defiling Hector's corpse
and refusing it due burial, Achilles changes from a hero of
godlike wrath to a potential object of divine anger (cf. XXIV.
113-114, 134-135). With the ransoming of Hector and his
funeral, the ordered hierarchy between gods and men is re-
stored.

Well and good, but what has all this got to do with the
Odyssey? The *Odyssey* is obviously a very different kind of
poem from the *Iliad*, and Odysseus a very different kind of
hero from Achilles. It would be premature at this point to
speculate on the nature of those differences. But a preoccupation common to both epics has emerged: in both wrath
plays a central role. Watkins has correctly grasped the complex character of *menis* in the *Iliad*, but his definition is equally
valid for the *Odyssey*:

> The association of divine wrath and a mortal by that very
> fact raises the mortal outside the normal ambiance of the
> human condition toward the sphere of the divine. . . . We
> must seek the meaning of μῆνις in the reciprocal relations
> between gods and men.[26]

Almost by definition, Odysseus is the man who provokes and
incurs anger—not only of Poseidon, Helios, and Zeus, but

[26] Watkins (1977), p. 190. Watkins, however, denies that divine wrath
might be a key word or motif in the *Odyssey*.

also, as we have seen, of Athena. And of these, only Athena's is called *menis* (3. 135). We will leave for a later chapter the question of what constitutes the θεῶν μήνιμα, the cause of divine wrath, against Odysseus. But the *menis* of Achilles and the name of Odysseus both point to the fact that wrath forms the crucial arena of both poems. Wrath in a sense defines the liminal area between gods and men.

Odysseus and the Heritage of Autolycus

Any discussion of Odysseus' name inevitably leads to a discussion of his relation to Autolycus. Odysseus' genealogical connection with the archtrickster of the Greek tradition,[27] as well as the many motifs in Odysseus' adventures that offer parallels to widespread folktales,[28] have led scholars to speculate about a pre-Homeric Odysseus who resembles a folklore figure common to almost all peoples. It is the Wily Lad, the folk hero who continually outsmarts and bedevils his opponents with his countless clever tricks and deceptions. Students of the subject maintain that, when this character of popular fantasy was incorporated into the Epic tradition, he was purged of some of his more questionable qualities and transformed into a heroic figure. Yet hints and traces of his plebeian origins survive in the *Odyssey*—most clearly in Odysseus' close connection with Autolycus—which do not quite jibe with our expectations of an Epic hero, and sometimes even contradict those expectations.

The clearest and most perceptive discussion of this process of the transformation of Odysseus from the hero of folktale

[27] For the traditions concerning Autolycus, see Roscher, s.v. "Autolykos," 1:1, 735-736.

[28] See, for instance, the discussions in L. Radermacher, "Die Erzählungen der Odyssee," *Sitz. Kais. Akad. Wiss. Wien* 178 (1916):1-59; R. Carpenter, *Folk Tale, Fiction and Saga in the Homeric Epics* (Berkeley, 1946); and D. Page, *Folktales in Homer's Odyssey* (Cambridge, Mass., 1973). For an exhaustive study of the variants of the Polyphemus story, see J. Glenn, "The Polyphemus Folktale and Homer's *Kyklopeia*," *TAPA* 102 (1971):133-81.

to the hero of Epic can be found in Maronitis' book.[29] His argument deserves to be taken seriously, if only because it raises some important questions about the interpretation of the Homeric poems. Since his work remains inaccessible even to most classicists because it has not been translated from the Demotic Greek, Maronitis' conclusions are worth summarizing.

Maronitis posits three stages in the evolution of the Odysseus figure: a pre-Epic, or what he somewhat unfortunately labels a "novelistic," phase, an Epic phase, and finally the Odysseus of the *Odyssey*. In the first, the Odysseus of folklore inherits Autolycus' talents for thievery, especially cattle-rustling, and the use of magic spells which allow him to carry out his thefts without being seen or caught. He embodies the gifts of Hermes, the trickster god. During the second stage, Odysseus is incorporated into the Epic, particularly into the traditional tales surrounding the Trojan War. Our evidence for the so-called Epic cycle is fragmentary and late, but the stories it contained must have preceded the Homeric poems in some form. Odysseus plays an important role in these tales, most spectacularly as the mastermind of the Trojan horse and as the winner in the contest over the arms of Achilles—incidents alluded to in the *Odyssey*. His cleverness and his inherited talent for trickery as well as deceit are, to a certain extent, put to the service of the united Greek cause against

---

[29] Maronitis (1973), pp. 150-96. Philippson (1947), pp. 8-22, is far less persuasive with her unduly sharp polarization between a pre-Homeric Odysseus who belongs to the dark chthonic world of Hermes—through his Autolycan background—and the Homeric hero who belongs to the clear Olympian sphere of Athena. Philippson finds the primitive Odysseus largely suppressed in the Homeric poems, but some older elements still obtrude, "unwillkürlich und wider den Willen des Dichters" (p. 14). Yet, paradoxically, she also asserts that the "Odysseus der Epen eine freie Schöpfung des Dichters ist" (p. 16), who is free enough to invent a whole new genealogy for his hero, substituting the Ithacan Laertes for the tradition—attested later, but Philippson argues, earlier—in which Sisyphus, Autolycus' rival for the title of archtrickster, was Odysseus' father. Philippson's discussion finally begs the question: if the poet was so free to cleanse the figure of Odysseus, why did he do such a bad job?

the Trojans; but some stories suggest Odysseus' reversion to the old Autolycan freebooter.[30] Finally, in the *Odyssey*, the traditional Odyssean guile is used largely in self-defense and for the preservation of the hero's companions and family. According to Maronitis, the poet of the *Odyssey* has cleansed his hero of the heavy burden of his Autolycan past by suppressing the more unsavory elements of Odysseus' character and reinterpreting negative qualities as positive virtues. The evolution of the figure of Odysseus can be summed up in the change in the meaning of Odysseus' name from the primitive Autolycan sense of the trickster—who causes trouble and vexation for his fellowmen and who provokes the hostility and distaste of decent people everywhere—to the Odyssean Odysseus who is, above all, the long-suffering victim of the undeserved and excessive anger of the gods.[31]

Maronitis' scheme has much to recommend it. No one can doubt that his account of the evolution of the figure of Odysseus goes a long way to explain the development of the most complex and contradictory hero of the Greeks. Fundamental questions, however, remain. For one thing, the Odysseus of the *Iliad* is far "cleaner" than the hero of the *Odyssey*.[32] Stanford notes that while Odysseus retains his reputation for cleverness in the *Iliad*, "his conduct is scrupulously honest and his words are studiously candid. If the *Iliad* were the only early record of Odysseus' career one would find it hard to understand how he had got his notoriety as a man of extreme wiliness. In contrast the *Odyssey* is a compendium of Ulyssean

---

[30] These traditions are collected by J. O. Schmidt, *Ulixes Posthomericus* (Berlin, 1885), pp. 7-27; and E. Bethe, *Homer: Dichtung und Sage. III: Die Sage vom Troischen Kriege* (Leipzig, 1927), pp. 55ff.

[31] On the basis of the linguistic variants of Odysseus' name ('Ολυσσεύς, 'Ολυττεύς, 'Ολυσσείδας, 'Ολισσεύς, cf. Latin Ulixes, Olyxes), P. Kretschmer, "Die vorgriechischen Sprach- und Volksschichten," *Glotta* 28 (1940):253, puts forward the attractive suggestion that the form, "Odysseus," is a creation of the Epic to justify the etymology from *odysasthai*. If this were true, then the double meaning of the hero's name would be coeval with the Epic.

[32] Surprisingly, Maronitis (1973) does not discuss the portrait of Odysseus as it emerges in the *Iliad*.

and Autolycan cunning."[33] Perhaps Stanford overstates the
case, but if the heroic environment of the *Iliad* has already
partially purified Odysseus, then presumably the poet of the
Odyssey could have continued the process of banishing the
skeletons in the closet of Odysseus' past. But he did not, nor
did he wish to do so.

The doubleness of Odysseus pervades his poem. It can be
found in his name, in his characteristic epithets, but, above
all, it informs his words and deeds. It is no accident that, after
the prologue, the very first image presented of Odysseus is the
most questionable and disturbing one in the entire *Odyssey*.[34]
Disguised as Mentes, Athena evokes for Telemachus an earlier
meeting with Odysseus:

εἰ γὰρ νῦν ἐλθὼν δόμου ἐν πρώτῃσι θύρῃσι
σταίη, ἔχων πήληκα καὶ ἀσπίδα καὶ δύο δοῦρε,
τοῖος ἐὼν οἷόν μιν ἐγὼ τὰ πρῶτ᾽ ἐνόησα
οἴκῳ ἐν ἡμετέρῳ πίνοντά τε τερπόμενόν τε,
ἐξ Ἐφύρης ἀνιόντα παρ᾽ Ἴλου Μερμερίδαο·
οἴχετο γὰρ καὶ κεῖσε θοῆς ἐπὶ νηὸς Ὀδυσσεὺς
φάρμακον ἀνδροφόνον διζήμενος, ὄφρα οἱ εἴη
ἰοὺς χρίεσθαι χαλκήρεας· ἀλλ᾽ ὁ μὲν οὔ οἱ
δῶκεν, ἐπεί ῥα θεοὺς νεμεσίζετο αἰὲν ἐόντας,
ἀλλὰ πατήρ οἱ δῶκεν ἐμός· φιλέεσκε γὰρ αἰνῶς.

Would that he would come now and stand at the outer
    gates of his house,
with helmet, shield, and two spears,
being the same as when first I knew him
in our house, drinking and enjoying himself

[33] Stanford (1963), p. 13.

[34] According to F. Dirlmeier, *Die Giftpfeile des Odysseus* (Heidelberg,
1966), the Ephyra story stands "völlig isoliert" (p. 16), and presents "ein
kantiges Gebilde, das nicht in unsere Odyssee passt" (p. 17), a glimpse of a
pre-Homeric Odysseus, not yet incorporated into the tale of Troy. But then
he claims: "Sie [the story of the poison arrows] einzufügen war ihm [the
poet] wichtiger als die Überlegung, ob sie zum Troia-Odysseus passte und
was sie im Zusammenhang des 1. Gesangs leistete" (p. 19-20). This story,
in fact, fits in very well with other aspects of Odysseus' character as it is
presented in the *Odyssey*. See below, pp. 95f.

on his return from Ephyra and Ilos, the son of
   Mermerus;
for Odysseus had gone there on a swift ship,
in search of a man-killing drug, so that he would have it
to smear on his bronze arrows; but Ilos refused
to give it, since he feared the gods who live forever;
but my father gave it to him, for he loved him terribly.
                                                                    (1. 255-264)

This first picture of Odysseus arouses our unease and suspicions, and the context makes clear that decent Homeric society
also took offense at the use of poison arrows. To put it mildly,
no overrefined sense of fairplay encumbers the Odysseus presented here.

The evolutionary explanation of the development of the
Odysseus figure is open to a crucial objection. It tends to
simplify and hence to flatten the complexities of Odysseus'
character as Homer presents them by assigning certain traits
to earlier and others to later strata. Such simplification becomes apparent in Maronitis' demonstrations of what he calls
the transformations of Odysseus. In one case, Maronitis maintains that the encounter between Odysseus and Ajax (11. 543-
567) is intended to absolve Odysseus of blame for Ajax' su-
icide after their contest over the arms of Achilles. According
to some traditions, Odysseus won by less than honorable—
one might call them Autolycan—means,[35] causing Ajax to go
mad and kill himself. The humane and generous words Odysseus addresses to the silent Ajax, with their verbal echoes of
the Iliadic quarrel between Achilles and Agamemnon, tend to
relieve Odysseus of the burden of guilt and suspicion which
characterized other traditions of his victory. There is un-
doubtedly much truth in Maronitis' interpretation, but he

---

[35] Cf. Pindar Nem. 8. 25-27, who gives Odysseus' victory over Ajax as an
example of the fact that "the greatest honor is opposed by nimble falsehood."
At the end of the Apology (41 b), Socrates claims to look forward to a possible
encounter with Palamedes and Ajax, "and any other men of old who died
through unjust judgment." In an epigram of Asclepiades (Anth. Pal. 7. 145),
Virtue mourns over Ajax' grave, because "among the Achaeans, Deception
of the guileful mind (δολόφρων 'Απάτα) is stronger than I."

skirts some of the more questionable implications of the meeting of these former antagonists. After all, Ajax remains silent and unforgiving as he goes off among the Dead. Yet Odysseus claims:

ἔνθα χ᾽ ὁμῶς προσέφη κεχολωμένος, ἤ κεν ἐγὼ τόν·
ἀλλά μοι ἤθελε θυμὸς ἐνὶ στήθεσσι φίλοισι
τῶν ἄλλων ψυχὰς ἰδέειν κατατεθνηώτων.

Then, nevertheless, he would have spoken, even though
    angry, or I to him;
but the heart in my own breast desired
to see the souls of others who had died.
(11. 565-567)

Maronitis is obliged to admit that the close of the scene constitutes something of an enigma,[36] but it is more than that. Ajax' unforgiving silence rekindles our suspicions. A number of other things accentuate our malaise: Odysseus' cocky assurance of his eventual success, his rather lame excuse for breaking off the encounter, and the curiosity that triumphs over his desire to make his peace with Ajax. Elsewhere, that curiosity regularly characterizes Odysseus; on occasion, it even endears him to us; here, it strikes one as slightly ignoble. Nor does any suggestion of reconciliation allay our unease. The final impression of this scene and Odysseus' role in it remain ambivalent.

Maronitis' analysis of the Polyphemus episode is open to similar objections. According to him, that episode forms the crowning step in the process of purification of Odysseus from his Autolycan heritage.[37] Here, the Autolycan characteristics—cleverness, trickery, and deception—are transformed from negative to positive qualities. They cease to be purely self-

[36] Maronitis (1973), pp. 176-77. The enigmatic quality of these lines has led some scholars to posit an interpolation of 11. 565-567 intended to form a transition to the supposedly spurious description of the Great Sinners in the Nekyia (11. 568ff.). Cf. K. Lehrs, *De Aristarchi studiis Homericis* (Leipzig, 1882), pp. 156-57. Eustathius 1968. 60, on the other hand, regards the lines as an example of "Homeric skill" (δεινότης Ὁμηρική).
[37] Maronitis (1973), pp. 181-96.

aggrandizing and self-serving; instead, they are put to the service of defensive and communal virtues. Odysseus' *doloi* are employed exclusively to bring about his own and his comrades' escape from the cannibal's cave. This adventure, then, is pivotal, for it results in Odysseus' becoming the object of Poseidon's unjust wrath, *odyssamenos*. Here, however, Maronitis neglects what cannot be neglected: the beginning of the episode. How did Odysseus get trapped in the monster's cave in the first place? Autolycan curiosity and greed played a critical role in creating Odysseus' predicament. One cannot overlook it with impunity. In sum, the diachronic view of the genesis of Odysseus requires us to ignore some traits at the expense of others and to gloss over inherent contradictions.

The whitewash of Odysseus in the *Odyssey* remains incomplete. The heritage of Autolycus may be played down to a certain extent, but it is by no means completely suppressed. Developmental explanations may help to explain how Odysseus got that way, but they finally interfere with a full understanding of Odysseus as the hero of the *Odyssey*. Once we have separated Odysseus into primitive Autolycan and more progressive "heroic" strata, we can no longer grasp the complex but highly integrated whole whose character is delineated by its very multiplicity.

The Heritage of Autolycus:
The Boar's-Tusk Helmet

After having failed to discover a satisfactory account of the Autolycan aspects of Odysseus' character within a developmental framework, we are still faced with the initial question. How should Odysseus' relationship to Autolycus be defined; to what extent is Odysseus true to his name and heir to the Autolycan character of the man who named him? To reject an evolutionary answer to a valid and important question— one that the Homeric text itself raises—is to become responsible for an alternative solution. The only safe and sure approach to such a solution is the venerable principle of "interpreting Homer from Homer." A passage from Book X of the *Iliad*, the so-called Doloneia, and the only other Epic passage that links Autolycus and Odysseus, suggests an answer to our question. To a certain extent, this answer confirms the speculation of scholars concerning the development of the Odysseus figure. However, it does so in Homeric terms which are at once simple and subtle. What is more important, it preserves the integrity of Odysseus' character.

At the beginning of the Doloneia, the most "Odyssean" book of the *Iliad*[38]—and, characteristically, the only one to take place wholly at night—the embassy to persuade Achilles to return to battle has just failed. Agamemnon lies sleepless and anxious, then calls together the Greek chieftains. When an expedition to spy on the Trojan camp is proposed, Diomedes volunteers and chooses Odysseus as his companion. In the meantime, the Trojans too have sent out a spy, Dolon, to discover the intentions of the Greeks. The nocturnal foray itself falls into two parts. It begins with the capture of Dolon; there follows the bloody attack on the sleeping Rhesus and his Thracians, a massacre that leads to the capture of Rhesus' splendid horses. The second incident belongs properly to Diomedes, the first, to Odysseus—as becomes evident from the distribution of the booty after the triumphant return of the heroes. Diomedes gets the Thracian horses (X. 566-569); Odysseus, the spoils of Dolon (X. 570-571).[39]

It is ironically appropriate that Odysseus, the man of *doloi* par excellence, should be pitted against an opponent named Dolon. The Doloneia as a whole is constructed on a pattern of contrast, parallelism, and reversal of expectations, a veritable "game of antitheses."[40] So, the greedy and insane boastfulness

[38] F. Klingner, "Über die Dolonie," in *Studien zur griechischen und römischen Literatur* (Zürich, 1964), pp. 32-33, compares the Doloneia to the various episodes from the Trojan War recounted in the *Odyssey*.

[39] Cf. F. Ranke, *Homerische Untersuchungen I: Doloneia* (Leipzig, 1881), pp. 44 and 47, who asserts that the poet ascribes to Odysseus "alles . . . wozu nur irgend ein wenig Klugheit gehört," but to Diomedes, "alle kriegerische Taten."

[40] See L. Gernet, "Dolon le loup," in *Anthropologie de la Grèce antique* (Paris, 1968), p. 162, who speaks of a "jeu d'antithèse" which structures the action of the Doloneia. Cf. Klingner (1964), p. 29.

of Dolon, who demands the horses of Achilles as his reward for spying on the Greeks, contrasts mightily with the unusual and uncharacteristic modesty of Odysseus, who not only does not set a price on his participation in the venture, but also demurely rejects the praise Diomedes heaps upon him, by saying that "the Greeks already know those things" (X. 250). The Greeks, moreover, go forth on their mission with no particular goal or ambition, but return with the superb horses of Rhesus, while Dolon not only fails to win his prize, but loses his life as well. In short, the trickster, Dolon, is out-tricked.[41]

A similar significance informs the bizarre outfits of the leading actors of the Doloneia.[42] The costumes are appropriate to the character of their wearers. For his spying mission, Dolon dons a wolfskin and a weasel cap, underlining his own disastrous combination of low cunning and insatiable greed.[43] Earlier, Menelaus had put on a leopardskin, while both Agamemnon and Diomedes wear lion pelts. As Reinhardt notes, the relation between Agamemnon and Menelaus, which is touchingly revealed in the king's concern for his beloved but weaker brother (X. 237-240), finds a subtle expression in their

---

[41] Stanford (1963), p. 15, calls Odysseus' conduct in the Doloneia an "example of deliberate self-restraint." Euripides' *Rhesus* makes explicit many of the implicit suggestions of the Homeric text and can almost be read as a commentary on the Doloneia. For example, Euripides underlines the irony of Dolon's name (159, 215) and heightens the Homeric wolfskin to a full-fledged wolf disguise (208-215). Finally, Dolon's boast in the play that he will return with the head of Odysseus and Diomedes (219-222) appears to allude to the manner of his own death in the *Iliad*. On the relation of the *Rhesus* to the *Iliad*, see B. Fenik, *Iliad X and the Rhesus*, Collection Latomus 73 (Brussels, 1964), who claims that all episodes in the *Rhesus* involving Dolon are directly derived from Book X of the *Iliad*.

[42] Fenik (1964), p. 60, n. 3, argues unconvincingly that "It is over-ingenious to seek any symbolism in the garbs themselves, or implied comparison between the persons wearing them." K. Reinhardt, *Die Ilias und ihr Dichter*, ed. U. Hölscher (Göttingen, 1961), p. 247, on the other hand, recognizes the symbolic value of the outfits and speaks of "Kostumierung."

[43] For the generally unpleasant character and reputation of the weasel in antiquity, see the testimonia collected in O. Keller, *Die Antike Tierwelt*, 2 vols. (Leipzig, 1909), 1:160-63.

respective outfits.[44] The lion, for the Greeks as for us, embodies heroic majesty, while the leopard, for all his attractiveness, is a creature of a lesser stature. Elsewhere, it is, of course, Paris, Menelaus' rival, who wears the leopardskin (III. 17). Diomedes, who represents the best qualities of heroic *arete* in those books in which Achilles is absent, is likewise well suited to the lionskin he wears. Finally, for the raid itself, Odysseus puts on a helmet that introduces yet another animal emblem. For this helmet is made of boar's tusks and described in unusual detail.[45] If the costumes of the other characters in the Doloneia have an emblematic value suitable to their wearers, then Odysseus' helmet must, on the contrary, be understood as a disguise. For the hero of supreme guile encounters his adversary, Dolon, not, as we might expect, in the guise of a fox or a wolf,[46] but as a wild boar, the beast who is known in the similes of the Epic as the animal most violent in destructive rage and might.[47] But just as Odysseus plays the fool when addressing the Trojans (III. 216-224), thus disarming his audience, he can in the Doloneia be said to dissemble his true character in order to trap his adversary. Such, after all, are the ruses of *metis*.

The full significance of the boar's-tusk helmet has not yet been exhausted, however, for it has an important bearing on the question of Odysseus' Autolycan heritage. Diomedes and Odysseus have come to the nocturnal conference of the Greeks unarmed and are obliged to borrow equipment from the guards for their expedition. It is from one of them, the Cretan Meriones, that Odysseus borrows a bow and spear as well as the

---

[44] Cf. Reinhardt (1961), p. 247.

[45] Similar helmets have been found in many Mycenean sites. See J. Borchhardt, *Homerische Helme* (Mainz, 1972), pp. 18-37, 47-52.

[46] Once again, Euripides makes the reversal explicit by having the charioteer of Rhesus dream of *two wolves* (i.e., Odysseus and Diomedes) attacking the horses (780-788).

[47] See especially XVII. 21-22, where the raging wild boar is described as having the greatest *thumos* in his breast and exalting in his strength (οὔ τε μέγιστος / θυμὸς ἐνὶ στήθεσσι περὶ σθένεϊ βλεμεαίνει). Cf. Aristotle *Hist. Anim.* 9. 44, 630a, 2-3.

helmet, which is described both in terms of its appearance and its history.

To be sure, several important objects in the Homeric poems, especially armor or weapons, are described by means of their history or genealogy. The most elaborate example of such a genealogy is the famous description of Agamemnon's scepter in Book II of the *Iliad*:

τὸ μὲν Ἥφαιστος κάμε τεύχων.

Ἥφαιστος μὲν δῶκε Διὶ Κρονίωνι ἄνακτι,
αὐτὰρ ἄρα Ζεὺς δῶκε διακτόρῳ ἀργεϊφόντῃ·
Ἑρμείας δὲ ἄναξ δῶκεν Πέλοπι πληξίππῳ,
αὐτὰρ ὁ αὖτε Πέλοψ δῶκ' Ἀτρέϊ, ποιμένι λαῶν·
Ἀτρεὺς δὲ θνῄσκων ἔλιπεν πολύαρνι Θυέστῃ,
αὐτὰρ ὁ αὖτε Θυέστ' Ἀγαμέμνονι λεῖπε φορῆναι,
πολλῇσιν νήσοισι καὶ Ἄργεϊ παντὶ ἀνάσσειν.

Hephaestus made it;
and Hephaestus gave it to Zeus, lord son of Cronus,
and then Zeus gave it to the Guide, slayer of Argus;
and the lord Hermes gave it to Pelops, driver of horses;
and Pelops in turn gave it to Atreus, shepherd of the people,
and Atreus, when he died, left it to Thyestes of many sheep;
but Thyestes in turn left it to Agamemnon to carry,
and to rule over many islands and all of Argos.
(II. 101-108)

The history of the scepter serves to characterize the kingly stature of its present heir, as Lessing demonstrates in his classic interpretation in the *Laocoön*. Similarly, the ash spear, which Achilles inherits from his father Peleus and which is the only original piece of armor he retains for his final confrontation with Hector, should, according to Shannon, be understood as a symbol of Achilles' mortality.[48] The history of an object

---

[48] Shannon (1975), p. 70. For other objects described in terms of their histories in Homer, see VII. 137-149, XI. 19-23, XV. 529-534, XVI. 140-144, and XVII. 194-197. The genealogy of Odysseus' bow (21. 11-41) will be examined below.

may, then, offer more than a merely ornamental anecdote; it may serve to characterize its owner in some important way. Such, it will be shown later, is the significance of Odysseus' bow. Indeed, it should not surprise us that the weapon that brings the action of the entire *Odyssey* to its climax is dignified with a complex and meaningful account of its origins. It may, however, seem peculiar that Homer lavishes so much attention on borrowed headgear. The lineage of the helmet runs as follows:

τήν ῥά ποτ' ἐξ 'Ελεῶνος 'Αμύντορος 'Ορμενίδαο
ἐξέλετ' Αὐτόλυκος πυκινὸν δόμον ἀντιτορήσας,
Σκάνδειαν δ' ἄρα δῶκε Κυθηρίῳ 'Αμφιδάμαντι·
'Αμφιδάμας δὲ Μόλῳ δῶκε ξεινήϊον εἶναι,
αὐτὰρ ὁ Μηριόνῃ δῶκεν ᾧ παιδὶ φορῆναι·
δὴ τότ' 'Οδυσσῆος πύκασεν κάρη ἀμφιτεθεῖσα.

Autolycus once took it from Eleon,
breaking into the close-built house of Amyntor, son of
  Ormenus;
then, in Scandeia he gave it to Amphidamas of Cythera;
and Amphidamas gave it to Molos as a guest-gift;
and he, in turn, gave it to his son Meriones to wear;
and on this occasion it covered the head of Odysseus.
(X. 266-271)

The verb used three times to describe the *paradosis* of the helmet is *doke*, "he gave." But in the first instance, the helmet was no gift; Autolycus stole it. Only here does Autolycus occur in the *Iliad*, and he is not explicitly identified as Odysseus' grandfather. Stanford rejects the notion that the poet of the Doloneia was unaware of the connection between Odysseus and Autolycus, even though "Homer gives no hint here of any relationship."

But two other explanations are possible. Homer may not have troubled to emphasize a universally known fact: if an English historian had to record that Henry VIII wore a helmet which Henry VII had once confiscated he would not need to remind his readers that these two were father and son. Or else a subtler reason may have influenced

Homer. He may have deliberately avoided any reference
to Odysseus' ancestry on the female side because it would
detract from Odysseus' prestige in the conventionally heroic atmosphere of the *Iliad*.[49]

Whatever the reasons for Homer's silence, in our passage, the
initial theft of the helmet reveals Autolycus' character to run
true to what we have heard of him in the *Odyssey*; he excelled
all men in thievery and equivocal oath (κλεπτοσύνῃ θ' ὅρκῳ
τε 19. 396). His method of operation remains the same.
The closest parallel to the elaborate history of the helmet
is the transmission of Agamemnon's scepter,[50] but a comparison reveals important differences. First, unlike the scepter,
the helmet is not assigned a divine origin. Then, too, while
the scepter is passed lineally from generation to generation,
the helmet moves laterally from person to person with no
apparent design. In its wanderings, the helmet proceeds from
Eleon to Cythera, to Crete, and finally, to Troy, whereas the
scepter remains a possession of the royal house and becomes
a symbol of the latter. The scepter, then, symbolizes Agamemnon's kingly inheritance. The boar's-tusk helmet also describes a legacy but of a rather different kind: Odysseus' inheritance of those Autolycan characteristics he received from
his grandfather. With a "natural" transmission along family
lines, Odysseus might well have inherited the helmet. In fact,
the helmet has had a more complicated and checkered history,
but finally it has reached its "natural" heir, Odysseus. A scholiast notes this mysterious coincidence: "It is a pretty reversal
that the helmet, having gone through so many hands, again
covers the offspring of Autolycus."[51]

It is tempting to speculate on the significance of this bizarre
coincidence. An apparently random chain of events turns out
to make unexpected sense, one that suggests that there is a
kind of order in the world which is hidden but also mean-

---

[49] Stanford (1963), p. 11.
[50] The similarity is noticed by Eustathius 803. 33-35.
[51] Schol. bT at X. 271: ἡδεῖα ἡ περιπέτεια, τὸ διὰ τοσούτων ἐλ-
θοῦσαν τὴν κυνῆν πάλιν σκεπάσαι Ὀδυσσέα τὸν ἐξ Αὐτολύκου.

ingful. Heraclitus, the most famous ancient proponent of such a hidden ordering of the cosmos, inevitably comes to mind. One of his fragments which "might . . . be taken as a general title for Heraclitus' philosophical thought"[52] fits the present case perfectly: "The invisible harmony is stronger than the visible one" (ἁρμονίη ἀφανὴς φανερῆς κρείττων DK B 54). However that may be, the curious tale of the helmet suggests that Odysseus' Autolycan heritage is not simple and linear, but complex and indirect. We may conclude that Autolycan qualities are in some sense present in the grandson, but that they are at least partly transmuted.

With the boar's-tusk helmet and its history, the poet gives us a concrete emblem of the relation between Autolycus and Odysseus. Once this overall significance has been grasped, we may try to examine the intervening steps in the helmet's transmission in the hope that they will reveal more about the character of Odysseus' Autolycan heritage. In this respect, however, the internal Homeric evidence is admittedly scant. Amyntor, from whom Autolycus originally stole the helmet, occurs in Book IX. 448ff. in the *Iliad* as Phoenix' father, who cursed his son for sleeping with his concubine. Then Amyntor set up a guard of his kinsmen to keep Phoenix imprisoned in the house, but on the tenth day Phoenix finally managed to escape. It is intriguing to consider that Phoenix, Amyntor's son, had trouble getting out of the very same house that Autolycus had previously broken into with apparent ease.[53] Homer tells us nothing more about Amphidamas nor about Molos, except that the latter was Meriones' father. There are, however, some later and fragmentary post-Homeric traditions that are suggestive, especially those about Autolycus. But caution and a healthy dose of skepticism must accompany their use, for while it is clear that countless traditional tales stand behind Homer and must have been common knowledge to

[52] C. H. Kahn, *The Art and Thought of Heraclitus* (Cambridge, 1979), p. 203.

[53] On the old controversy concerning the identification of the Amyntor in Book IX with the one in Book X, see the Scholia at X. 266, Eustathius 804. 21-23, and the discussion in *RE* s.v. "Amyntor," (1894), 1:2009-2010.

his audience, any attempt at their recovery opens unto the
realm of surmises rather than certainties. With that caveat, I
believe it is possible to put together not, indeed, a complete
picture, but at least a suggestive outline concerning the origins
of the mysterious helmet.

The traditions concerning Autolycus link him closely to
Hermes. In the *Odyssey*, as we have seen, Hermes grants
Autolycus his thievish talents, but elsewhere the god is not
only Autolycus' patron, but also his father.[54] Hermes' name
is absent from the helmet passage in the *Iliad*, but his influence
can be detected in the rare verb, ἀντιτορέω, to pierce or bore
through, which describes Autolycus' break-in to the house of
Amyntor. In the *Hymn to Hermes*, the god's characteristic
activity is precisely this "boring through."[55] There, Apollo
says of Hermes:

πολλάκις ἀντιτοροῦντα δόμους εὖ ναιετάοντας
ἔννυχον οὔ χ᾽ ἕνα μοῦνον ἐπ᾽ οὔδεϊ φῶτα καθίσσαι
σκευάζοντα κατ᾽ οἶκον ἄτερ ψόφου. . . .

Often you have bored through prosperous houses
at night and brought more than one man down,
gathering his goods without a sound. . . .
                          (283-285)

Earlier, Hermes himself had threatened to rob the rich shrine
of Apollo at Delphi: "I myself will go to pierce through the
great house of Pytho" (εἶμι γὰρ εἰς Πυθῶνα μέγαν δόμον
ἀντιτορήσων *H.H.* 178).[56] Autolycus' method of breaking

[54] Cf. the Scholia at 19. 432. See also Ovid *Metamorphoses* 11. 315, where
Autolycus is described as *patriae non degener artis*, 'not unworthy of his
paternal art,' which has just been defined as *furtum ingeniosus ad omne*,
'clever at all kinds of theft.'

[55] I owe this important observation to Christopher Dadian, who is currently
working on the *Hymn to Hermes*.

[56] Compare *Hymn to Hermes* 42, where Hermes "pierces the life out" of
the tortoise: αἰῶν᾽ ἐξετόρησεν ὀρεσκῴοιο χελώνης; and 119, δι᾽ αἰῶνας
τετορήσας, of Hermes' slaughter of the cattle of Apollo. The repeated notion
of piercing or boring through points to Hermes' function as liminal god who
both oversteps and mediates between different spheres, e.g., life and death,
gods and men. In Homer ἀντιτορέω occurs only once again when Diomedes

and entering is identical to that of Hermes, and like his patron, Autolycus is known as a virtuoso cattle-rustler and thief. He is also said to have the power to make himself and other things invisible—a useful talent in his line of work. Now tradition has it that Hermes has a cap of invisibility, which on one occasion at least he lent to Perseus when the latter went off to kill the Gorgon.[57] In the *Iliad* (V. 844-845), Athena puts on a similar cap to make herself invisible to Ares. Could the boar's-tusk helmet in our passage in some sense "stand for" the magic cap of invisibility?

An answer to this question requires us to follow the advice of Kuiper: "Whoever wishes to investigate the true nature of this cap made of leather [X. 261-262] must enter the far reaches of mythology."[58] The dearth of evidence precludes absolute certainty in such an investigation, but what evidence there is does not seem to contradict our conclusion. Two additional points deserve mention. Of Scandeia and Amphidamas, the next link in the transmission of the helmet, nothing more of significance is known. However, an ancient etymology connects Cythera with κευθεῖν, 'to hide,'[59] so that the name of the island might be interpreted as 'hiding place.' Furthermore, there is a bizarre notice in Plutarch (*De defectu orac.* 14) referring to a ritual he claims to have witnessed in Crete

---

wounds Aphrodite (V. 337), a moment in which the boundaries of mortality and immortality are, for an instant, transgressed and reasserted (cf. V. 339-342).

[57] The testimonia are collected in Roscher, 1:1, 735-736.

[58] K. Kuiper, "De Idomeneo ac Merione," *Mnemosyne* 47 (1919):47. Philippson (1947), p. 14, rejects out of hand such a line of speculation: "Es wird auch nicht gesagt, dass diesem Helm zauberhafte Eigenschaften—etwa, dass er sein Träger unsichtbar macht—innewohnen." Keller (1909), p. 393, records a custom of the Aestii, an ancient people who lived in what is now Prussia, who wore helmets with boars on them in the belief that such headgear would make their wearers invisible.

[59] Cf. Hesychius *Etym. Mag.*, and the *Suda* s.v. Κυθηρεία; also Eustathius 1598. 51. This etymology has more recently been revived by H. Güntert in *Kalypso* (Halle, 1919), p. 187, but has been rejected by both Frisk and Chantraine in their etymological dictionaries. What counts, of course, is not whether the etymology is correct, but whether it was perceived to be valid within the Homeric tradition.

in which a headless statue, said to be of Molos, was displayed. Headlessness, hiding places, and cap of invisibility—they all add up to an intriguing pattern whose general significance can still be retrieved, even if some of the details remain lost to us. We should remember in this context that Dolon dies by decapitation. It may be considered corroborating evidence, or at least an indication that the present interpretation is on the right track, that Gernet, who approaches the Doloneia from a completely different angle, detects the same nexus of associations in the figure of Dolon: animal disguises, hiding, headlessness, and invisibility.[60]

When we turn to the final link in the chain of transmission, we reach more solid ground. The *Iliad* itself offers ample information concerning Meriones—a Cretan warrior not quite of the first rank—which can be shaped into a plausible portrait. Meriones is first mentioned in the Catalogue of Ships as leader of the Cretans along with Idomeneus (II. 651). At the mustering of the troops in Book IV, Idomeneus marshals the forward ranks, while Meriones takes charge of the rear (IV. 254)—which suggests that Meriones is Idomeneus' junior partner. At times a near equal to the Cretan chieftain, on other occasions Meriones appears to be merely Idomeneus' vassal or underling (ὀπάων, θεράπων). This apparent contradiction, however, does not require theories of multiple authorship or conflicting sources for its resolution, although such stratagems have been tried.[61] Common sense will serve as well, and the inconsistency is most likely due simply to the differences in the two men's ages. After all, when he is not in the company of Idomeneus, Meriones frequently forms part of a group of younger warriors (e.g., IX. 83, XIII. 93). In Book XIII. 249, Idomeneus calls Meriones "dearest of companions" (φίλταθ' ἑταίρων), an expression that reminds us of the relationship between Achilles and Patroclus (cf. XIX. 315). But, unlike Patroclus, Meriones has an independent authority

---

[60] Gernet (1968), p. 165. See also H. Jeanmaire, *Couroi et Courètes* (Lille, 1939), pp. 400-401.

[61] See Kuiper (1919), pp. 35-54; also Kroll in *RE* s.v. "Meriones," XV (1931), pp. 1031-1035.

as can be seen from the fact that he does not share Idomeneus'
tent. On the contrary, it appears that Meriones' tent lies at
some distance from the Cretan leader's, perhaps even at the
far end of the Cretan forces. For when Meriones meets Idomeneus, who rebukes him for holding back from battle, Meriones explains that he has lost his spear and is now on the
way to get another from his camp "which is not nearby" (XIII.
268). Moreover, Meriones has moments of independent glory.
A conversation with Idomeneus reveals Meriones' special excellence in ambushes (XIII. 249ff.) But Meriones' finest hour
occurs during the funeral games for Patroclus; in an upset
victory—which astonishes the onlookers—he beats Teucer with
a masterful feat of bowmanship and wins the prize (XXIII.
850ff.). Teucer, who shoots first, manages to snap the cord
that holds the bird, but Meriones then hits the bird in its free
flight.

The *Odyssey* adds nothing to the above portrait of Meriones, although Nestor says that those who accompanied
Idomeneus returned home safely (3. 191). Diodorus (V. 79,
4) reports that Idomeneus and Meriones were buried together
in Cnossus and were there honored with hero cults. The same
author also tells of Meriones' travels to Sicily after the fall of
Troy and the foundation there of a rich temple devoted to the
Cretan cult of the Mothers (V. 79, 6). Later tradition offers
various accounts of Meriones' genealogy. According to Apollodorus (III. 3, 1), Meriones' father was a bastard son of
Deucalion, Idomeneus' father; that would make Meriones
Idomeneus' illegitimate nephew. Diodorus, on the other hand,
makes Meriones Idomeneus' cousin by calling both Molos
and Deucalion sons of Minos (V. 79, 4). An odd passage in
Alcidamas, *Ulysses* 4, describes the sons of Molos who go to
Menelaus for the arbitration of a quarrel concerning their
father's inheritance. That tradition presumably considers Meriones and Idomeneus as brothers.[62] All of these accounts of
Meriones' background and birth tend to explain the somewhat

[62] Cf. *RE* s.v. "Molos," 15:1(1933), p. 14.

unusual character of the relationship between Meriones and Idomeneus that emerges from the *Iliad*.

Readers of the *Odyssey* will find this composite picture of Meriones strangely familiar. In fact, it offers striking parallels to certain elements of the Cretan tales told by the disguised Odysseus on his return to Ithaca, especially in his various false accounts of his origins. A brief review of those tales will help to make this clear.

Odysseus gives the following story to Athena in Book 13: he had fled from Crete after murdering Orsilochus, the son of Idomeneus, in a night ambush. That was because Orsilochus had tried to deprive him of his due share of the booty from Troy on the grounds that he had not served Idomeneus faithfully; instead, he had led his own contingent (13. 257ff.). Later, in Book 14, Odysseus introduces himself to Eumaeus as Kastor, illegitimate son of the rich Cretan Hylax. Cut off from his patrimony by the legitimate heirs, Kastor restores his fortunes by way of an advantageous marriage. The gods grant him the courage and daring which proves itself most spectacularly in ambushes. Then war and piracy increased his wealth, until he became a man to be reckoned with among the Cretans. At that point, however, Idomeneus forced him to take an unwilling part in the Trojan expedition (14. 192-242). Finally, in his first interview with Penelope in Book 19, Odysseus gives yet another account of his origins, presenting himself this time as Aithon, younger brother of Idomeneus, who played host to Odysseus on his way to Troy (19. 172-198).

In all these lying tales, the stranger's purported Cretan origins, close relationship, and near equality with Idomeneus all remind us of Meriones. But while Meriones' loyalty to Idomeneus in the *Iliad* is never thrown into question, Odysseus' account to Athena is redolent of insubordination and even criminal treachery toward the Cretan chief. As Kastor, Odysseus again presents himself as an unwilling participant in the Trojan War. We may recall the story, not mentioned in Homer, but reported by Proclus in his summary of the *Cypria* (Allen 103), where Odysseus himself tried to avoid joining the expedition against Troy by feigning madness.[63] The manner of Orsilochus' murder recalls Meriones' expertise in ambush. Of course, nocturnal ambush also plays a role in Odysseus' clever tale to coax a warm cloak out of Eumaeus (14. 468-506). On a chilly night in Troy while lying in ambush, Odysseus managed to furnish the Cretan stranger with a cloak by means of a ruse. Eumaeus gets the point of the story and offers a blanket and cloak to the disguised Odysseus to ward off the cold night air. The piquancy of the ploy is enhanced if we remember that, in the remarkably similar setting of the Doloneia, Odysseus alone of the heroes goes forth without a cloak but acquires at the end the wolf pelt of Dolon.[64] In his initial conversation with Penelope, Odysseus retains his Cretan disguise but at the same time suppresses much that might have appeared seamy in his earlier false tales. At the same time, he elevates himself to the closest family relation to the Cretan king—Idomeneus.

Outstanding skill in archery has played no part in Odysseus' Cretan tales, although Cretans were generally known as good bowmen in antiquity. But the hero of the *Odyssey* has an intriguing relationship to the expert archer of the *Iliad*. For Meriones' prize for his wonderful exhibition shot is none other than ten *double-axes*. Double-axes, of course, form a crucial element in Odysseus' own master-shot and the climax of the *Odyssey*. Now, it is well known that in the *Iliad* Odysseus does not appear as a bowman. But in the passage from the Doloneia that prompted these reflections, Odysseus borrows not only the helmet but also a bow from the same Meriones. Only in the *Odyssey* do we learn why Odysseus came to Troy without his bow. Its history too will require further investi-

[63] The incident may be alluded to at 24. 119.

[64] Cf. L. Muellner, *The Meaning of Homeric* EYXOMAI *Through its Formulas* (Innsbruck, 1976), p. 96, n. 43, who poses the question that must be asked: "Is epic too unsophisticated for a cross-reference here in the *Odyssey* to another version of this tale in which Odysseus himself needed a χλαῖνα ...?" The cumulative evidence suggests that the answer must finally affirm the possibility of just such subtle cross-reference.

gation, but, in any case, archery provides yet another link between Meriones and Odysseus.

There is a modern critic who seems to suspect something of the complex interconnections between Odysseus and the figure of Meriones. In his book on the Doloneia, Shewan cryptically remarks that Eumaeus, upon hearing the disguised Odysseus' tale, must have thought to himself: "You must be Meriones himself!"[65] Unfortunately, Shewan has nothing more to say on the subject. There is, however, an interesting piece of ancient testimony in an unlikely place connecting Odysseus and Meriones . . . and helmets (Plutarch *Life of Marcellus* 20. 3):

> There is a city of Sicily, called Engyium, not large but very ancient, and famous for the appearance there of goddesses, who are called Mothers. The temple is said to have been built by the Cretans, and certain spears were shown there, and bronze helmets; one of these bore the name of Meriones, and others that of Ulysses (that is, Odysseus), who had consecrated them to the goddesses.
>
> (trans. B. Perrin)

Plutarch's statement suggests that the connection between Odysseus and Meriones is not purely "literary," but that it finds a reflection in the traditional lore embodied in cult. I must leave to others the exploration of these "far reaches of mythology." The evidence, however allusive, is sufficient to show that the intricate cluster of associations linking Meriones and Odysseus is no mere coincidence. This, in turn, implies that, on the literary level, the relationship between the *Odyssey*, the Doloneia, and the *Iliad* may be far more complex than is generally recognized.

But let us return to the question of the boar's-tusk helmet

---

[65] A. Shewan, *The Lay of Dolon* (London, 1911), p. 169. More recently, the nexus of associations linking Odysseus and Meriones through the Cretan tales has been studied in a somewhat different context by S. Lowenstam, "The Typological Death of Patroklos" (Ph.D. diss., Harvard University, 1975), pp. 140ff.; and by D. Petegorsky in an unpublished paper entitled "The Cretan Tales, the Doloneia, and the Bow of Odysseus." Their conclusions give me greater confidence in my own.

from which we began. The Autolycan inheritance of Odysseus, of which the helmet is an emblem, seems to surface most clearly in Odysseus' lying tales. The "thievery and equivocal oath" of the grandfather are not transmitted to his grandson without change. Rather, they are transmuted into a gift for lies and deceptive speech: Cretan tales. And this is the very talent for which Athena praises her favorite: "deceptive and thievish tales, which are dear to you from the bottom of your heart" (ἀπατάων / μύθων τε κλοπίων, οἵ τοι πεδόθεν φί-λοι εἰσιν 13. 294-295). By means of this modification, the helmet of Autolycus fits the head of Odysseus.

Our investigation of the name and origins of Odysseus has offered fruitful insights into the nature of the hero. But his multiplicity demands that our approach to him be similarly multiple. It is time to set Odysseus in the wider context of the other heroes of Epic and to view his accomplishments within the larger framework of heroic possibilities.

THE BOW OF ODYSSEUS

Like the boar's-tusk helmet, the bow of Odysseus has a history behind it. And, as with the helmet, the story of the bow deepens our understanding of Odysseus' character. But while the helmet of Autolycus gave an account of Odysseus' inheritance of certain ancestral traits, the bow, in a different manner, defines Odysseus in relation to other heroes of the Epic. By comparing and contrasting them with Odysseus, it assigns to the latter a unique place in their constellation.

At the beginning of Book 21, Penelope enters the palace storeroom to fetch the bow of Odysseus in preparation for the test that will end with the slaughter of the suitors. Its history is outlined in some detail in a lengthy digression "structured with consummate artistry."[66] Iphitus, the son of the famous archer, Eurytus, had given Odysseus his father's bow

---

[66] G. K. Galinsky, *The Herakles Theme* (Oxford, 1972), p. 11. The passage is structured on the principles of ring-composition. Cf. W.A.A. van Otterlo, *De Ringcompositie als Opbouwprincipe in de epische Gedichten van Homerus, Verhandel. der Ned. Akad. Wetensch., Afd. Letterkunde* 51, 1, (1948), pp. 24-26; and Gaisser (1969), pp. 21-23.

as a guest-gift on the occasion of their meeting in Messene. Odysseus had gone there as a young man on a public mission to retrieve some herds that the Messenians had rustled. At the same time by chance, Iphitus was searching for twelve mares who ultimately proved to be the cause of his death. According to a tradition reported by Eustathius and other ancient commentators on the passage, but not mentioned in the Homeric text, Autolycus—who keeps turning up like a bad penny— had stolen Iphitus' horses and sold them to Heracles.[67] Whether the mares were bought or stolen, Heracles evidently decided to keep them and impiously murdered poor Iphitus in clear violation of the sacred rights of guests:

αἳ δή οἱ καὶ ἔπειτα φόνος καὶ μοῖρα γένοντο,
ἐπεὶ δὴ Διὸς υἱὸν ἀφίκετο καρτερόθυμον,
φῶθ' Ἡρακλῆα, μεγάλων ἐπιίστορα ἔργων,
ὅς μιν ξεῖνον ἐόντα κατέκτανεν ᾧ ἐνὶ οἴκῳ,
σχέτλιος, οὐδὲ θεῶν ὄπιν αἰδέσατ' οὐδὲ τράπεζαν,
τὴν ἥν οἱ παρέθηκεν.

Afterwards, those mares became his death and destiny,
when he came to the mighty-hearted son of Zeus,
the man, Heracles, privy to great deeds,
who killed him while a guest in his house—
wretch, who respected neither the anger of the gods nor
   the table
which he had set before him.

                                                    (21. 24-29)

Before his death, however, Iphitus had given the bow to Odysseus as a gift. When he set out for Troy, Odysseus left it at home as a pious *mnema* or memorial to their friendship which had been so prematurely terminated (21. 38-41).

Odysseus' bow, then, has an illustrious prehistory; it is in fact the bow of one of the most famous archers of the past. Such an ancestry lends dignity—and class—to what will be the focal point of the *Odyssey*'s dénouement. One might leave it at that and be satisfied, but there is more to be said, and

67 Cf. Scholia B.Q. at 21. 22; Eustathius 1899. 37-39.

the additional features are precisely what make the bow of Odysseus significant. We must not, however, ignore two oddities in the story thus far. First, as Galinsky says of the passage, "this is one of the most devastating indictments of Herakles in literature."[68] The murder of Iphitus could not be presented in a more brutal or condemnatory fashion. Moreover, the mere presence of Heracles in the narrative is surprising, for it runs counter to the traditional Epic chronology which places Heracles one, if not two, generations before the heroes of the Trojan War. The poet seems to show an awareness of the inconsistency by emphasizing that Odysseus was still very young (παιδνὸς ἐών 21. 21). Prinz correctly speaks of "an intentional blurring of the tradition,"[69] but fails to ask, "to what purpose?"

A passage in Book 8 at the games of the Phaeacians offers a clue to the answer and to the meaning of Odysseus' bow. After his winning discus-throw, Odysseus is in a good and garrulous mood, boasting to his hosts of his skill in archery (8. 215-228). At Troy, Odysseus claims, only Philoctetes surpassed him. But, then, Odysseus modestly adds, he would not dare to measure himself against the great archers of the past, neither Heracles nor Eurytus, who even challenged the gods. Heracles once wounded both Hera and Hades with his arrows, as Dione recounts to her daughter Aphrodite, who has just

---

[68] Galinsky (1972), p. 12. In the context, Heracles' brutal violation of the laws of hospitality stands in emphatic contrast to Odysseus' pious regard for them. Cf. K. Bielohlavek, "Zu den ethischen Werten in Idealtypen der griechischen Heldensage," WS 70 (1957):28; "Mit ihrer Darstellung des Mordes an Iphitos als einer am Gastfreund begangenen besonders schweren Freveltat geht die Odyssee über die ablehnende Haltung der Ilias gegenüber Herakles noch weit hinaus." For the tension between Heracles and the Homeric heroes, see U. von Wilamowitz-Moellendorff, Euripides Herakles, 2nd ed. (Darmstadt, 1959), 2:42-45.

[69] F. Prinz, s.v. "Herakles," RE Suppl. 14 (1974), p. 190. Prinz adds: "Iphitos scheint vom Odysseedichter oder seinen Vorgängern in der Sagenbildung wohl nur um des Bogens willen verwendet, wenn nicht sogar erfunden zu sein." Cf. on this question, P. Friedländer, Herakles, Philologische Untersuchungen 19 (Berlin, 1907), p. 73; and L. Radermacher, Mythos und Sage bei den Griechen (Munich, 1943), pp. 87-88.

been wounded by Diomedes. Dione ends her tale by roundly condemning Heracles' outrageous conduct:

σχέτλιος, ὀβριμοεργός, ὃς οὐκ ὅθετ᾿ αἴσυλα ῥέζων,
ὃς τόξοισιν ἔκηδε θεούς, οἳ Ὄλυμπον ἔχουσι.

Wretch, accomplisher of monstrous deeds, who cared
    nothing for the evil he did,
and who wounded with his arrows the gods who live on
    Olympus.
                                                              (*Il.* V. 403-404)

Eurytus, on the other hand, appears to have challenged the gods directly to a contest of archery. As a result, he never reached old age, but Apollo killed him in anger at his provocation.[70]

Now, while Homer nowhere explicitly states that Philoctetes inherited Heracles' bow, it seems clear that both he and his audience knew that tradition well. The *Iliad* alludes unmistakably to the rest of the story: Philoctetes' wound, his exile on Lemnos, and his later return to Troy (II. 716-726). The Catalogue of Ships says only that "Soon the Argives by their ships would remember lord Philoctetes" (II. 724-725). According to the fuller tradition, Philoctetes and his bow—the bow of Heracles—were essential to the destruction of Troy.[71] We can, then, add to the genealogy of Odysseus' bow a second parallel genealogy: Eurytus' bow is inherited by Iphi-

---

[70] Homer seems to betray no awareness of the traditions surrounding the *Sack of Oechalia*, ascribed to the poet Creophylus, in which Eurytus, along with his sons (who would, of course, include Iphitus), were killed by Heracles for refusing his daughter Iole to Heracles in marriage. Cf. Scholia B.Q. at 21. 22 and Eustathius 1899. 38 and 1593. 30-31. See also W. Burkert, "Die Leistung eines Kreophylos," *MH* 29 (1972):81; and Friedländer (1907), p. 74. This version of the story informs Sophocles' *Trachiniae*.

[71] See Proclus' summary of the *Little Iliad* (Allen 106) and the testimonia on later sources collected in Roscher, s.v. "Philoctetes," 3:2, 2313. In several versions, it is Odysseus, with either Diomedes or Neoptolemus, who goes on the mission to bring Philoctetes back to Troy. More often than not, Odysseus is said to retrieve the bow by means of trickery. In Sophocles' *Philoctetes*, Neoptolemus refuses to go along with Odysseus' deceit. The resultant impasse is only broken by the appearance of Heracles *ex machina*.

tus who gives it to Odysseus, while Heracles' bow is inherited by Philoctetes. This parallel genealogy and parallel rivalry—Heracles/Eurytus–Philoctetes/Odysseus—suggests that the Odysseus of the *Odyssey* ought to be viewed as both a parallel and a rival to the greatest hero of the Greek tradition, Heracles. But he must also be understood as a contrasting figure.[72] An elaborate comparison between Heracles and Odysseus is thus established, though its precise terms remain obscure. But the epiphany of the *eidolon* of Heracles indicates how the opposition should be understood.

With his observation of the so-called Great Sinners—Tityus, Tantalus, and Sisyphus—Odysseus' encounters with the dead in Book 11 draw to a close. But the last of the shades Odysseus notices before "green fear" compels him to retreat is Heracles—or his *eidolon*, since he himself (αὐτός) has joined the gods in their feasts along with his immortal wife, Hebe (11. 601-604).[73] The image of Heracles which offers itself to Odysseus' eyes is both haunting and hair-raising:

ἀμφὶ δέ μιν κλαγγὴ νεκύων ἦν οἰωνῶν ὥς,
πάντοσ᾽ ἀτυζομένων· ὁ δ᾽ ἐρεμνῇ νυκτὶ ἐοικώς,
γυμνὸν τόξον ἔχων καὶ ἐπὶ νευρῆφιν ὀϊστόν,
δεινὸν παπταίνων, αἰεὶ βαλέοντι ἐοικώς.

Round about him was the shrill cry of the dead, like
    birds,
scurrying in fear in all directions; but he was like gloomy
    night,
holding a naked bow with an arrow poised,
eyes blazing terribly, and always on the point of
    shooting.
                                          (11. 605-608)

---

[72] Cf. Galinsky (1972), p. 11, who comments that Heracles "serves as a foil for Odysseus."

[73] For the old controversy surrounding these lines, see D. Page, *The Homeric Odyssey* (Oxford, 1955), pp. 25-26 and notes; also E. Rohde, "Nekyia," *RM* 50 (1895):625-631. The apotheosis of Heracles described here contradicts the words of Achilles in XVIII. 117-119: "Not even the might of Heracles escaped death, / even he, who was dearest to lord Zeus, son of Cronus; / but fate overtook him and the harsh wrath of Hera."

Intensifying the horrifying image is the ghastly golden sword-belt Heracles wears, which depicts wild beasts, combats, battles, and murders.[74] Odysseus interrupts his own narrative to describe the sight. In a rare aside, he expresses the wish that such a horrible object had never been made and the hope that none like it may ever be manufactured again. No matter what one thinks of this passage and the many problems surrounding it, the smoldering violence of this Heracles is memorable and grippingly effective. Only one other moment in the *Odyssey* equals it: the beginning of Book 22, when Odysseus, bow in hand, reveals himself to the suitors.[75]

The grim figure of Heracles in the Nekyia immediately recognizes Odysseus and, somewhat surprisingly, addresses him in tears, drawing a parallel between his own hard lot and labors and the fate of Odysseus.[76] Although born a son of Zeus, Heracles was bound to obey an inferior, Eurystheus, and to perform many difficult labors. The parallelism, however, does not quite work, for neither divine parentage nor service to an inferior characterizes Odysseus' lot.[77] On the other hand, Heracles and Odysseus both participate in a sack of Troy (cf. *Il.* V. 642, XIV. 250-251; cf. XX. 145-148), both endure a delayed *nostos* because of an angry god (XIV. 253-256, XV. 25-30), and both accomplish the supreme heroic feat, the descent into Hades. The circumstances surrounding these two descents are, to be sure, quite different. Heracles goes down to fetch the hound of Hell, Cerberus, and enjoys

---

[74] Could these be depictions of the "Labors of Heracles"?

[75] As Galinsky (1972), p. 14, comments on 11. 605-608: "This is how Odysseus will appear to the suitors in Book 22." The expression, νυκτὶ ἐοικώς, 'like night' (606), occurs only once again in the Homeric corpus describing Apollo's appearance as he rains arrows down on the Achaeans in *Il.* I. 47.

[76] Cf. A. Thornton, *People and Themes in Homer's Odyssey* (Dunedin, 1970), p. 79: "The poet here presents Odysseus and Heracles as a pair in fate: the two who went to Hades alive, the two great archers."

[77] We may be reminded, rather, of Achilles, who himself draws a parallel between his fate and that of Heracles (XVIII. 117-121). It is noteworthy that the epithet θυμολέοντα, 'lion-hearted,' is reserved in Homer to Heracles (V. 639, 11. 267), Achilles (VII. 228), and Odysseus (4. 724 = 4. 814).

the help of Athena and Hermes on his mission (11. 623-626), while Odysseus' purpose is different—to learn the means of his return. No god assists him.

What links this passage from the Nekyia to the ones we have examined previously is once more the establishment of a parallelism and a contrast between Heracles and Odysseus. The relationship set up between the two heroes can be characterized by the contrast between the dark violent brutality of Heracles, the βίη Ἡρακληείη, as he is appropriately called in the formulaic language of the Epic,[78] and the *metis* and humanity of Odysseus. But we must not forget that *metis* is always an ambivalent quality; its darker aspects embrace trickery and deceit—*doloi*. In a transfer whose significance must not be overlooked or ignored, the *Odyssey* poet reassigns poison arrows, a dirty trick or *dolos* par excellence, from the figure with whom they are traditionally connected, Heracles, to his own hero, Odysseus (1. 260-264).[79] In his essay on the poison arrows of Odysseus, Dirlmeier preemptorily asserts that it is somehow improper to discern any connection between Heracles, Odysseus, and poison arrows:

> There is no Odysseus-type who is comparable to the Heracles whom Odysseus sees in the underworld. . . . To come to the point, the Ephyra incident [1. 260-264] should not under any circumstances be interpreted as if Odysseus were there for a moment assimilated to Heracles, who is in possession of poison arrows; the Hydra-poison . . . is mythical; the Ephyra-poison, on the other hand, "historical."[80]

The issue has nothing to do with mythical versus "historical" material; and the only impropriety lies in not following the evidence of the Homeric text. The opposition between Her-

---

[78] The expression occurs only here in the *Odyssey* but appears eight times in the *Iliad*.

[79] The poison for Heracles' arrows comes from the blood of the Hydra. Cf. Sophocles *Trachiniae* 574, 714-718, and Euripides *Heracles* 422.

[80] Dirlmeier (1966), p. 9. Heracles is, in fact, once mentioned in connection with Ephyra in the Catalogue of Ships (II. 659).

acles and Odysseus is carefully developed throughout the *Odyssey* with great subtlety and tact. That opposition culminates
in the poet's stripping Heracles of his traditional attribute—
the use of poison arrows—and transferring it to Odysseus,
thereby heightening the contrast between the two figures. The
man of *metis* rivals, if indeed he does not surpass, the hero
of force.

In this context, it is well to remember that the adventure
told at greatest length in Odysseus' wanderings relates what
happened in the Cyclops' cave. It recounts the triumph of
metis over brute force, *bie*. The strands which emanate from
the story of Odysseus' bow tell the same tale.

It is significant that no single one of the passages discussed
would have made this point in isolation. Like pieces in a jigsaw
puzzle which appear a meaningless jumble unless joined, the
full story of the bow emerges only when passages occurring
at widely different intervals are fitted together. Once joined,
however, the disparate pieces convey a message that touches
a central nerve of the *Odyssey*: that its hero, *polytropos* Odysseus, the man of *metis*, represents a radically different kind
of Epic hero.

ODYSSEUS AND ACHILLES

The web of allusions to Heracles, the greatest of the heroes
of the past, the *proteroi andres*, points to the peculiar character of Odysseus and the elevation of *metis* to heroic stature.
As we have seen, the poet of the *Odyssey* has considerably
coarsened and denigrated the features of the older hero in
order to throw into relief the *bie/metis* dichotomy with which
he is concerned. The more important confrontation between
Achilles and Odysseus has a similar foundation and function
in the poem, but it is both more thoroughly elaborated and
handled in a subtler fashion. Homer does not caricature the
figure of Achilles but gives him the honor due his greatness.
In the final analysis, however, the humane heroism of Odysseus, based as it is on intelligence and endurance, is set above
the quicksilver glory of Achilles.

The rivalry between Odysseus and Achilles surfaces explicitly three times in the *Odyssey*: in Demodocus' first song (8. 73-82) and in the two Nekyias. In turn, it implies a poetic rivalry between the *Iliad* and the *Odyssey*. The intimate connection between subject matter and poetics emerges most clearly but also most mysteriously in the first juxtaposition of Achilles and Odysseus: the first song Demodocus performs before the hero and the Phaeacians.[81]

The blind bard of the Phaeacians sings three songs in all. The adulterous adventures of Ares and Aphrodite, accompanied by dancing and recounted in direct discourse, are framed by two *klea andron*, incidents drawn from the Trojan expedition, which follow feasting and are summarized in indirect discourse. These three performances offer a triptych, examples of the range of the art of the Epic poet. Odysseus requests the final song, the tale of the wooden horse, while the first, concerning the quarrel of Odysseus and Achilles, is prompted by the Muse:

> Μοῦσ' ἄρ' ἀοιδὸν ἀνῆκεν ἀειδέμεναι κλέα ἀνδρῶν,
> οἴμης τῆς τότ' ἄρα κλέος οὐρανὸν εὐρὺν ἵκανε,
> νεῖκος Ὀδυσσῆος καὶ Πηλεΐδεω Ἀχιλῆος,
> ὥς ποτε δηρίσαντο θεῶν ἐν δαιτὶ θαλείῃ
> ἐκπάγλοις ἐπέεσσιν, ἄναξ δ' ἀνδρῶν Ἀγαμέμνων
> χαῖρε νόῳ, ὅ τ' ἄριστοι Ἀχαιῶν δηριόωντο.
> ὣς γάρ οἱ χρείων μυθήσατο Φοῖβος Ἀπόλλων
> Πυθοῖ ἐν ἠγαθέῃ, ὅθ' ὑπέρβη λάϊνον οὐδὸν
> χρησόμενος· τότε γάρ ῥα κυλίνδετο πήματος ἀρχὴ
> Τρωσί τε καὶ Δαναοῖσι Διὸς μεγάλου διὰ βουλάς.

[81] In the course of the slow birth of this book, the substance of this section was formulated before the appearance of Nagy's masterful study, *The Best of the Achaeans* (Baltimore, 1979), from which I have greatly benefited. Our analyses converge on a good many points, but differ decisively on certain fundamental issues. Rather than recast my argument, which I think has an integrity of its own, I have taken up our differences in the Appendix. Two other studies on the first song of Demodocus have also proved useful: W. Marg, "Das erste Lied des Demodocus," in *Navicula Chiloniensis: Festschrift für Felix Jacoby* (Leiden, 1956), pp. 16-19; and Rüter (1969), pp. 247-254. My interpretation of this intriguing passage is also indebted to theirs, but in the last analysis differs in its conclusions.

The Muse roused the bard to sing the *klea andron*,
from the lay[82] whose fame then reached wide heaven,
the quarrel of Odysseus and Achilles, the son of Peleus,
how once they fell out in a flourishing banquet of the
   gods
with violent words; but Agamemnon, lord of men,
rejoiced in his heart that the best of the Achaeans were
   quarreling;
for thus had Phoebus Apollo prophesied to him
in holy Pytho, when he crossed the stone threshold
to consult the oracle; for then truly did the beginning of
   woe roll down
upon Trojans and Danaans alike, through the plans of
   great Zeus.

(8. 73-82)

The incident is summarized only in the sketchiest fashion. Agamemnon had gone to Delphi, presumably before the beginning of the expedition against Troy, to inquire about the success of the undertaking. The oracular response must have been something like: "When the best of the Achaeans quarrel, then Troy will be taken." Observing Achilles and Odysseus quarreling at a feast, Agamemnon rejoices, thinking, on the basis of the prophecy, that the fall of Troy is near at hand. We can easily reconstruct that much. But where and when did the quarrel occur? What were the issues? How did it end? All this is left tantalizingly vague.

Demodocus' words do not, after all, unambiguously indicate the occasion of the quarrel. The "beginning of woe which rolled over both Greeks and Trojans" may refer not to the scene of the dispute but merely to the occasion of the oracle itself.[83] Neither the oracle nor the quarrel is reported in Pro-

---

[82] It is unclear whether οἴμης is a partitive genitive ("from the lay whose fame reached heaven") or whether it is simply attracted into the genitive case: "the lay, whose fame reached heaven." The first would emphasize that Demodocus performs part of a larger whole. Nagy (1979), p. 18n., translates *oime* as "story-thread" and discerns an underlying image of weaving.

[83] On the ambiguity of τότε (8. 81), see Marg (1956), pp. 23-24 and Rüter (1969), p. 248. Marg calls the "Formulierung sehr merkwürdig."

clus' summaries of the *Cypria*, recounting events preceding the opening of the *Iliad*, or in the *Aethiopis*, which covered events after the *Iliad* up to the death of Achilles. Yet most modern interpreters of the passage have tended to set the quarrel near the beginning of the war. Searching for an occasion, some have fixed on an incident in the *Cypria* when the assembled Greek host feasted on Tenedos, before crossing over to the Troad.[84] There, Proclus says, "while they were feasting . . . Achilles, who was invited last, had an argument with Agamemnon."[85] As reported, the quarrel involves not Odysseus, but Achilles and Agamemnon. It seems to be a doublet of the dispute between them at the beginning of the *Iliad* and presumably centered similarly on an offense to Achilles' sense of honor.[86] The only reason to connect Odysseus with the disagreement on Tenedos is a fragment from a play of Sophocles, the *Syndeipnoi*, or *Feasters* (Fr. 566 Pearson), in which Odysseus evidently attempts to shift Achilles' attention away from the supposed insult at the feast.[87] Achilles had announced his intention to return home, and Odysseus accuses him of cowardice. If Fragment 567 is assigned to Achilles, then he responded by insulting Odysseus' lineage from both Autolycus and Sisyphus. The words exchanged are surely harsh, but they are also peripheral; the real *neikos* on Tenedos remains between Agamemnon and Achilles.[88]

[84] See especially P. Von der Mühll, "Zur Frage, wie sich die Kyprien zur Odyssee verhalten," in *Ausgewählte kleine Schriften* (Basel, 1976), pp. 148-54. Von der Mühll, p. 154, believes that Demodocus' song is derived from the Tenedos incident in the *Cypria* and must be a later addition to the *Odyssey*, since the *Cypria* is post-Homeric. He does not consider the possibility that the traditions incorporated into the *Cypria* are pre-Homeric.

[85] Proclus, 104 (Allen).

[86] Cf. Aristotle *Rhetoric* 2, 24, 6, who alludes to the incident: ". . . because he was not invited Achilles was wroth with the Achaeans at Tenedos; whereas he was really wroth because he had been treated with disrespect, ὡς ἀτιμαζόμενος ἐμήνισε (trans. J. H. Freese [Cambridge, Mass., 1939], p. 331).

[87] For the context of the fragment, see Plutarch *Quomodo adul.* 36, 74a.

[88] Cf. A. C. Pearson, ed., *The Fragments of Sophocles*, 3 vols., (Cambridge, 1917), 2:199: "The banquet at Tenedos must not be identified with the occasion briefly described in Hom. ϑ 75-82, in spite of the words ἐν δαιτὶ ϑαλείῃ: for (1) the quarrel mentioned in the *Odyssey* took place at a later

After dismissing Tenedos and the episode from the *Cypria* as a possible *locus* for the dispute between Odysseus and Achilles, many scholars still insist that it occurred early on, near the beginning of the Trojan expedition.[89] Yet the reasoning is poor: if Achilles' dispute with Odysseus had taken place *after* the quarrel of Achilles and Agamemnon in the *Iliad*, then Agamemnon would have had to remember the oracle on the earlier occasion. But the *Iliad* mentions no such prophecy; hence the incident recounted by Demodocus must have happened *before* the beginning of the *Iliad*.[90] The point, then, of Demodocus' tale becomes the fact that Agamemnon misunderstood the oracle and rejoiced prematurely—over the wrong quarrel.[91] There is nothing in our text to support the hypothesis that Agamemnon was mistaken; and the consequences of this view are completely out of keeping both with

---

period of the siege, and (2) the altercation at Tenedos was between Achilles and Agamemnon, not, as in the *Odyssey*, between Achilles and Odysseus." Von der Mühll (1976), the main proponent of Tenedos as the site of the dispute, explains Agamemnon's rejoicing (χαῖρε νόῳ) as due to his involvement in the quarrel, i.e., that Odysseus took his side in the dispute (p. 151). That, of course, dispenses with the oracle. Von der Mühll also admits that he can find no convincing explanation for how a quarrel arising from an offense to Achilles' honor could be linked to a dispute concerning courage and intelligence, force and guile, as the scholiasts on the passage report (see below).

[89] Cf. Marg (1956), p. 24; Rüter (1969), p. 248; and Nagy (1979), p. 64, speaks of Agamemnon's "premature conclusion" and places the quarrel before Achilles' withdrawal from battle, hence before the beginning of our *Iliad*.

[90] Marg (1956), p. 24: "Die hier vom Dichter angenommene, wenn auch übergangene Situation muss natürlich vor dem Agamemnon-Achilleus-Streit liegen; sonst könnte Agamemnon das Orakel nicht so fehldeuten."

[91] Cf. Rüter (1969), p. 248: "je früher im Krieg unsere Szene, um so grösser die Selbsttäuschung Agamemnons." Also G. M. Calhoun, "Homer's Gods—Myth and Märchen," *AJP* 60 (1939):11, n. 25: "This is quite clearly a story based on the motif of the misunderstood prophecy." The same interpretation was already put forth by "some" in antiquity. See Porphyry *Quaestiones Hom. ad Od. Pert.*, 72, 21 (Schrader) and Scholium H.Q. at 8. 77. For Nagy (1979), p. 64, Agamemnon's misunderstanding of the oracle consists in his premature joy "at a sign that presaged the destruction of Troy" while he remained "unaware of the intervening pain yet to be inflicted on the Achaeans by the withdrawal and then by the death of Achilles."

the immediate and wider context of Demodocus' song. The motif of the misunderstood prophecy is, of course, common enough throughout Greek literature, but that cannot be the focus of this tale which must remain fixed on the *neikos* itself. Ancient commentators had nothing to go on but the words of the *Odyssey* itself in their attempt to solve the riddle of Demodocus' song.[92] We, also, are in the same shoes as the Alexandrians. But they came up with a far more convincing and plausible explanation both for the timing of the quarrel and its contents. According to them, it occurred toward the end of the Trojan War, after the death of Hector, with which the *Iliad* ends. The issue between Achilles and Odysseus was whether Troy would be taken by force or by guile. The scholiasts paraphrase the differences between the two heroes in terms of a contrast between ἀνδρεία and σύνεσις, between 'courage' and 'intelligence,' βία and δόλος, 'force' and 'trickery,' or τὰ σωματικά and τὰ ψυχικά, 'bodily things' and 'spiritual things.'[93] But to speak Homerically is to speak of a contrast between *bie* and *metis*. At bottom, the confrontation between Odysseus and Achilles parallels the contrast between Odysseus and Heracles.

The old interpretation of the quarrel allows us to connect the first song of Demodocus closely to the last;[94] for what was first debated in words is decided by the event. The wooden horse, the stratagem of Odysseus, which the hero himself calls a *dolos* (8. 494), proclaims that the final victory belongs to *metis*. The taking of Troy through *dolos* wins for Odysseus

[92] Marg (1956), p. 20, calls the scholiasts' interpretation of the passage "reine Rekonstruktion aus der Odysseestelle," which proves that "der alexandrinischen Homererklärung keine Überlieferung über das Thema vorlag."

[93] Scholia H.Q.V. at 8. 75 and B.E. at 8. 77; cf. Eustathius 1586. 25-28. See also Nagy (1979), pp. 45ff. concerning the *bie/metis* dichotomy as the crux of the conflict between Achilles and Odysseus.

[94] Thornton (1970), pp. 43-44, while insisting that the quarrel took place at the beginning of the war, recognizes the close connection between the last song of Demodocus and the first, which she calls a "counterpiece" to it. "The first song of Demodocus therefore prepares for his third song in which Odysseus' guile triumphs."

the epithet πτολίπορθος "city-sacker," which he shares with
Achilles.[95] After the third song, Odysseus is moved to tears
as he had been after the first. A breathtaking simile describes
Odysseus' weeping (8. 522-531). The tears of city-sacking
Odysseus are likened to those of a woman helplessly watching
her husband being killed while defending his children and city
from destruction. The capture of the city is seen through the
eyes of the most helpless victim.[96] The αἰνότατος πόλεμος,
"the most terrible war" (8. 519), of the narrative of the sack
of Troy and the ἐλεεινότατον ἄχος, "the most pitiful grief"
(8. 530), of the simile are one and the same, two sides of the
same image. The fall of Troy is the *pema* which rolls over
both Greek and Trojan alike (8. 81-82). The first song of
Demodocus complements the last. Together, they articulate a
central theme of the *Odyssey*: the confrontation of *bie* and
metis in the persons of Achilles and Odysseus, a contestation
leading to the ultimate triumph of *metis*.

Mysteries remain, however. The story of the wooden horse
occurs in the Epic Cycle and references to it abound in later
Greek art and literature. But the "Quarrel of Achilles and
Odysseus"—an epic theme if ever there was one—is not attested in Proclus or anywhere else apart from the unique passage under discussion. The song which proclaims that its "fame
then reached heaven" has never been heard since. This suggests that, unlike his third song, the first song of Demodocus
may not be traditional but has been woven out of whole cloth,
and is an invention of the poet.[97] But this cannot be quite

---

[95] πτολίπορθος is restricted to Odysseus in the *Odyssey* (eight times). But
in the *Iliad* the epithet is used of Ares and Enyo (XX. 152, V. 333), and in
two instances it is applied to *fathers* of heroes (II. 728, XX. 384). Of contemporary heroes, however, it is confined to Achilles and Odysseus (XXI.
550, XXIV. 108, VIII. 372, XV. 77, II. 278, X. 363).

[96] See H. Foley, "Reverse Similes and Sex Roles in the Odyssey," *Arethusa*
11 (1978):7. Nagy (1979), p. 101 comments: "The resemblance with Hektor
is unmistakable" as is the "parallel to the specific situation of Andromache
at the end of the *Iliou Persis*."

[97] Marg (1956), p. 21 calls it an "Augenblickserfindung." For Nagy's position, see Appendix. See also J. Griffin, *Homer on Life and Death* (Oxford,
1980), p. 185, for a possible parallel in Thetis' story of the Olympian con-
spiracy against Zeus.

correct either. Every element in Demodocus' account has a
parallel in traditional material, more precisely, in the *Iliad*
itself.[98] The song Demodocus performs appears, then, to be
an amalgam of familiar material in a new configuration. To
what purpose?

To answer this question, we must examine the unmistakable
echoes of the *Iliad* and see how they are recombined. The
Iliad, of course, begins with the quarrel of Agamemnon and
Achilles, who also exchange violent words. The strife breaks
out between the two chieftains who, Nestor says, "surpass
the Greeks in counsel and fighting" (I. 258). It is again Nestor
who recognizes that their dispute is, basically, a duel for supreme honor, with power and rank on the side of Agamemnon
opposed by Achilles' accomplishment of warlike deeds (I. 280-
281). As the proem tells us, the quarrel leads finally to countless sufferings for the Greeks (I. 2-5). "And the will of Zeus
was accomplished" (I. 5; cf. 8. 82).

The verbal and thematic similarities between the beginning
of the *Iliad* and the tale of Demodocus are most striking, and
I do not believe them to be coincidental. Even those elements
appearing to differ from the account of the quarrel of Achilles
and Agamemnon ultimately seem to derive from the *Iliad*. The
dispute which erupts in the *Odyssey* takes place at a feast,
θεῶν ἐν δαιτί. The setting at a banquet suggests the immediate impulse to the quarrel: who—Achilles or Odysseus—
should receive the portion of honor? The content of the debate
centers on the question of whether Troy should be taken by
force or guile. But the setting in the *Odyssey* makes clear that
the dispute is ultimately a contest for supremacy. To be sure,
the initial rupture between Agamemnon and Achilles occurs
at an *agora* rather than a feast, but their reconciliation is
immediately followed by a disagreement between *Achilles and
Odysseus* about whether to have a feast (XIX. 155ff.). Im-
petuously, Achilles wants to go into battle immediately and
refuses to eat, while Odysseus insists that the army must eat

---

[98] For Iliadic reminiscences, see Marg (1956), pp. 25-26 and Rüter (1969),
pp. 248-251, whom I follow closely. Cf. Nagy (1979), pp. 23ff. The story
of the contest between Ajax and Odysseus over the arms of Achilles, which
is alluded to in the *Odyssey* (11. 554-555), may also have played a role.

before fighting. At the end, Odysseus asks Achilles to give way to him, even though Achilles is mightier; but he, Odysseus, surpasses him in intelligence, since he is "older and knows more" (XIX. 217-219). A tension between Achilles and Odysseus—perhaps inevitable, given the character of the two—is already apparent in the Embassy scene in Book IX of the *Iliad*.[99] There, Odysseus makes the "official" speech, giving Agamemnon's terms for a reconciliation. Tactfully, Odysseus omits the end of Agamemnon's own speech in which the king had insisted that Achilles give in and submit to Agamemnon's greater power and rank. Instead, Odysseus substitutes an appeal to Achilles to pity the Greeks and promises him great glory if he should fight Hector (IX. 158-161; cf. IX. 300-306). Odysseus' discretion fails on this occasion. Achilles' rejection of Agamemnon's overtures is preceded by the famous response which not only makes the claim that his own speech will be direct and straightforward, but also implies that Odysseus' has been substantially less than honest:

ἐχθρὸς γάρ μοι κεῖνος ὁμῶς Ἀΐδαο πύλῃσιν
ὅς χ' ἕτερον μὲν κεύθῃ ἐνὶ φρεσίν, ἄλλο δὲ εἴπῃ.

Hateful to me as the gates of Hades is the man
who hides one thing in his heart and says another.
                                                (IX. 312-313)

Odysseus has done just that. A natural tension emerges here between Achilles' self-proclaimed simplicity and the *polymechanie* of Odysseus.

Thus, almost every element in Demodocus' first song appears to be inspired by the *Iliad*. If in some sense the three songs of the Phaeacian bard, taken together, represent the range of possibilities open to the Epic poet, then his first song seems to demonstrate the poet's freedom to transform traditional themes and motifs into something new.[100]

---

[99] The scholium at IX. 347 refers to our passage (τὸ ἐν Ὀδυσσείᾳ ζητού-μενον "νεῖκος Ὀδυσσῆος καὶ Πηλείδεω Ἀχιλῆος"). Cf. Rüter (1969), p. 250, and especially Nagy (1979), pp. 49ff. on the Embassy scene.

[100] Compare the comments of K. Reinhardt, "Das Parisurteil," in *Tradition*

There is, however, one important component of Demodocus' tale which has no parallel in the *Iliad* and is not mentioned
anywhere else: the oracle given to Agamemnon that Troy
would fall when the best of the Achaeans quarreled.[101] Of
course, oracles and prophecies concerning the fall of Troy
abound both in the *Iliad* and in the Cyclic poems. But this
particular one is not attested. It is, I believe, nothing other
than an invention inspired by the opening situation of the
Iliad. Within the context of Demodocus' song, its significance
lies not in Agamemnon's misunderstanding of an ambiguous
prophecy, but in the playful implication that the *Iliad* presents
the "wrong" quarrel. The misapprehension of the oracle lies
not with Agamemnon, but with us, the audience of the *Iliad*,
who wrongly believed that Agamemnon and Achilles were the
"best of the Achaeans."

According to the *Odyssey*, the best of the Greeks are necessarily Achilles and Odysseus. The definition of "best" no
longer centers on rank, power, and strength, as it did in the
dispute between Agamemnon and Achilles, but rather on two
modes of existence, two conceptions of the world and man's
relation to it, embodied in Achilles and Odysseus,[102] and
summed up in part in the contrast between *bie* and *metis*.

In pitting the two heroes of their respective Epics against
each other, Homer, both playfully and seriously, suggests an
alternate *Iliad*. Marg correctly apprehends the playful implications: "A game is being played here: a poem which is very
similar to the *Iliad*, and yet is not the *Iliad*."[103] But when he
poses the obvious question—"why does the poet not allow
Demodocus to sing the *Iliad* openly?"—he answers that it
would not do, since any closer allusion to the *Iliad* here would
break the dramatic framework. I, frankly, do not understand

---

und Geist (Göttingen, 1960), p. 20: ". . . indem das grosse Epos die ihm
vorausliegenden Geschichten umformt, hebt, verfeinert, schafft es ihm ge-
mässe epische Situationen, die in seinem Stil, in seiner Tonart die alten Motive
neu zum Klingen bringen."

[101] Cf. Marg (1956), p. 25: "das Apollonorakel hat keine Parallele."

[102] Cf. Rüter (1969), pp. 249ff.

[103] Marg (1956), p. 26.

what that means, nor can I concur with Marg's conclusion that Demodocus' song is intended as an indirect praise of the *Iliad*.[104] The serious implications of the alternate *Iliad* outlined by Demodocus go far beyond a courtly gesture and point rather to a poem whose scope is more global and whose issues are more fundamental than those of the *Iliad*. The poet hints at the wider compass of his alternate *Iliad* by speaking of a *pema* which touches both Greeks and Trojans alike, while the proem of the *Iliad* dwells solely on the sufferings of the *Greeks*.[105] Demodocus' first song alludes to a poem that never existed, was never composed. It looks back at the *Iliad* through the eyes of the *Odyssey*, an *Iliad* recast in the light of the themes and issues of the *Odyssey* and its hero.

The confrontation of Achilles and Odysseus entails a confrontation of the *Iliad* and the *Odyssey*. If the Epic can be defined as the poetry of praise,[106] then the praise of Odysseus in the *Odyssey* vies with the praise of Achilles in the *Iliad*. In setting up his hero as an equal—if not superior—to Achilles, the poet of the *Odyssey* stakes the highest claim to the excellence of his own poem.[107] The remaining scenes juxtaposing

---

[104] Marg (1956), p. 28, goes on to conclude from what he takes as indirect praise of the *Iliad* that the poet of the *Odyssey* cannot be the poet of the *Iliad*: "Sein eigenes Gedicht kann der Dichter nicht so loben." This involves him in a contradiction, since he has just claimed: "Die Odyssee stellt sich so stolz neben die Ilias, sieht sich von gleicher Gültigkeit vor dem Himmel, den Göttern." In any case, the Epic poet, whose business it is to give *kleos aphthiton*, imperishable fame, to the heroes and their deeds, has no need for modesty concerning his enterprise.

[105] Cf. Eustathius 1586. 35, who explains Διὸς μεγάλου διὰ βουλάς (8. 82) as follows: "these plans are that Troy is to be destroyed with much toil on the part of both armies, and not, indeed, that Achilles be honored, as is the case in the *Iliad*." (αἵπέρ εἰσι, τὸ πολλῷ πόνῳ ἑκατέρων τῶν στρατευμάτων ἁλῶναι τὴν Τροίαν, καὶ οὐ δή ποτε τὸ τιμηθῆναι τὸν Ἀχιλλέα ὅπερ ἐν Ἰλιάδι ἐφαίνετο).

[106] Nagy (1979), pp. 222ff.

[107] Cf. Marg (1956), p. 22: "Odysseus gegenüber Achilleus: die Besten, Gestalt gegen Gestalt—fast Gedicht gegen Gedicht." Compare also Rüter (1969), p. 253: "Indem der Dichter der Odyssee . . . den Helden seines Epos dem grössten Helden der Ilias ebenbürtig sein lässt, meldet er, wie wir meinen, zugleich für sein Gedicht den Anspruch an, ebenbürtig neben die Ilias zu treten." Unfortunately, Rüter then (p. 254) proceeds to call this equation of the hero and the poem dedicated to him a "naive Literaturauffassung."

Odysseus and Achilles in the *Odyssey* all focus on the problem of praise, *kleos*, and the terms of praise suitable to Odysseus. After Demodocus' songs and Odysseus' tears, Alcinoos asks the stranger's name and the cause of his weeping. Has he, by any chance, lost a close relative at Troy, or a noble companion? "For a friend who is pleasing and wise is by no means inferior to a brother" (8. 585-586). The ghost of Achilles hovers over these words; Alcinoos' striking formulation inevitably reminds us of Achilles and his beloved companion, Patroclus. The evocation of Achilles and his fate at this very moment of the narrative should give us pause to contemplate the difference between the two heroes. No, Odysseus is no Achilles; their stories and their destinies point in different directions.

At long last, Odysseus answers Alcinoos' question:

εἴμ' Ὀδυσεὺς Λαερτιάδης, ὃς πᾶσι δόλοισιν
ἀνθρώποισι μέλω, καί μευ κλέος οὐρανὸν ἵκει.

I am Odysseus, son of Laertes, who for all wiles
am famous among men, and my fame reaches heaven.

(9. 19-20)

The self-revelation of Odysseus forms the climax to Demodocus' songs which presented the victory of Odyssean *metis*. In announcing himself to Alcinoos and the Phaeacians, Odysseus lays claim to the highest *kleos*, based on the fame of his *doloi*. The fame of Demodocus' song already reaches heaven (8. 74). To be complete, the triumph of Odyseus' *metis* must be celebrated in song; it must receive its due share of *kleos*, the fame by which song grants immortality to great accomplishments. *Kleos*, as Nagy points out, cannot exist outside the medium of its transmission: ". . . the usual translation of κλέος, 'fame,' is inadequate: it merely designates the consequences rather than the full semantic range. *The actions of the gods and heroes gain fame through the medium of the Singer, and the Singer calls his medium κλέος.*"[108] The confrontations of Achilles, Odysseus, and also Agamemnon in

[108] Nagy (1974), p. 250.

the first and second Nekyia center on the question of *kleos*.[109]
Undying fame has already been assured to Achilles. But what
kind of *kleos* is appropriate to Odysseus?

At Alcinoos' request, Odysseus recounts his meeting with
the shades of three heroes of the Trojan expedition. Ajax, the
last, remains silent, while Agamemnon bitterly recounts the
details of his murder at the hands of Aegisthus and warns
Odysseus of the wiles of women. The *psyche* of Achilles now
approaches in the company of his beloved Patroclus and other
heroes. In tears, Achilles asks what brings Odysseus to Hades
"where the insubstantial dead abide" (11. 475-476)—or does
Odysseus "devise some even greater deed?" (11. 474). Odysseus explains his mission to consult the seer Teiresias, for he
has yet to reach home, but "always has evils" (11. 482). In
contrast to his own unrelenting plight, Odysseus praises the
unparalleled felicity of Achilles, who "was honored as a god
in his lifetime and now rules over the assembled dead" (11.
482-486).

"Speak to me not of death," begins Achilles' famous reply.
He would rather be the serf of a poor man than rule over all
the dead (11. 489-491). Achilles now claims to prefer life on
any terms, no matter how lowly. We inevitably remember the
well-known choice of Achilles from the *Iliad*:

εἰ μέν κ᾽ αὖθι μένων Τρώων πόλιν ἀμφιμάχωμαι,
ὤλετο μέν μοι νόστος, ἀτὰρ κλέος ἄφθιτον ἔσται·
εἰ δέ κεν οἴκαδ᾽ ἵκωμι φίλην ἐς πατρίδα γαῖαν,
ὤλετό μοι κλέος ἐσθλόν, ἐπὶ δηρὸν δέ μοι αἰὼν
ἔσσεται, οὐδέ κέ μ᾽ ὦκα τέλος θανάτοιο κιχείη.

If I stay here and fight by the city of the Trojans,
my homecoming is gone, but my fame will be
    imperishable.
But if I go home to my own paternal land,
my fine fame is gone, but long my life
will be, nor will death soon overtake me.
                                        (IX. 412-416)

---

[109] Cf. Rüter (1969), pp. 251ff.; also Wender (1978), pp. 41-44; and Nagy
(1979), pp. 35ff.

The choice offered to Achilles allows of no middle ground: *either* a short, glorious life with no return *or* a long life of obscurity at home. The terms of Achilles' choice present no alternate route to immortal fame than glorious death in battle. The road to *kleos* appears to require the passport of premature death. In his passionate response to Odysseus' words of praise, Achilles regrets his former choice, but can only embrace the other extreme: the lowliest, most obscure existence he can imagine.

The fate of Agamemnon seems to confirm the absence of any possible compromise. While Agamemnon does survive Troy, his murder by his wife's lover upon his return constitutes the most pitiful and inglorious death for one who was the most powerful king among the Greeks. In the second Nekyia, Achilles commiserates with Agamemnon, and wishes that, instead of his disgraceful end, the king had died like him, fighting before Troy with his honor intact (24. 30-31), "and great glory would have redounded to his son thereafter" (24. 33). But Agamemnon's "most pitiful death" (24. 34) has somehow deprived him of that *kleos*. He will, indeed, earn a measure of remembrance through song. But it will not be a song of *kleos*, but rather, as Agamemnon himself predicts, a στυγερὴ ἀοιδή, a "hateful song," heaping shame and bad repute on the race of women—even those who are virtuous (24. 200-202; cf. 11. 433-434).[110]

As Odysseus had done before him, Agamemnon now lauds the fate of Achilles:

> ὄλβιε Πηλέος υἱέ, θεοῖς ἐπιείκελ' Ἀχιλλεῦ. . . .

> Happy son of Peleus, you who are like the gods, Achilles. . . .

> (24. 36)

Describing to Achilles his death in battle and splendid funeral, where the Muses themselves sang a *threnos* and gods and men

---

[110] For the "hateful song" as the converse of the song of praise, see Nagy (1979), p. 255n.

joined in the mourning (24. 60-64), Agamemnon concludes
with the pronouncement:

ὣς σὺ μὲν οὐδὲ θανὼν ὄνομ' ὤλεσας, ἀλλά τοι αἰεὶ
πάντας ἐπ' ἀνθρώπους κλέος ἔσσεται ἐσθλόν,
Ἀχιλλεῦ.

So, not even in death have you lost your name, but always
you will have a fine *kleos* among all men, Achilles.

(24. 93-94)

In Book 1, Odysseus' own son Telemachus contrasts the
glory his father would have earned in dying before Troy with
the lack of *kleos* his long absence entails:

. . . εἰ μετὰ οἷς ἑτάροισι δάμη Τρώων ἐνὶ δήμῳ,
ἠὲ φίλων ἐν χερσίν, ἐπεὶ πόλεμον τολύπευσε.
τῷ κέν οἱ τύμβον μὲν ἐποίησαν Παναχαιοί,
ἠδέ κε καὶ ᾧ παιδὶ μέγα κλέος ἤρατ' ὀπίσσω.
νῦν δέ μιν ἀκλειῶς ἅρπυιαι ἀνηρείψαντο.

. . . if he had succumbed in Troy among his comrades,
or in the arms of his friends, when he had finished the
    war—
then all the Greeks would have made him a tomb,
and for his son also he would have won great *kleos*.
But now the whirlwinds have snatched him away without
    kleos.

(1. 237-241)

The same wish Achilles had expressed for Agamemnon—to
die gloriously at Troy—is repeated by Odysseus on his skimpy
raft when Poseidon sends the mighty storm against him:

τρισμάκαρες Δαναοὶ καὶ τετράκις οἳ τότ' ὄλοντο
Τροίῃ ἐν εὐρείῃ, χάριν Ἀτρεΐδῃσι φέροντες.
ὡς δὴ ἐγώ γ' ὄφελον θανέειν καὶ πότμον ἐπισπεῖν
ἤματι τῷ ὅτε μοι πλεῖστοι χαλκήρεα δοῦρα
Τρῶες ἐπέρριψαν περὶ Πηλείωνι θανόντι.
τῷ κ' ἔλαχον κτερέων, καί μευ κλέος ἦγον Ἀχαιοί·
νῦν δέ με λευγαλέῳ θανάτῳ εἵμαρτο ἁλῶναι.

Three and four times blessed are the Danaans, who died
   then
in wide Troy, bringing favor to the sons of Atreus.
Would that I too had died and met my fate
on that day, when the greatest number of Trojans
hurled against me their bronze spears around the dead
   son of Peleus.
Then I would have received funeral honors, and the
   Achaeans would have maintained my *kleos*;
but now I am destined to perish by a miserable death.
                                              (5. 306-312)

To have died defending the body of Achilles would have assured Odysseus' *kleos*, which now is threatened by a miserable
death at sea, just as Agamemon's was by his pitiful murder
(5. 312; cf. 24. 34).

Agamemnon, Telemachus, and even Odysseus, in a moment
of despair, appear to accept the harsh uncompromising polarities of Achilles' choice: *nostos*, homecoming, and *kleos* are
regarded as mutually exclusive. From this perspective, the
story of Odysseus, the *Odyssey*, offers an alternative: a new
kind of *kleos* founded precisely on Return and long life. The
traditional *kleos* of an Achilles demands spectacular martial
accomplishments, unflinching courage, and a splendid death
on the field of battle. The *kleos* of Odysseus, on the other
hand, resides in endurance and survival and on the accomplishment of the Return through the aid of *metis*.

After hearing an account of the final stages of that Return,
culminating in the slaughter of the suitors, Agamemnon breaks
into words of praise, reminiscent of his earlier apostrophe of
Achilles:

ὄλβιε Λαέρταο πάϊ, πολυμήχαν' Ὀδυσσεῦ . . .

Happy son of Laertes, Odysseus of many devices . . .
                                      (24. 192; cf. 24. 36)

This, at the very end of the poem, is the seal to the promise
of *kleos*, both for Odysseus and for his Penelope, whose fame
will never perish; "and the gods themselves will make a pleas-

ing song about them for mortals" (24. 196-198). The *Odyssey*, the song of praise for Odysseus, fulfills that promise.

ODYSSEUS AND POLYPHEMUS

So far, I have attempted to approach Odysseus from various angles—his name, his Autolycan heritage, and his relation to two other heroes of the Epic, Achilles and Heracles. It would be possible to discuss each of his adventures in order to reveal Odysseus' character in action, but I will limit myself to one incident: the episode in the cave of Polyphemus. Such a choice may appear arbitrary and in need of justification. It is not, for example, Odysseus' most disastrous adventure in terms of the number of men lost. That prize must go to the brief visit to the Laestrygonians, where eleven ships and their crews are destroyed. One could, of course, argue that the *consequence* of the Cyclops incident—the wrath of Poseidon—is most crucial to Odysseus' fate. Considering, however the great detail with which the story is related, the incident derives its interest from more than its outcome alone.

To put it most simply, what happens in Polyphemus' cave constitutes the most "Odyssean" of all the adventures. Here, Odysseus is still unhandicapped by the Cyclops' curse, and the anger of Poseidon has not yet begun. Moreover, we have seen that Athena, Odysseus' patroness, is significantly absent from the entire episode. In another context, Odysseus himself comments:

ῥηΐδιον δὲ θεοῖσι, τοὶ οὐρανὸν εὐρὺν ἔχουσιν,
ἠμὲν κυδῆναι θνητὸν βροτὸν ἠδὲ κακῶσαι.

It is easy for the gods, who live in broad heaven,
either to glorify a mortal man or to make him wretched.
(16. 211-212)

While it may well be easy for the gods to intervene, here, at least, neither divine protection nor divine enmity influence the action. If we want to see Odysseus plain, here is where we must look. Then, too, this episode differs from most of the

later adventures because the encounter with Polyphemus is
not foretold to Odysseus by anyone. When Odysseus approaches the Sirens, or passes through Scylla and Charybdis,
or becomes stranded on Thrinacia, he has been warned of the
dangers by Teiresias or Circe. But Odysseus is in no way
prepared for what he will find when he enters the cave of
Polyphemus. He extricates himself from the cave by his wits
alone, without any divine assistance, or the help of foreknowledge, nor yet with the hindrance of Poseidon's wrath. As a
result, the Cyclops episode has a unique place among Odysseus' adventures and stands as his masterpiece. Here, and
preeminently here, we find him the quintessential man of *metis*.

The confrontation between Polyphemus and Odysseus re-
states the opposition between *bie* and *metis* in the clearest as
well as the broadest terms. Odysseus makes good his escape
from the cave of the Cyclops by means of many *doloi*, tricks
both verbal (especially the ploy with the name) and nonverbal
deceptions.[111] But the fuller range of meaning of *metis*, as
defined by Hesychius, is exploited throughout the adventure:
σύνεσις, βουλή, τέχνη, γνώμη, δόλος, ἀπάτη—"understanding, counsel, art or skill, intelligence, trickery, deception." Odysseus' *metis* here represents more than the re-
sourcefulness and guile necessary for getting out of the ogre's
cave alive; it also stands for the arts and skills of civilization,
the *technai*, which are contrasted with the Cyclopes' lack of
technology and civilized life. The narrative continually draws
attention to this contrast, not only in the story, but also through
the similes, whose cumulative effect carries out the message
of the tale: "Odysseus' defeat of the Cyclops is thus," as Segal
puts it, "a great victory of his human intelligence over the
vast, primitive forces . . . the sheer *bia* . . . of untamed nature."[112]

[111] Cf. G. Hunger, "Die Odysseusgestalt in Odyssee und Ilias" (Diss., University of Kiel, 1962), p. 6: "Nirgends triumphiert die δόλος des Odysseus,
in der Form eines verwegenen μῆτις, in der Odyssee so kraftvoll und mit-
reissend wie in der Höhle des Polyphem."

[112] C. P. Segal, "The Phaeacians and the Symbolism of Odysseus' Return,"
Arion 1, 4 (1962):34. Similarly, K. Reinhardt, "Die Abenteuer der Odyssee,"

At the beginning, Odysseus and his men come to a deserted island which is described in idyllic terms: a good harbor, good climate, and fine soil for cultivation (9. 116-141). While only a short distance away, the Cyclopes are incapable of exploiting the island's potential wealth, since they have no ships to cross the narrow channel, nor, indeed, do they engage in agriculture. They confine themselves to a purely pastoral economy. The newcomers find plentiful food as they turn to hunting the wild goats who inhabit the island. Hunting, it should be noted, is yet another activity foreign to the Cyclopes. After feasting on their kill and on the wine brought along from the Cicones, Odysseus and his men see smoke, a sure sign of habitation, arising on the land opposite. The Cyclopes possess the art of fire-making, but, characteristically, they do not utilize it for cooking, but presumably only for light and warmth.

Later, on Circe's island, the sight of smoke similarly invites exploration on the part of Odysseus' company. But there, not curiosity but the loss of all sense of orientation demands that they approach the goddess (10. 190ff.).[113] On that occasion, Odysseus sends a search party *ahead* while he himself remains by the ship. So too, immediately after the Cyclops adventure, Odysseus keeps his own ship outside the harbor of the Laestrygonians and thereby escapes destruction. The outcome of the visit to Polyphemus has taught Odysseus to balance curiosity with caution. We should remember also that on the island of the goats, unlike at Thrinacia, the company is not stranded, nor is it driven to explore by hunger. Yet the next day, Odysseus calls an *agora* and announces his intentions to his men:

ἐλθὼν τῶνδ' ἀνδρῶν πειρήσομαι, οἵ τινές εἰσιν,
ἤ ῥ' οἵ γ' ὑβρισταί τε καὶ ἄγριοι οὐδὲ δίκαιοι,
ἦε φιλόξεινοι, καί σφιν νόος ἐστὶ θεουδής.

in *Tradition und Geist* (Göttingen, 1960), p. 67, characterizes the conflict as "ein Kampf zwischen Gesittung mit Intelligenz vereint und Barbarei mit roher Kraft."

[113] Cf. Reinhardt (1960a), p. 64-65.

I will go and test these people, to learn what sort they
    are,
whether, in fact, they are violent and wild and unjust,
or hospitable and godly in their minds.
(9. 174-176)

The last two lines are pronounced twice again by Odysseus,
on his arrival on Scheria (6. 120-121), and when—unwit-
tingly—he has reached Ithaca (13. 201-202), but on these
occasions in the form of a weary question.[114] By then, Odysseus' thirst for adventure and curiosity will have diminished.[115]
In Phaeacia, he will find hospitable and kindly folk, but on
Ithaca, a mixture of violent and brutal men—the suitors—
and those who have remained loyal. Once home, Odysseus
will "test" both friend and foe alike, but for a specific purpose:
to determine their fidelity. Here, however, Odysseus' curiosity
serves no practical purpose, nor is it decreased when he begins
to suspect the worst, which he soon does.

As they approach, Odysseus and his party see a huge cave
by the side of the sea, which is the home of the monster
Polyphemus. In the *Odyssey*, only subhuman (Scylla, Polyphemus)[116] or superhuman (Calypso and the Nymphs) creatures make their homes in caves. Before setting out, Odysseus
brings along the wine of Maron, "thinking," as he says, "that
they might encounter a savage brute who knows neither justice
nor laws" (9. 213-215). The Greek reads: "Suddenly my mighty
thumos thought. . . ." In Homer, *thumos* can mean heart or
mind, and it is the seat of various kinds of mental and emotional impulses. Here, it almost means intuition. Throughout

---

[114] The formula is also used by Alcinoos when he inquires about Odysseus'
wanderings (8. 575-576). Cf. W. Krehmer, "Zur Begegnung zwischen Odysseus und Athene" (Inaugural-Dissertation, University of Erlangen-Nürnberg,
1973), pp. 61-63.

[115] See Reinhardt (1960a), p. 66, who traces the transformation of Odysseus
from "Abenteuerfreudige zum Abenteuer Überstehenden, zuletz zum Abenteuer Fürchtenden."

[116] Consider the *Hymn to Hephaestus* XX. 3-4, where men are described
as "Formerly living in caves in the mountains, like beasts" before they acquired the arts of Hephaestus.

the Polyphemus story, *thumos* becomes a key word worth noticing. Sometimes, as here, it represents a kind of uncanny foresight which is not unconnected with *metis*; at other times, it suggests impulses whose consequences may be disastrous. At this point, however, Odysseus' ominous intuition, based perhaps on the forbidding appearance of the cave, [117] in no way lessens his initial curiosity. After entering the cave, Odysseus' men try in vain to persuade him to leave. As he relates the tale to Alcinoos, Odysseus agrees that it would have been far better to take their advice. But at the time, he refused because he wanted to "see this monstrous creature and try to get a guest-gift out of him" (9. 229). It seems, then, that Odysseus' desire to get home and to save his companions— of which the proem spoke so emphatically—is attenuated by his curiosity and by his interest in gifts, or as Stanford comments on the passage, Odysseus' motives are his "inquisitiveness and acquisitiveness."[118]

One must recall that guest-gifts in the Homeric world are far more than acquisitions or mere souvenirs. Finley notes that "The whole of what we call foreign relations and diplomacy, in their peaceful manifestations, was conducted by gift-exchange."[119] Throughout the *Odyssey*, the exchange of gifts and adherence to the laws of hospitality are the hallmarks of civilized conduct. The wine Odysseus was inspired to bring along and which will become an essential tool in the blinding of Polyphemus is a symbol precisely of peaceful diplomacy among civilized men—even in wartime. That wine, Odysseus recounts, was one of the many gifts that Maron, a priest of Apollo, gave him in exchange for his safety and that of his family after the attack on the Cicones (9. 196-205).[120] The

---

[117] Cf. Bona (1966), pp. 83-85.

[118] Stanford (1965), at 9. 229.

[119] M. I. Finley, *The World of Odysseus*, 3rd ed. (New York, 1978), p. 66. For the theme of gift-giving in the Cyclops episode, see A. Podlecki, "Guests-gifts and Nobodies in Odyssey 9," *Phoenix* 15 (1961):125-33.

[120] Cf. C. Calame, "Le mythe des Cyclopes dans l'Odyssée" in *Il Mito Greco: Atti del Convegno Internazionale Urbino 1973*, ed. B. Gentili and G. Paioni (Rome, 1977), p. 381, n. 12: "Dans le cas de Maron, l'échange civilisé que Polyphème a refusé à Ulysse est réalisé."

Cyclops' complete ignorance of such civilized behavior and commerce is a sure sign of barbarism. As they wait in the cave for the ogre's return, Odysseus' party conduct a primitive sacrifice with the Cyclops' cheese (9. 231). The point of this peculiar sacrifice, as well as the *agora* Odysseus convoked before setting out (9. 171), can only be to emphasize the absence of such political and religious institutions among the Cyclopes. After Polyphemus returns, blocks the door to the cave with a huge boulder, and attends to his evening chores, he catches sight of his visitors and immediately accuses them of being pirates. For those who lack all notions of commerce or communal enterprise, whether hostile or peaceable, outsiders can only be private trouble-makers—pirates. The distinction between legitimate and illegitimate trade, never entirely clear in the Homeric world, simply does not exist for the isolated Cyclopes.

Odysseus gamely replies to Polyphemus' insults: they are heroes returning from the Trojan War, which—crowning barbarism—makes no impression on the monster, who knows nothing of the "greatest *kleos* on earth" (9. 264). They come, Odysseus adds, as suppliants. Then, perhaps a bit too eagerly, Odysseus puts in a request for appropriate gifts and reminds his host of the proper respect due the gods who look after guests and suppliants. The blatant violations of the normal procedures for welcoming strangers are already ominous. Polyphemus has offered his guests no food nor displayed any curiosity concerning their names and backgrounds. The Cyclops' response increases the threatening atmosphere:

νήπιός εἰς, ὦ ξεῖν᾽, ἢ τηλόθεν εἰλήλουθας,
ὅς με θεοὺς κέλεαι ἢ δειδίμεν ἢ ἀλέασθαι·
οὐ γὰρ Κύκλωπες Διὸς αἰγιόχου ἀλέγουσιν
οὐδὲ θεῶν μακάρων, ἐπεὶ ἦ πολὺ φέρτεροί εἰμεν.

You're a fool, stranger, or else have come from afar,
you who bid me to fear the gods and avoid their anger.
The Cyclopes pay no attention to Zeus of the aegis,
nor the blessed gods, since we are much stronger.
(9. 273-276)

Polyphemus mindlessly boasts that they are stronger than the gods. His second mistake is to believe that force is the only measure of superiority; he ignores the existence of a power that can overcome those whose strength is greater: *metis*. The Cyclops does display a certain low cunning, however, when he asks Odysseus where he has moored his ship. But Odysseus immediately perceives this transparent ploy and counters the "test" by saying that their ship has been wrecked. This is only the first of Odysseus' *doloi*. Yet, while still unaware of how difficult it will be to escape from the Cyclops' cave, but always on guard and sizing up potential dangers, Odysseus prepares for all contingencies. Such foresight is the very hallmark of *metis*.

Suddenly, Polyphemus reveals his full bestiality by devouring two men. The horrified observers are paralyzed and without resources: ἀμηχανίῃ δ' ἔχε θυμόν (9. 295). As soon as the monster falls asleep, Odysseus begins to plot in his "great-hearted *thumos*." His first impulse is to kill the Cyclops, but then another *thumos* restrains him. If Polyphemus dies, they will all be trapped; so he must be incapacitated but still able to move the enormous boulder from the mouth of the cave. Moreover, time is of the essence, since each mealtime signals the loss of two more men. The best plan comes to Odysseus' *thumos*—the idea of blinding Polyphemus with a stake.

The stake becomes the *mechane* that dissolves their previous *amechanie*.[121] Both the blinding itself and the enormous pike of Polyphemus are described in images drawn from *technai*. The latter is likened to the mast of a cargo vessel, while the simile depicting the piercing of the monster's eye comes from the art of shipbuilding; and the burning of the eye-socket is likened to the tempering of steel by a blacksmith.[122] These

---

[121] For *mechane* and *amechanie* in relation to the vocabulary of *metis*, see Detienne and Vernant (1974), *passim*. Compare Aristophanes *Knights* 758-759, where the clever man, adept at resources, is described as the one who can find a means out of a hopeless situation: ποικίλος γὰρ ἀνὴρ / κἀκ τῶν ἀμηχάνων πόρους εὐμήχανος πορίζειν.

[122] 9. 321-324; 384-388; 391-394. Compare the similar image and effect

striking similes point again to the absence of such arts among
the Cyclopes and to the fact that the *technai* are an important
component of *metis*.

The evening before, contrary to his usual custom, Polyphemus has brought all his sheep into the cave, including the
rams. That turns out to be a stroke of good luck; or rather,
it pinpoints Odysseus' ability to exploit whatever may be at
hand for his purposes—the wine, the stake, the sheep, even
the willow-branches on which the Cyclops sleeps. After two
more men are eaten, Odysseus offers Polyphemus some wine.
This is the same wine that was, as we have seen, the product
of civilized exchange. Now it is used to wash down a can-
nibalistic dinner which forms a grotesque parody of the con-
ventions regarding hospitality. As the monster grows tipsy,
he asks Odysseus' name so that he "may give him a guest-
gift" (9. 356). The Cyclops follows Homeric etiquette only
when drunk—only to pervert it by offering as his gift to eat
Odysseus last. Odysseus' famous answer, Outis, "Nobody,"
prevents the other Cyclopes from coming to the aid of Polyphemus as he screams in pain. But the pun is really the point
of the story.[123] For *outis* becomes *me tis* in certain types of
clauses; and *metis* is our hero's outstanding characteristic.
Polyphemus' neighbors inquire:

τίπτε τόσον, Πολύφημ', ἀρημένος ὧδ' ἐβόησας
νύκτα δι' ἀμβροσίην, καὶ ἀΰπνους ἄμμε τίθησθα;
ἦ μή τίς σευ μῆλα βροτῶν ἀέκοντος ἐλαύνει;
ἦ μή τίς σ' αὐτὸν κτείνει δόλῳ ἠὲ βίηφιν;

---

in Hesiod *Theog.* 862-867, where the thunderbolt of Zeus which consumes
Typhoeus is likened to the smelting of metals.

[123] W. B. Stanford, *Ambiguity in Greek Literature* (Oxford, 1939), p. 105:
"This is the only place in Homer where ambiguity and paronomasia motivate
a whole episode." Instead of "Nobody," the widespread folk-tale variants of
the name trick offer "Myself"—which, of course, works quite as well in
getting rid of inquisitive neighbors. Cf. Page (1955), p. 5, and S. Schein,
"Odysseus and Polyphemus in the Odyssey," *GRBS* 11 (1970):79-81. But
for Homer, the Outis trick is more than a clever ploy with a practical purpose;
it reveals the nature of his hero clearly.

Why are you bellowing, Polyphemus, so noisily in
   distress
through the immortal night and keep us awake?
Does someone (*me tis*) drive away your flocks against
   your will?
or does someone (*me tis*) kill you by guile or force?
                                              (9. 403-406)

Polyphemus within:

   ὦ φίλοι, Οὖτίς με κτείνει δόλῳ οὐδὲ βίηφιν.

   Friends, Outis is killing me by guile, not force.
                                              (9. 408)

To which they respond:

   εἰ μὲν δὴ μή τίς σε βιάζεται οἶον ἐόντα,
   νοῦσόν γ᾽ οὔ πως ἔστι Διὸς μεγάλου ἀλέασθαι,
   ἀλλὰ σύ γ᾽ εὔχεο πατρὶ Ποσειδάωνι ἄνακτι.

   If indeed no one (*me tis*) does you violence in your
      solitude,
   truly, there is no escaping an illness from great Zeus;
   but go now and pray to your father, lord Poseidon.
                                              (9. 410-412)

The lovely word play, *metis biazetai*, sums up the story. The
metis of Odysseus has overcome the *bie* of the Cyclops. Odysseus' heart laughs at "how his name and flawless *metis* has
outtricked" Polyphemus (9. 414).
   Now, as the blinded and raging monster sits by the entrance
to his cave, Odysseus must still figure a way to get past him;
as he says, "I wove all *doloi* and *metis* as if it were a matter
of life and death" (9. 422-423). The hero's plotting results in
the successful escape under the sheeps' bellies, punctuated by
Polyphemus' speech to his ram. The Cyclops, ironically, reveals himself more humane when conversing with his animal
than in human society.[124] The scene has added significance if

[124] Cf. Eustathius 1639. 17, who cites in this context the proverb of "like
to like."

we recall a passage from the *Iliad*, in which Priam, watching
from the ramparts of Troy, offers his impression of Odysseus:

αὐτὸς δὲ κτίλος ὣς ἐπιπωλεῖται στίχας ἀνδρῶν·
ἀρνειῷ μιν ἔγωγε ἐΐσκω πηγεσιμάλλῳ,
ὅς τ᾽ οἰῶν μέγα πῶϋ διέρχεται ἀργεννάων.

Like a ram he ranges through the ranks of men;
I liken him to a fleecy ram,
who goes through a great flock of white sheep.
                                            (III. 196-198)

The escape is made good in silence, but Odysseus does not
forget to take on board the sheep which were their salvation.
These animals will soon be sacrificed to Zeus, who will already
be plotting the death of Odysseus' companions (9. 551-555).

Once on board, Odysseus announces to Polyphemus that
his sufferings are the gods' just punishment for his mistreatment of his guests. Odysseus presents himself as the avenger
of the monster's cruelty and impiety, as a representative of
civilized norms taking proper revenge on uncivilized behavior.
Little does Odysseus know that the gods will take a very
different view of the incident. After Polyphemus almost shat-
ters their ship, Odysseus' companions beg the hero to keep
silent lest at the end they perish. But, once again, just as at
the beginning they had urged him to leave the cave, they are
unable to convince their leader's great-hearted *thumos* (9.
500). Addressing the Cyclops with an angered *thumos*, Odysseus insists on revealing his name. Polyphemus is thunder-
struck: on the basis of an oracle, he had heard that a certain
Odysseus would some day blind him. But he had expected a
big, strong man, not a little *nobody* (9. 513-515).

The revelation of his name has disastrous consequences for
Odysseus, for it permits the Cyclops to curse him (9. 530-
531; cf. 504-505). Why, then, does the hero give himself away?
It is in fact inconceivable that Odysseus should *not* reveal
himself after his masterful accomplishment. With no assistance, relying only on his *metis*, Odysseus managed to extricate

himself from an apparently hopeless situation. His final act
of self-assertion snatches this accomplishment from oblivion—from Outis, Nobody.

Two later allusions to the Cyclops story help to bring out
its significance and its special place among the adventures. In
Book 12, as his ship nears the narrows between Scylla and
Charybdis, Odysseus encourages his frightened men with the
following words:

> ὦ φίλοι, οὐ γάρ πώ τι κακῶν ἀδαήμονές εἰμεν·
> οὐ μὲν δὴ τόδε μεῖζον ἔπι κακὸν ἢ ὅτε Κύκλωψ
> εἴλει ἐνὶ σπῆϊ γλαφυρῷ κρατερῆφι βίηφιν·
> ἀλλὰ καὶ ἔνθεν ἐμῇ ἀρετῇ βουλῇ τε νόῳ τε
> ἐκφύγομεν, καί που τῶνδε μνήσεσθαι ὀΐω.

Friends, we are not unacquainted with evils;
this is no greater evil than when the Cyclops
trapped us with force and violence in his hollow cave.
Yet even there, by my courage, counsel, and intelligence
we escaped, and I think that somehow these things will
    be remembered.

                                                      (12. 208-212)

Odysseus considers the Cyclops' cave to be the worst situation
they have encountered, and he views their escape on that
occasion as the triumph of his intelligence over brute force.
In the last phrase, Odysseus refers to the continued memory
of the deed and hence to his own fame.[125] The final reward
for such accomplishments is eternal fame—*kleos*—as their
memory is handed down by the poets. We can now understand
better why Odysseus had to shout out his name to Polyphemus, and why he had to claim credit for a deed on which his
kleos rests.

The second allusion, whose interpretation is more complex,
occurs at the beginning of Book 20, on the eve of Odysseus'
final revenge against the suitors. This passage has been studied

---

[125] Vergil's famous "forsan et haec olim meminisse iuvabit" (*Aeneid* I. 203)
imitates these words, but in a very different spirit.

in the context of Epic scenes depicting deliberation or decision-making.[126] In fact, the opening of Book 20 offers an example unique in Homer embracing both major types of deliberation in close succession; and its final resolution—the epiphany of Athena—is also atypical.[127] Yet the significance of the evocation of the Cyclops adventure at this moment in the narrative has received little attention, even though its proper understanding offers a key to the sequence of events that follows.[128]

Odysseus lies sleepless in the forecourt of his own palace, his mind filled with thoughts of vengeance. When he hears the servant girls giggling and running out to join the suitors, he wonders whether to strike them dead on the spot for their outrageous behavior—or to wait. Speaking to himself, Odysseus urges patience:

τέτλαθι δή, κραδίη· καὶ κύντερον ἄλλο ποτ᾽ ἔτλης,
ἤματι τῷ ὅτε μοι μένος ἄσχετος ἤσθιε Κύκλωψ
ἰφθίμους ἑτάρους· σὺ δ᾽ ἐτόλμας, ὄφρα σε μῆτις
ἐξάγαγ᾽ ἐξ ἄντροιο ὀϊόμενον θανέεσθαι.

Endure, my heart, you have endured worse once before,
on the day when the Cyclops in his overpowering
    strength

[126] C. Voigt, *Überlegung und Entscheidung bei Homer* (Berlin, 1933), pp. 69-74. Voigt discerns two major types of deliberation in Homer, the first involving alternative courses of action (usually expressed in the form μερμηρίζειν ἤ . . . ἤ) and a second type, involving only a consideration of the means to an already adopted end (μερμηρίζειν ὅπως).

[127] J. Russo, "Homer against his Tradition," *Arion* 7 (1968):291ff., calls this passage a "dramatic and creative departure from the traditional pattern or type," and considers it a paradigm of Homer's ability to recombine traditional material into something innovative.

[128] Eustathius 1880. 57ff. does try to account for the introduction here of the Cyclops incident rather than another adventure by noting that, while Scylla and the Laestrygonians were most pitiful and dreadful adventures, they were also woes about which nothing could be done (*apraktos*); "but in the case of the Cyclops, Odysseus was able to defend himself and endured until he found the right moment (*kairos*); even as here, he will, at the right moment, pay back the evil maids."

ate my companions; but you endured until intelligence
(*metis*)
brought you out of the cave, even though you thought
you would die.

(20. 18-21)

Odysseus again attributes his escape from Polyphemus to his
metis. But what happened in the cave is also viewed as an
exemplar of endurance and self-restraint. Odysseus, we remember, had to curb his first impulse to kill the Cyclops.
Here, too, he restrains his immediate impulse to strike down
the serving girls and persuades himself to hold out until the
next day. Now the sequence appears to come to an end. We
expect Odysseus to drift off to sleep. But no, he still lies in
the grip of restless anxiety. His tossing and turning is described
in a peculiar simile of a sausage, tossed and turned over a fire
by a man anxious to have it ready (20. 24-30). This wonderful
if bizarre image illustrates Odysseus' extreme impatience for
revenge and his anguished anxiety as to how it will all be
accomplished.

Suddenly, Athena appears out of the blue, and in a mocking
tone asks Odysseus why he is still awake; after all, he is in
his own house with his own wife and child. Odysseus responds
that he is troubled as to how he—one against so many—will
be able to slaughter the suitors. But there is an even greater
anxiety: even if he should succeed in killing them with the
approval of Zeus and Athena, how can he hope to escape
afterwards? Athena avoids answering Odysseus' question but
replies instead:

σχέτλιε, καὶ μέν τίς τε χερείονι πείθεθ' ἑταίρῳ,
ὅς περ θνητός τ' ἐστὶ καὶ οὐ τόσα μήδεα οἶδεν·
αὐτὰρ ἐγὼ θεός εἰμι, διαμπερὲς ἥ σε φυλάσσω
ἐν πάντεσσι πόνοις.

Wretch, any man would trust a worse comrade,
one who is a mere mortal and does not have as many
counsels;

but I am a god who guards you continually
in all trials.

(20. 45-48)

Then, promising her support, Athena advises Odysseus to get
some sleep.

Some of the unspoken issues in this scene require explication. At first, the memory of the Cyclops encourages Odysseus
to restrain himself. But the recollection of that adventure also
induces extreme anxiety in the hero's mind, which is only
allayed by Athena's epiphany. In the cave of Polyphemus,
Odysseus extricated himself with no help from the goddess.
Now, he is not only one against the many suitors, but the
consequences of even his successful eradication of the suitors
are formidable. If the result of blinding the Cyclops was the
totally unexpected anger of Poseidon, the consequences of
slaughtering 108 young men from the best families are fairly
predictable. Odysseus' unspoken fear that he may once again
have to act without divine assistance and his anxiety that the
consequences of his actions will be even more disastrous than
Polyphemus' curse motivates the entrance of the goddess. Athena
responds not to Odysseus' specific questions but to his unspoken fears. Scolding Odysseus for his distrust of her, she
penetrates the essential question in the hero's mind by promising her complete support and indicating that the next day
will bring no repetition of the Cyclops incident.

To sum up, for Odysseus the Cyclops adventure has two
significant aspects. It marks the triumph of intelligence and
self-restraint over force and impulse; and it constitutes a feat
accomplished without divine assistance.

CYCLOPES AND PHAEACIANS

The proem informs us that Odysseus "saw the cities of many
men and learned their minds." In turn, Odysseus receives his
definition through the marvelous creatures and societies he
encounters in his wanderings; the world of fantastic adventures progresses toward a definition of human society. In the

Cyclops story, as we have seen, the familiar conflict between *bie* and *metis* expands to embrace the polarities of nature and culture. But these, in turn, point beyond themselves to define the specifically human in terms of the sub- and super- human. It is necessary to reexamine the Cyclops episode within this larger perspective. The encounter with Polyphemus is prefaced by an outline of what used to be called the "manners" of the Cyclopes (9. 106-115). Kirk has noted that this first description presents "an extraordinary mixture of the divine and the brutish."[129] As a people, the Cyclopes are violent and lack common rules of conduct (*themistes*); they do not even have public meetings (*agorai*) in which communal decisions are made; "but living in caves on the mountain peaks, each one lays down rules for his wives and children, nor do they pay any attention to one another" (9. 113-115).[130] Polyphemus, who has no family and lives farthest away from the others, is simply an extreme example of the general isolation in which the Cyclopes live.[131] When his neighbors approach at the sound of Polyphemus' screams, they do so because their nocturnal peace has been broken rather than any great concern for their fellow. The Cyclopes neither sow nor plow, since they lack even the most rudimentary arts of agriculture. But their lives, prepolitical and primitive as they are, also have an idyllic aspect: "trusting in the immortal gods," all things grow for them without labor, as in the golden age, and Zeus grants them sufficient rainfall.[132]

A number of commentators have noticed the contradictions inherent in this combination of primitive barbarism and the paradisiacal. Kirk, for example, sees in all this "a kind of orderly confusion of attitudes" involving "various aspects of

[129] G. S. Kirk, *Myth* (Cambridge, 1970), p. 165.

[130] Compare the description of the Cyclopes in Euripides' *Cyclops* 113ff. and, especially, the characterization (130): ἀκούει δ᾽ οὐδὲν οὐδεὶς οὐδενός.

[131] Eustathius 1622. 24 calls Polyphemus ἀθεμίστων ἀθεμιστότερος, "most lawless of the lawless."

[132] Eustathius 1617. 36 compares the land of the Cyclopes to the "island of the blessed."

nature and culture."[133] As we have seen, the poet is at pains to emphasize the contrast between nature and culture throughout the Polyphemus episode; and a comparison with folk-tale parallels reveals that Homer has chosen to underline the ogre's brutishness by having him eat his victims raw rather than cooked, by adding the incident with the wine, and by substituting a wooden stake for the traditional metal spit as the instrument of the monster's blinding.[134] The point of these changes is clear enough. Yet when Kirk tries to schematize the different characteristics of the Cyclopes on a grid of nature / culture, the results turn out to be peculiarly unsatisfactory. He finds himself obliged to use categories like "super-civilized," "civilized," "relatively civilized," "uncivilized," and "super-uncivilized."[135] The emerging pattern becomes blurred rather than focused, and Kirk concludes with some rather vague statements concerning the ambiguities of nature and culture. After reading Kirk's analysis, one cannot help but feel that his scheme is misconceived, that the coordinates of his discussion are somehow wrong. At least, they are unhomeric. I believe that by shifting the coordinates, we can recognize in the description of the Cyclopes a pattern that serves to define the subhuman rather than nature. But the full significance of that pattern does not reveal itself in isolation; it emerges only when we draw in its counterpart—the superhuman. Homer himself invites us to do so.

Just before the beginning of the Cyclops adventure, Odys-

---

[133] Kirk (1970), p. 168.

[134] Cf. Schein (1970), pp. 73-79.

[135] Kirk (1970), p. 169. Cf. the similar table of Calame (1977a), p. 388, where the categories are "civilisation" (under which rubric, Calame lists only traits of Odysseus); "sauvagerie," "non-sauvagerie," and "non-civilisation" (which applies only to the Cyclopes). Compare Calame's "L'univers cyclopéen de l'Odyssée," *Živa Antika* 27 (1977):315-22, where he puts forth a tripartite scheme rather than the polarity of nature and culture: "la pensée grecque saisit la position de la civilisation non pas comme simple contraire de la nature, mais comme intermédiaire entre l'âge d'or que vivent les dieux et la sauvagerie propre aux bêtes" (p. 317). This scheme, fundamentally correct, only receives its complete configuration by the addition of the Phaeacians. See below.

seus and his companions land on an island that is inhabited
only by wild goats and whose rich potential remains unex-
ploited by the nearby Cyclopes because of their inability to
engage in the arts of shipbuilding, hunting, and agriculture.
We have already discussed the role of the island in the narrative structure of the Cyclops story, but the island's significance transcends its utility to the plot of the *Odyssey*. There
are sufficient indications in the poem to show that this deserted
island is none other than Hyperia, the former home of the
Phaeacians.[136] At an earlier time, the Phaeacians fled to Scheria
under the leadership of Nausithoos in order to escape the *bie*
of the marauding Cyclopes (6. 4-6). Thus, the Phaeacians,
who used to be neighbors of the Cyclopes, form a silent presence throughout the Cyclopodeia—in more ways than one,
since they also make up the audience of Odysseus' tale.

The contrast between the supercivilized Phaeacians and the
barbaric Cyclopes has, to be sure, been remarked. As Segal
puts it:

> The fullest antithesis of the Phaeacians is the Cy-
> clopes. . . . The high civilization of the Phaeacians, their
> social development, shipbuilding and sailing, entertain-
> ment of guests, stand in the greatest contrast with the
> isolation of the individual Cyclopes, their lack of ships
> and primitive means of sustenance, their scorn for the
> gods and divinely sanctioned rights.[137]

Yet the Phaeacians are not simply an idealized human society.
As the Cyclopes are underdeveloped in the *technai* of civilization, so are the Phaeacians overdeveloped. Their magic ships,
which travel to their destinations swift as thought and without
toil, the immortal golden watchdogs made by Hephaestus, the
golden youths who hold the lamps in the great hall,[138] and

---

[136] See J. S. Clay, "Goat Island," *CQ* 30 (1980):261-64.

[137] Segal (1962), p. 33. Eustathius 1617. 59-60 compares the presence of
a *politeia* among the Phaeacians to its absence among the Cyclopes.

[138] Compare the "automatic" golden tripods (XVIII. 373-377) and the
golden serving maids of Hephaestus (XVIII. 417-421) in the *Iliad*.

the magic fertility of Alcinoos' orchard—all these belong to divine rather than human technology.

The Phaeacians and the Cyclopes appear at opposite poles of the super- and sub- human. Yet all of Odysseus' wanderings take place in a world "which will be alternately superhuman or subhuman,"[139] or, more accurately, in which these opposing traits are continually combined and recombined. Thus, both the brutish Cyclops and the goddess Calypso live in caves. The cannibalism and immense stature of the Cyclops are shared by the Laestrygonians, who, on the other hand, have a city, king, and *agora*, and are capable of a communal effort—be it only to destroy intruders. On the floating island of Aeolus, Odysseus receives the same hospitable treatment he later gets from the Phaeacians. There, too, he tells his story to his host and receives a *pompe*, a means of return, in the bag of the winds. While possessing a city with walls, Aeolia has only one social unit, as do the Cyclopes. It is the family; and that situation in isolation necessarily leads to incest. These and other combinations which Odysseus encounters suggest that the sub- and super- human may have more in common than one originally suspects.

Such is also the case with the apparently disparate Phaeacians and Cyclopes. According to Vidal-Naquet:

> In a sense, they [the Phaeacians] are indeed, as has been said, the opposite of the Cyclopes. All their human virtues, the practice of hospitality, piety, the art of gift-giving and of feasting, are indeed the counterparts of the barbarism of the Cyclopes. But there is even more to be said: the former proximity and the present distance between the Phaeacians and the Cyclopes betray more subtle relationships.[140]

The former geographical proximity of these very different peoples points beyond a simple polar opposition to a more

---

[139] P. Vidal-Naquet, "Valeurs religieuses et mythiques de la terre et du sacrifice dans *l'Odyssée*," in *Le chasseur noir* (Paris, 1981), p. 47.

[140] Vidal-Naquet (1981), p. 64. Vidal-Naquet develops several of the correspondences I have outlined here.

complex and problematic interrelationship. The innate violence of the Cyclopes compelled the Phaeacians to emigrate. As a result of their previous closeness, both Cyclopes and Phaeacians share a complete isolation from what we may call ordinary human life; the Cyclopes because of their lack of technology and also curiosity, the Phaeacians, by choice. Peaceful commerce and its converse, war, are foreign to both peoples. Hence both, for different reasons, are unheroic. Polyphemus has not even heard about Agamemnon's expedition; the Phaeacians, on the other hand, know all about the Trojan War, and they entertain themselves with accounts of *klea andron* after dinner. In their games, however, they are best at running and dancing rather than in the rougher sports of boxing and wrestling (8. 246-247).[141] Moreover, they do not compete at all in the martial arts of archery and spear-throwing:

αἰεὶ δ᾽ ἡμῖν δαίς τε φίλη κίθαρίς τε χοροί τε
εἵματά τ᾽ ἐξημοιβὰ λοετρά τε θερμὰ καὶ εὐναί.

But always feasting, the lyre, and dancing are dear to us,
and changes of clothing, warm baths, and beds.
(8. 248-249)

It seems safe to conclude, then, that the softness of the Phaeacians and the brutality of the Cyclopes are equally remote from the heroic.

An even closer and more mysterious bond, however, unites the Phaeacians and the Cyclopes. When Odysseus suddenly appears at the hearth of Alcinoos, the king wonders if the stranger may not be a god, although this would be contrary to their usual custom. For previously, the gods always revealed themselves without disguise among the Phaeacians,

οὔ τι κατακρύπτουσιν, ἐπεί σφισιν ἐγγύθεν εἰμέν,
ὥς περ Κύκλωπές τε καὶ ἄγρια φῦλα Γιγάντων.

nor do they hide themselves, since we are near them,
just as the Cyclopes and the wild race of giants.
(7. 205-206)

---

[141] Compare the Scholia at 8. 100 and 102.

The proximity of which Alcinoos speaks is usually understood as "closely related" in genealogical terms.[142] Poseidon, to be sure, is both Alcinoos' grandfather and Polyphemus' father. We also learn from Athena's genealogical sketch (7. 56ff.) that Alcinoos' great-grandfather, Eurymedon, was king of the Giants, but "he destroyed a reckless people and perished himself" (7. 60).[143] The peace-loving, sybaritic Phaeacians turn out to have some surprising connections—not only their former geographical closeness to the Cyclopes, but also a close lineal relation to the Giants.

But Alcinoos' ἐγγύθεν suggests even more than that. In the context of his statement, he seems to speak of an especially privileged position vis-à-vis the gods. The Phaeacians, whose standing epithet is ἀγχίθεοι, "near to the gods," enjoy not only undisguised intercourse with the gods, but also the magic ships from Poseidon, the splendid products of divine technology, and the "shining gifts of the gods" in Alcinoos' garden. Yet the Cyclopes, while characterized by grossly impious behavior, culminating in cannibalism, also receive a privileged status from the very gods they ignore. Thus, Zeus makes their land fertile (9. 111), and Poseidon immediately hearkens to the curse pronounced by his son. The curse reestablishes the ancient link between the Cyclopes and the Phaeacians who fled from their *bie*. It also fulfills the oracle given to Nausithoos (8. 564-570; 13. 172-178), pronounced, no doubt, on the occasion of the Phaeacian migration from their old home in Hyperia to Scheria.[144] The circle draws to a close.

[142] See Ameis-Hentze, *Homers Odyssee* (Leipzig, 1908), at 7. 205; also Stanford (1961). G. W. Nitzsch, *Erklärende Anmerkungen zu Homers Odyssee* (Hanover, 1840), at 7. 205 remarks: "So unähnlich sie sonst den frevelhaften Giganten und Kyklopen waren, dennoch nennen sie sich den Göttern so nahe verwandt wie diese." Compare the glosses on ἀγχίθεοι offered by the Scholia at 5. 35.

[143] Hence there are no Giants in the *Odyssey*. But consider the Laestrygonians, who are likened to Giants (10. 120). According to a later tradition (Scholia to Apollonius Rhodius IV. 992), both the Phaeacians and the Giants sprang from the blood of the mutilated Uranus.

[144] For the practice of consulting an oracle before sending out a colony, see H. Parke and D. Wormell, *The Delphic Oracle*, 2 vols. (Oxford, 1956), 1:49-81.

The prehistory of the Phaeacians and the Cyclopes as well as their mysterious interconnections go beyond the simple opposition between barbarism and civilization or nature and culture. Both the divine technology of the Phaeacians and the barbaric *bie* of the Cyclopes have common bonds which unite them more closely to each other than to the simply human. Both the Phaeacians and the Cyclopes are indeed "near the gods": the Phaeacians live like the gods; the Cyclopes act the way the gods sometimes do.

It may appear that we have moved some distance from the center of our discussion, the character of the *Odyssey's* hero. In fact, we have only enlarged our focus in order to obtain a better perspective. The properly human in the *Odyssey*—and that means in large part Odysseus and the Ithaca to which he strives to return—defines itself in opposition to both the sub-human and the superhuman. It accepts the necessity of toil, suffering, and mortality, but also offers the possibility of endurance and heroism and also of justice. Homer's Odysseus, for all his enigmatic and even questionable qualities—or perhaps because of them—shows himself to be not only the best of the Greeks. He finally embodies the best possibilities of the human in its precarious position between god and beast.

CHAPTER III

GODS AND MEN

Wer, mit einer anderen Religion im Herzen, an diese
Olympier herantritt und nun nach sittlicher Höhe, ja
Heiligkeit, nach unleiblicher Vergeistigung, nach erbar-
mungsvollen Liebesblicken bei ihnen sucht, der wird un-
mutig und enttäuscht ihnen bald den Rücken kehren
müssen.

Whoever approaches these Olympians with another religion in his heart, searching among them for moral
elevation, even for sanctity, for disincarnate spirituality,
for charity and benevolence, will soon be forced to turn
his back on them, discouraged and disappointed.

(Nietzsche, *Geburt der Tragödie* 3,
Trans. W. Kaufmann)

The preceding chapter has traced the multifaceted and elusive
qualities of Odysseus, the man of many wiles and the object
of Athena's anger. We have by no means lost sight of the
starting point and ultimate goal of the present study: an appreciation of the role of the wrath of Athena in the structure
and thought of the *Odyssey*. But before confronting the issue
of the nature and cause of the goddess' wrath, we will need
the framework of a broader understanding of the Homeric
gods, both in themselves and in their relations with men. Only
from the vantage of such a larger perspective can the full
significance of Athena's wrath in the *Odyssey* emerge.

To be sure, I do not hope to tread an unbeaten path, nor
even to break new ground in a field well-sown with controversy. But a general sketch of some of the powers and limitations of the Homeric gods and their interactions with the
heroes of the epic constitutes a necessary preliminary to the
interpretation of the relationship between Athena and Odysseus.

To speak about Homer's gods means first to acknowledge their utter strangeness to us. It is symptomatic of the alien world we are entering that Wilamowitz felt obliged to defend the title of his book, *Der Glaube der Hellenen*.[1] "Religion," he realized, had no Greek equivalent—but then neither does *Glaube*.[2] The proper Greek expression, νομίζειν θεούς, is characteristic in its ambiguity.[3] At the center of all religious experience, R. Otto places the encounter with the Holy, the shattering and awe-inspiring experience of an ineffable *mysterium tremendum*, with the uncanny "*Ganz Anderes*."[4] Even a great defender of Homeric religion concedes that the Greeks seem to lack precisely those qualities that are essential to our notions of religion: "a sense of the eternal," "ineffable exaltation," "consecration," "holiness," "moral earnestness," "communion," and "the bliss of oneness" with the divine.[5] Burkert correctly emphasizes that in the Olympian religion "the normal sacrificial cult is a cult without revelation or epiphany."[6] The Homeric hero may on occasion encounter his gods in fear, wonder, or even suspicion, but such an experience is not accompanied by ecstasy. Fundamental to Ju-

[1] 2 vols. (Berlin, 1931), 1:12ff.

[2] Cf. K. Reinhardt, "Walter F. Otto," in *Vermächtnis der Antike* (Göttingen, 1960), p. 378: "Wer vom "Glauben" der Griechen spricht—wie Wilamowitz in seinem letzten Werk ... beweist schon damit, dass er von ganz irrtümlichen Voraussetzungen ausgeht." Wilamowitz rather lamely proposed *pistis*, but compare G. Kittel, ed., *Theologisches Wörterbuch zum Neuen Testament*, (Stuttgart, 1949-1978), 6:178-79: "Zu Termini der religiösen Sprache sind die Bildungen mit πιστ- im klassischen Griechisch nicht geworden ... in keinem Sinne ist πιστός ... zur Bezeichnung der religiösen Grundhaltung des Menschen geworden."

[3] The expression does not occur in Homer. For its history, see W. Fahr, ΘΕΟΥΣ ΝΟΜΙΖΕΙΝ Spudasmata 26 (Hildesheim, 1969).

[4] *Das Heilige*, 9th ed., (Breslau, 1922), pp. 12ff. On the absence of *Heiligkeit* in Homeric religion, see also Nägelsbach (1840), p. 31.

[5] W. F. Otto, *The Homeric Gods*, trans. M. Hadas (New York, 1954), p. 3. See now also Griffin (1980), pp. 144-78, for a thoughtful discussion of "the numinous and sublime side of the Homeric gods," which is free of Otto's rather Dionysian rhetoric. Griffin's excellent study, especially the two last chapters, covers much of the terrain of the present section, and I wholeheartedly commend it to the reader.

[6] Burkert (1977), p. 290.

deo-Christian theology is God's creation of man "in His own image." Individual heroes may, to be sure, have a divine parent, but the striking absence of such a creation of men by the gods in Homeric religion means that the relation between gods and men cannot be founded on the possibilities of intimacy and interdependence of the relationship between creator and creature.[7] At the center of Judaism is the giving of the Law on Mount Sinai; for Christianity, it is the Resurrection. But no such central revelation informs the beliefs of the Greeks.

Given their strangeness, the simplest way of dealing with the Homeric gods is to ignore them or to explain them away as much as possible.[8] One can consider the divine machinery "primarily a sort of adornment," "an embroidery or appliqué of ornamental design"[9] superimposed on the fabric of the Epic and fundamentally empty of religious content. Even in antiquity, the frivolity and immorality of the gods was already widely criticized and led to Homer's expulsion from Socrates' ideal *polis*.[10] But moderns have found the coexistence of the sublime and the ridiculous particularly jarring. Universal gods who protect the moral and cosmic order appear to coalesce side by side with immoral divinities who seek nothing but the immediate gratification of their Olympian but all-too-human appetites. One therefore frequently finds the argument that Homer introduces these gods into the Epic from time to time merely to advance his plot, to lend grandeur to his heroes,

[7] Cf. Burkert (1977), p. 290; and Snell, (1975), p. 34.

[8] For example, G. Murray, *The Rise of the Greek Epic*, 4th ed. (Oxford, 1934), p. 265, disposes of the problem easily by claiming the Homeric religion is "not really religion at all." Cf. C. M. Bowra, *Tradition and Design in the Iliad* (Oxford, 1930), p. 222: "This complete anthropomorphic system has of course no relation to real religion or to morality." A. Lesky's "Homeros," *Sonderausgabe der RE* (Stuttgart, 1967), pp. 39-54, is very revealing for a common modern attitude toward Homer's gods; in his section on "Religion," Lesky devotes little space to the Olympians, while abstract conceptions like *themis* and *moira* as well as Homeric psychology receive lengthy treatment.

[9] G. M. Calhoun, "Homer's Gods: Prolegomena," *TAPA* 68 (1937):15, 16. For the term, "divine machinery," see Alexander Pope, "Preface to the Iliad" in Vol. 7 of the Twickenham Edition of the *Poems of Alexander Pope* (London, 1967).

[10] *Republic* 398a-b, 607a. Cf. Xenophanes Fr. 11 B *DK*.

and to provide occasional comic interludes. Accordingly, the gods form a conventional and useful part of the poet's narrative, but no coherent theology is either intended or discernible.

Modern investigators of Homeric psychology have, to be sure, put forth some explanation of Homer's gods—but they usually end up explaining away what they set out to give an account of. According to this approach, Homer possesses no unified conception of the soul and therefore has no means of expressing psychic phenomena such as decision-making. Divine intervention, then, serves as an externalization and projection of the internal psychological processes which the poet is incapable of expressing as such.[11] The unspoken assumptions on which these views rest cannot be dealt with here, but we can easily see to what interpretation of the Homeric gods they lead.

The intervention of Athena in the first book of the *Iliad* (I. 194-222) constitutes the standard example.[12] As Achilles reaches for his sword and prepares to fall upon Agamemnon, Athena suddenly appears to him alone and advises restraint. The psychological explanation—that Athena represents Achilles' second thoughts, which the hero decides to follow rather than yielding to his immediate impulse to strike Agamemnon down on the spot—suggests itself with a certain ease. It surely renders the scene more palatable to a modern audience; nothing miraculous has occurred. But such an interpretation does not differ fundamentally from the ancient allegoresis of the passage cited by Eustathius.[13] More important, it will not work

[11] Snell (1975), pp. 18ff. Cf. E. R. Dodds, *The Greeks and the Irrational* (Berkeley, 1951), p. 14: "The Homeric poets were without the refinements of language which would have been needed 'to put across' adequately a purely psychological miracle." See also M. Nilsson, "Götter und Psychologie bei Homer," *Archiv für Religionswissenschaft* 22 (1924):374ff. For a critique of this line of interpretation, see J. Russo and B. Simon, "Homeric Psychology and the Oral Epic Tradition," *Journal of the History of Ideas* 29 (1968):483-98; and N. Austin, *Archery at the Dark of the Moon* (Berkeley, 1975), pp. 82ff.

[12] Snell (1975), pp. 35ff.; Dodds (1951), p. 14; Nilsson (1924), pp. 373ff.

[13] See, for example, the remarks of Eustathius at *Il.* I. 195.

for a good many divine interventions in Homer and thus can be only a partial explanation at best. One example should suffice. At the beginning of the fifteenth book of the *Odyssey*, Athena appears to Telemachus as he sleeps in Sparta. The purpose of her epiphany here is to bring the young man home, just as her arrival in Book 1 had provided the impulse for his journey. The goddess' remarks can only partially be rationalized as projections of the young hero's inner fears. Moreover, such a view tends to blur rather than illuminate the workings of the gods. Athena's avowed intention (13. 412ff.) is to get Telemachus back to Ithaca at top speed and to warn him of the ambush awaiting him on the way. The state of affairs in Ithaca that Athena sketches for him—the suitors destroying his patrimony and his mother on the verge of remarriage—can indeed be viewed as the product of the young man's fevered anxieties and his unconscious distrust of his mother. But the final section of Athena's speech (15. 27-42) warns Telemachus of the trap the suitors have laid for his return; it gives specific instructions for bypassing their ambush; and it tells him to proceed immediately to Eumaeus' hut, where the reunion with Odysseus will take place. This part of the goddess' speech, in which she conveys concrete information beyond Telemachus' power to know, for a purpose of which he cannot be aware, will not yield to any purely psychological explanation.[14] To view the Greek gods as "projections of mental activity" may perhaps give a clue to their remotest origins. But a long road leads from such obscure and primitive beginnings to the Olympians of Homer.[15] A recent variant of the psychological approach considers the gods to be expressions of social or cultural norms and pressures.[16] It

[14] Otto (1954), pp. 182-84, gives just such a psychological rationalization—but at the price of ignoring the entire second half of Athena's speech.

[15] Cf. Nilsson (1924), p. 390. Nilsson, in fact, always keeps a clear view of his interests as a historian of Greek religion and those of the Epic poet.

[16] See, for example, A.W.H. Adkins, "Homeric Gods and the Values of Homeric Society," *JHS* 92 (1972):1-19; and also Griffin (1980), pp. 145ff. for a discussion of the inadequacies of such approaches.

)

too is finally open to similar objections—that it minimizes and rationalizes the divine in Homer.

Historians of religion have, for the most part, made short shrift of Homer, interested as they are in the origins and development of Greek religious beliefs to which the highly sophisticated Homeric pantheon seems to provide little access. The great shift in the study of religion from mythology to cult in the nineteenth century served to push Homer even farther into the background. Anthropology, the comparative study of religions among primitive peoples, and the tangible evidence of archeology came to play a far more important role. The revived interest in mythology stimulated by the work of Lévi-Strauss has produced some provocative results in the area of Greek religious thought, but thus far it has been unable to synthesize the Homeric material as a whole. It has been more successful in dealing with the more transparent theogonic and aetiological myths drawn from the works of Hesiod and others and with some of the lesser divinities, such as Dionysus and Hermes, who are somewhat peripheral to the Homeric pantheon.[17] Moreover, the structuralist approach, with its commitment to a synchronic perspective, is admittedly limited in its ability to interpret an individual text.

Access to the Homeric gods remains difficult. We can only begin again from the beginning with a humble phenomenology, delineating their characteristics, their powers, and their limitations. We must not fear to repeat what may have been said before, but hope, nonetheless, that with a fresh start, some deeper coherence will emerge. *Die Götter sind da*, according to Wilamowitz, but what is their mode of being present? In the Epic, they are there first and foremost as dramatis personae, whose actions, comings and goings, and appear-

---

[17] See, for example, M. Detienne, *Les jardins d'Adonis* (Paris, 1972); *Dionysos mis à mort* (Paris, 1977); and L. Kahn, *Hermès passe* (Paris, 1978). I have, of course, cheerfully exploited the many good insights of Detienne, Vernant, Vidal-Naquet, and their *équipe* whenever they throw light on the Homeric texts. P. Pucci, "Lévi-Strauss and Classsical Culture," *Arethusa* 4 (1971):109, speaks of the fact that "the personal achievement" and the "individual gesture" of the poet "necessarily disappears in structural analysis."

ances seem to follow certain rules, and whose principles of conduct and abilities differ from those of the mortal actors. It is these we must attempt to discover, not on the basis of modern psychology or theology or anthropology, but on the bare evidence of the text of Homer's poems.

We may perhaps start with the general epithets for the gods as a group. In the formulaic language of the Epic, these major epithets all have their counterparts in the standard epithets for men. This suggests that in Homer the gods are, above all, defined in opposition to men. To the most common epithet, a negative formation, ἀθάνατοι, deathless ones, corresponds a positive, θνητοί, or καταθνητοί, mortals. Reflection on the gods appears to be preceded by reflection on men, on the human condition and on mortality.[18] The gods inhabit Olympus (τοὶ Ὄλυμπον ἔχουσιν, τοὶ οὐρανὸν εὐρὺν ἔχουσιν), while men are confined to the earth (οἳ ἐπὶ χθονὶ ναιετάουσιν, ἐπὶ ζείδωρον ἄρουραν). Doomed to death, mankind is wretched and miserable (δειλοί, ὀϊζυροί), but the gods remain blessed and "live easy" (μάκαρες, ῥεῖα ζώοντες).

Exemption from death, however, does not exempt the gods from passion, though it strips them of its tragic consequences. In the second song of Demodocus, the discovery of the adultery of Ares and Aphrodite causes "unquenchable laughter among the blessed gods" (8. 326). We, the audience, are allowed for a moment to share in that careless Olympian laughter. Only here in Homer are the gods called "givers of good things" (δωτῆρες ἐάων 8. 325). That "good thing" is the delight (τέρψις) the song evokes in the listening Phaeacians and in Odysseus, who has wept before at the tale of Troy and will weep again. It is this same momentary forgetfulness of the grief and care which is the human condition that Hesiod calls the "gift of the Muses" (*Theog.* 102-103).

[18] Cf. Griffin (1980), p. 168: "it is by contemplating the gods and seeing in them a nature like their own, but delivered from the restrictions which hamper and limit them, that men understand what they are themselves." This formulation is the opposite of my own, but perhaps only proves that gods and men acquire their definition through mutual oppositions.

In the world of the Epic, marital infidelity does not evoke mirth. Clytemnestra's adultery leads to Agamemnon's ignominious death which he ceaselessly bemoans even in Hades. Penelope's potential infidelity hangs like a cloud over the whole *Odyssey*. At the moment of her reunion with Odysseus, she herself recalls the exemplar of Helen "from whom, from the beginning, grief came upon us also" (23. 224). By contrast, the illicit love of Ares and Aphrodite gives rise to neither war nor death. The penalty Hephaestus exacts is left vague, but Penelope's arrogant suitors pay for their misdeeds with their lives.

The sublime frivolity of the gods in Homer is the shocking and paradoxical result of profound and logical reflection on their immortality. This darkly brilliant insight into the consequences of divine immortality transcends any supposed desire on the part of the poet to lighten or vary his narrative with comic interludes. As a result, any attempt to "distinguish . . . the cosmic gods and the comic gods,"[19] or to trace the evolution of a "purer" conception of divinity on the one hand and a light-hearted "Götterburleske"[20] on the other, means to mistake the point of departure of Greek reflection on the gods. That starting point lies not in the ascription of justice or goodness or wisdom, but rather in the absolute and primary predication of immortality to anthropomorphic divinities— which, in turn, entails their ultimate lack of seriousness. To be sure, Homeric gods can suffer and feel pain on occasion, but their wounds, whether physical or spiritual, are quickly healed. Deathless, they cannot risk their lives for anything more precious than life, be it honor, the love of a friend, or the love of home. Their inability to sacrifice themselves for something higher constitutes a limitation on the gods. Left to themselves, the gods are often petty, vindictive, and incon-

---

[19] Calhoun (1937), p. 21.

[20] See, for instance, G. M. Calhoun, "The Higher Criticism on Olympus," *AJP* 58 (1937):257ff.; and W. Nestle, *Vom Mythos zum Logos* (Stuttgart, 1940), pp. 29-30. Griffin (1980), p. 199, n. 57, rightly calls attempts to separate the "high" and the "low" aspects of the gods "not only a doomed enterprise but also a profoundly wrong one."

stant. Paradoxically, it is through their involvement with their inferiors, earthbound men, destined to die, that the gods acquire a measure of earnestness. The superhuman, then, turns out to be less than the human in an essential respect.

IMMORTAL AND UNAGING FOREVER

> . . . μόνοις οὐ γίγνεται
> θεοῖσι γῆρας οὐδὲ κατθανεῖν ποτε,
> τὰ δ᾽ ἄλλα συγχεῖ πάνθ᾽ ὁ παγκρατὴς χρόνος.
> (*Oedipus at Colonus* 607-609)

Exemption from death, then, forms the primary characteristic of Homer's gods. But the gods are not only immortal; they are also unaging. To be a god in the language of the Epic means to be "immortal and unaging for all time" ἀθάνατος καὶ ἀγήρως ἤματα πάντα.[21] While many stories are told of the birth and childhood of the gods, none is told of their senescence. The Olympians reach their prime quickly and remain forever fixed in the perfection of maturity. The specific point of maturity forms a principle of differentiation among the Olympians. Thus, Hermes is the eternal youth, Apollo, the *kouros*, and Zeus, the father.

Yet agelessness and immortality are not simply synonymous, as the tale of Tithonus recounted in the *Hymn to Aphrodite* reveals. In contrast to Zeus' beloved, Ganymede, who was translated to Olympus and made "immortal and ageless," Tithonus, though immortal, soon began to age and grew eternally weaker and weaker. For the dawn-goddess, Eos, had asked Zeus to make her lover immortal, but she forgot to ask for eternal youth (*H. Aphr.* 202-238). From this example, Aphrodite draws the conclusion, as she explains to her mortal lover, Anchises:

---

[21] *Il.* VIII. 539; XII. 323; XVII. 444; *Od.* 5. 136, 218; 7.94, 257; 23. 336. Cf. *Hymn to Demeter* 242 and 260, where Demeter would have made Demophon "immortal and ageless," were it not for Metaneira's interference. While consigning Demophon to mortality, the goddess grants him τιμὴ ἄφθιτος, "imperishable honor." See Nagy (1979), pp. 181ff. This section appeared in slightly different form in *CJ* 77 (1981-82):112-17.

οὐκ ἂν ἐγώ γε σὲ τοῖον ἐν ἀθανάτοισιν ἑλοίμην
ἀθάνατόν τ᾽ εἶναι καὶ ζώειν ἤματα πάντα.
ἀλλ᾽ εἰ μὲν τοιοῦτος ἐὼν εἶδός τε δέμας τε
ζώοις, ἡμέτερός τε πόσις κεκλημένος εἴης,
οὐκ ἂν ἔπειτά μ᾽ ἄχος πυκινὰς φρένας ἀμφικαλύπτοι.
νῦν δέ σε μὲν τάχα γῆρας ὁμοίιον ἀμφικαλύψει
νηλειές, τό τ᾽ ἔπειτα παρίσταται ἀνθρώποισιν,
οὐλόμενον καματηρόν, ὅ τε στυγέουσι θεοί περ.

If this were to be your lot among immortals, I should not
    choose
for you immortality and eternal life.
But should you live on such as you now are
in looks and build, and be called my husband,
then no grief would enfold my prudent heart.
But now you will soon be enveloped by leveling old age,
that pitiless companion of every man,
baneful, wearisome, and hated even by the gods.
                                    (239-246, trans. Athanassakis)

Since Aphrodite cannot guarantee Anchises' youthfulness,[22]
she would rather do without him. In the same poem, we are
told that the tree nymphs "resemble neither gods nor men,"
but "live a long time"—presumably without aging. Finally,
however, their souls "leave the light of the sun" at the same
moment that the trees which are born with them wither and
die (257-272). Perhaps analogous are the herds of the Sun in
the *Odyssey* who, while they can be slaughtered, are exempt
from the natural cycle of giving birth and decaying (γόνος δ᾽
οὐ γίγνεται αὐτῶν, / οὐδέ ποτε φθινύθουσι 12. 130-131).
In the case of the gods, immortality and agelessness coincide,
but these examples prove that they are separable phenomena.

As we have seen, immortality is an absolute predication of
the Homeric gods and requires no further explanation. (Only
later do the Greeks begin to fret about whether gods who
have come into being can be eternal. Homer never seems to

---

[22] An essential but unspoken premise of the *Hymn to Aphrodite* is that the
era of the apotheosis of mortals is irrevocably past.

pose the problem.)[23] Their agelessness, however, is secondary
and is based on a conception of divine physiology closely
analogous to the physiology of mortals. Men are born, flourish, and decline. When Apollo dissuades Poseidon from fighting over mortals, he likens them to leaves:

ἐννοσίγαι’, οὐκ ἄν με σαόφρονα μυθήσαιο
ἔμμεναι, εἰ δὴ σοί γε βροτῶν ἕνεκα πτολεμίξω
δειλῶν, οἳ φύλλοισιν ἐοικότες ἄλλοτε μέν τε
ζαφλεγέες τελέθουσιν, ἀρούρης καρπὸν ἔδοντες,
ἄλλοτε δὲ φθινύθουσιν ἀκήριοι.

Earthshaker, you would not call me sensible
if I were to fight with you for the sake of mortals,
wretches, who like leaves at one moment
flourish luxuriantly, as they eat the fruit of the fields,
but wither at another and die.

(XXI. 462-466)

Men not only resemble vegetative nature in their growth and
decline; they are also intimately linked to that same vegetative
cycle through their consumption of grain, "the fruit of the
field," for sustenance. The word Apollo uses in this passage
for men is *brotoi*, which in the language of the Epic is frequently connected with expressions involving the eating of
grain.[24] That men are *brotoi* because they eat grain is due to
the fact that βροτός, 'mortal,' resembles a rare Homeric word
for blood, βρότος, which occurs in two formulaic phrases,
ἔναρα βροτόεντα 'bloody spoils,' and the tautological βρό-
τον αἱματόεντα 'bloody gore.' Chantraine translates the word

---

[23] The Epic, of course, does not deal with tales of the birth of the gods,
which seem to belong to the province of Hymn poetry.

[24] For the linking of *brotoi* with what men eat, consider the expressions:
"*brotoi* who eat the fruit of the field" (οἳ ἀρούρης καρπὸν ἔδουσιν VI.
142); "*brotoi* who eat grain upon the ground" (βροτοί . . . ἐπὶ χθονὶ
σῖτον ἔδοντες 8. 222); "mortal *brotoi* on the barley-giving earth" (θνητοῖ-
σι βροτοῖσι ἐπὶ ζείδωρον ἄρουραν 3. 3; 12. 386). Compare also 5. 196-
197, where Calypso sets before Odysseus "all kinds of food to eat and drink,
such as *brotoi* men eat." She, by contrast, consumes ambrosia and nectar.

as "sang qui a coulé d'une blessure."[25] Its etymology remains
obscure, but it does not appear to be related to βροτός which
comes from *mrt-, 'mortal.'[26] Untroubled by scientific etymology, the Epic joins these apparent homonyms to suggest a
conception of what it means to be mortal. Mortals are "those
who have blood in their veins," and this blood is conceived
of as being produced by their eating of grain. The notion of
blood as a life-sustaining substance is evident in the Nekyia,
where the dead must first drink blood before they can regain
consciousness and speak to Odysseus. Blood, the consumption
of grain, and mortality are thus linked to form a definition of
human life.

The physiology of the gods corresponds to and mirrors that
of men, as becomes clear from the passage describing the
wounding of Aphrodite in the *Iliad*:

ῥέε δ᾽ ἄμβροτον αἷμα θεοῖο,
ἰχώρ, οἷός πέρ τε ῥέει μακάρεσσι θεοῖσιν·
οὐ γὰρ σῖτον ἔδουσ᾽, οὐ πίνουσ᾽ αἴθοπα οἶνον,
τοὔνεκ᾽ ἀναίμονές εἰσι καὶ ἀθάνατοι καλέονται.

The *ambroton* blood of the goddess flowed,
ichor, such as flows through the blessed gods;
for they eat no grain, nor drink shining wine;
therefore they are bloodless and called immortals.

                                          (V. 339-342)

The bodies of the gods contain *ichor*, "immortal blood," *ambroton aima*, which means at the same time "bloodless blood."
Because they do not partake of the food of mortals which

---

[25] *Dictionnaire étymologique de la langue grecque* (Paris, 1968-1980), s.v.
βρότος.

[26] M. Leumann, *Homerische Wörter* (Basel, 1950), pp. 124-27, suggests
that βρότος is a poetic neologism formed from ἄμβροτος, meaning 'immortal.' In the verses from *Iliad* V cited below, ἄμβροτον is the equivalent
of 'bloodless.' Hence, Leumann argues, βρότος came to mean 'blood' on the
basis of this very passage or its prototype. I believe with Leumann that βρότος
is a poetic formation, but wonder if the derivation of βρότος from βροτός
may not be primary. It does not seem beyond the mental capacity of the
Homeric age to connect blood with mortality.

generates blood, they themselves are *anaimones*.[27] The gods nourish themselves on "red nectar"—analogous to the wine of men—and "ambrosia," immortal or bloodless food.

Attempts to draw any significant distinctions between the functions of nectar and ambrosia have failed, nor have etymological speculations, especially in reference to the linguistic origins of nectar, produced scholarly consensus.[28] But what matters to our discussion is that, in Homer, nectar and ambrosia do not in and of themselves render the gods immortal, but they prevent them from aging and exempt them from the natural cycle of growth and decay.[29] This, I believe, is the original Homeric conception of the meaning of nectar and ambrosia. In the later Greek tradition, it becomes blurred and diluted, and the rationale behind it is lost.[30] Yet even some

[27] Cf. J.-P. Vernant, "À la table des hommes," in *La cuisine du sacrifice en pays grec*, ed. M. Detienne and J.-P. Vernant (Paris, 1979), p. 61.

[28] See, for example, Güntert (1919), pp. 158-63; P. Kretschmer, "NEKTAP," *Anz. der Oester. Akad. der Wissensch. Phil.-hist. kl.* 84 (1947):13-26; P. Thieme, "Nektar" and "Ambrosia," in *Indogermanische Dichtersprache*, ed. R. Schmitt (Darmstadt, 1968), pp. 102-112 and 113-32; and S. Levin, "The Etymology of νέκταρ: Exotic Scents in Early Greece," *SMEA* 13 (1971):31-50.

[29] Thieme (1968), on the basis of an etymological argument deriving nectar from the root *nek*, 'death' and *tṝ*, meaning 'to cross over (into safety),' defines nectar as "das über die [Todes-] Vernichtung Hinweg rettende" (p. 111). Yet Thieme's own examples of the power of nectar—to ward off hunger, age, and decay—reveal its efficacy as a preservative rather than as an agent of immortality—just like ambrosia. Of ambrosia, which he translates as "Lebenskraft," Thieme notes: "Es ist offensichtlich, dass bei Homer die Vorstellung der "Unsterblichkeit" keineswegs notwendig mit ἀμβροσίη verbunden ist" (p. 125). Citing Wilamowitz ("Ohne Nektar altern selbst die Götter"), Thieme adds: "Dies gilt natürlich auch für Ambrosia" (p. 126). Both Güntert and Kretschmer consider ambrosia and nectar to be synonymous; and there is nothing in the Homeric texts to contradict that view.

[30] For later examples in which ambrosia and nectar make men immortal, see, for instance, Theocritus *Id.* XV. 106-108, where Aphrodite makes Berenike immortal by dripping ambrosia into her chest. Similarly, in Ovid's *Metamorphoses* XIV. 606-607, Venus makes Aeneas a god by applying ambrosia mixed with nectar. Thetis, in the *Argonautica* IV. 869-872, tries to make Achilles immortal by anointing him with ambrosia by day and placing him in a fire by night (cf. Apollodorus 3. 13, 6). A similar twofold process underlies Demeter's thwarted attempt to render Demophon immortal in the

later texts still show an awareness of the Homeric distinction between immortality and agelessness. For instance, according to Hesiod (*Theog.* 793-798), a divinity who has violated the sacred oath by the Styx is deprived of nectar and ambrosia for one year. The god does not, of course, die but enters a state of suspended animation (κακὸν κῶμα) and remains without breath as well as speech (ἀνάπνευστος καὶ ἄναυδος). In the *Hymn to Demeter*, the infant Demophon does not eat grain, but Demeter anoints him with ambrosia, "as if he were the offspring of a god" (236-237). Yet this is not sufficient to render him immortal.[31] Again, though mortal, the long-lived nymphs of the *Hymn to Aphrodite* (259-272) eat "immortal food" ἄμβροτον εἶδαρ, which seems to keep them from aging. In the same poem, Eos nourishes Tithonus *after* he has already begun to age σίτῳ τ᾽ ἀμβροσίῃ, "grain and ambrosia," as if this mixture might perhaps slow down the inevitable process of decay to which Tithonus is doomed (228-232). Pindar, as often, reflects both the original Homeric notion of the power of ambrosia and nectar and the later conception of them as the food of immortality. Thus, in *Pythian* 9. 63, Gaia and the Horai make Aristaeus immortal by dripping ambrosia and nectar on his lips (θήσονταί τέ νιν ἀθάνατον). But in the first *Olympian*, Tantalus' theft of ambrosia and nectar is motivated not by the desire to become immortal, but to become *aphthiton* (ἄφθιτον θέν νιν l. 63). The root *phthi-* suggests the natural cycle of growth and decay which defines the human condition and links it to the vegetative

---

Hymn to Demeter 236-240. As to the possible origins of the change in conception of the power of nectar and ambrosia, Aristotle, *Metaphysics* III. 4. 12, 1000a9ff., attributes to "those around Hesiod" the notion that "whatever does not eat of nectar and ambrosia is mortal" (οἱ μὲν περὶ Ἡσίοδον . . . τὰ μὴ γευσάμενα τοῦ νέκταρος καὶ τῆς ἀμβροσίας θνητὰ γενέσθαι φασίν).

[31] The critical step in Demophon's immortalization (καί κέν μιν ποίησεν ἀγήρων τ᾽ ἀθάνατόν τε 242)—placing him in the fire—is interrrupted by Metaneira (242-258). In Apollodorus 1. 5, 1-2, the child is burnt up. For the belief, see J. G. Frazer, ed., *Apollodorus*, 2 vols. (Cambridge, Mass., 1921) II. 311-317.

process. Its negation (*aphthi-*) signifies precisely the exemption from that process enjoyed by the gods.[32] The original efficacy of ambrosia and nectar lies in their power as preservatives and age-retardants rather than as agents of immortality. Significantly, the goddess who pours nectar and ambrosia for the gods in Homer (IV. 2-3) is called Hebe, which does not simply mean "youth," but rather the flowering or peak of the process of growth. Elsewhere, Ganymede, whose eternal youth and beauty are emphasized, shares this function (XX. 232-235; cf. *H. Aphr.* 206). In the *Odyssey*, we hear that ambrosia is brought to Zeus from beyond the Planktai by doves of whom we are told:

ἀλλά τε καὶ τῶν αἰὲν ἀφαιρεῖται λὶς πέτρη·
ἀλλ' ἄλλην ἐνίησι πατὴρ ἐναρίθμιον εἶναι.

But the smooth rock always takes away one of them;
and the father inserts another to make up their number.

(12. 64-65)

In some mysterious way, the process of supplying the gods with ambrosia involves loss and renewal; and we can only guess how Zeus' "insertion" differs from the natural cycle of birth, growth, decay, and death.

The use by the gods of nectar and ambrosia on the bodies of men demonstrates their power as preservatives. For example, when Thetis pours nectar and ambrosia into the nostrils of the dead Patroclus, she neither brings him back to life nor makes him immortal (XIX. 38-39). Rather, the goddess retards the natural rotting of the corpse, just as Aphrodite later anoints the body of Hector with "rosy ambrosial oil" to prevent its corruption (XXIII. 186-187). Similarly, when Achilles refuses all food after the death of his comrade, Athena, at the behest of Zeus, relieves his natural hunger by dripping nectar and ambrosia into his chest (XIX. 352-54). In a more lighthearted context, the goddess Eidothea relieves the discomfort of Menelaus and his men, wrapped in sealskins, as they lie in wait for Proteus. Good naturedly, the goddess

[32] Cf. Nagy (1979), pp. 178ff.

applies a little ambrosia to their nostrils to neutralize the putrid smell of the rotting skins (4. 444-446). Finally, to prepare Penelope for her dramatic appearance before the suitors and the yet unrecognized Odysseus, Athena washes and anoints her with an ambrosial cosmetic as she sleeps, thereby erasing the effects of Penelope's long years of waiting and mourning for Odysseus (18. 188-196). The suitors immediately become inflamed with desire at the sight of her beauty, though Penelope claims that it had perished long ago, when Odysseus left for Troy. Athena's beauty treatment retards or even reverses the process of aging and decay to which all mortal flesh is heir.

Exempt from death and exempt from the inevitable decay of all vegetative and animal nature, the Homeric gods remain frozen in an eternal prime: "immortal and unaging." The formula to describe this state occurs only once in Homer without immediate reference to the gods: to describe the deathless and unaging golden dogs who guard the palace of Alcinoos (7. 94).[33] The gods most closely resemble these beautiful imitations of nature, the product of art, the divine art of Hephaestus. Elsewhere in Homer, such immortal works of art are called *aphthita*, "imperishable."[34] The beautiful works of the gods and the gods themselves are contained in an imperishable work of art that imitates nature: the poem that confers immortality, *kleos aphthiton*, and, like nectar and ambrosia, eternal youth on its participants.

DIVINE KNOWLEDGE: *Moira*

Immortality, as we have seen, is the most prominent attribute of the Homeric gods. Their physiology, based on a diet of ambrosia and nectar which produces *ichor* rather than blood,

[33] In a variant of the formula, the aegis of Athena is once called ἀγήρων ἀθανάτην τε (Il. 447).

[34] The gods themselves are called *aphthitoi* in the *Hymn to Hermes* 326, but the expression does not occur in Homer. For the relationship of *aphthi-* to both the gods and works of art—especially the art of the Epic—see again Nagy (1979), pp. 175-89.

ensures their eternal youthfulness. In almost all other respects, the gods reveal themselves to be only relatively superior to men. They are larger and more beautiful than mortals and stronger; they can move faster and shout louder. And, as I pointed out in the first chapter, the gods can see farther than men; as a result, they know more.

It is now time to resume that earlier discussion and to undertake an analysis of the nature of divine knowledge. What do the gods know and how? What are the limitations of their knowledge, and how does it differ from that of men? According to Homer, the divinely inspired seer of the *Iliad*, Chalcas, knows "those things that are, those things that will be, and those things which were before" (τά τ' ἐόντα τά τ' ἐσσόμενα πρό τ' ἐόντα I. 70). There exist, then, three distinct spheres of knowledge: (1) knowledge of the present or visual knowledge based on eyewitness; (2) knowledge of the past, of which the Muses are the special patrons; and (3) knowledge of the future or prophetic knowledge.[35] According to our earlier analysis, the first two are closely related, both depending on seeing or prior sight. The knowledge of the gods is vastly superior to that of mortals because their powers of vision are greater. But, despite the pious statements of Menelaus that "the gods know all" (4. 379, 468), Homer's gods do not appear omniscient in practice. Poseidon, for example, learns of the gods' decision to allow Odysseus to return home only by inference when he sees Odysseus on his raft (5. 286-287); Hera succeeds in tricking Zeus in the fourteenth book of the *Iliad*—if only for a time; and, most strikingly, Helios, who supposedly "hears and sees all," does not know what has happened to his cattle until word is brought by the nymph Lampetie (12. 374-375).[36] A gulf appears to exist between men's beliefs about the gods and their reality.

The importance of the gods' ability to recognize one another

---

[35] Cf. *Theogony* 33 and the discussion of M. Treu, *Von Homer zur Lyrik*, Zetemata 12 (Munich, 1968), pp. 123ff. Treu, however, does not perceive that the knowledge of the future differs from the other two modes of knowing.

[36] Cf. the Scholia at 12.374 and also the Scholia at III. 277. Consider also the discussion of Nägelsbach (1840), pp. 18-21.

has already been discussed. When the Muses transmit such knowledge to the poet, his art becomes possible. Ordinary men may surmise that "some god" has intervened, but the poet knows which one; and since he is privy to the councils of the gods on Olympus, he also knows their intentions. Like the gift of the Muses, the gift of prophecy, the knowledge of what will be, derives from the gods. The gods have knowledge of the future and may, on occasion, share that knowledge with select mortals—who then become seers or prophets. Yet a prophecy, whether delivered by a god or a divinely inspired mortal, differs both in form and in content from the preceding types of divine knowledge based on visual perception.

A statement about the future retains a certain degree of vagueness even when pronounced by a divinity. Ambiguity, conditional or alternative statements seem to characterize the prophetic utterance.[37] This typical vagueness of prophecy is well illustrated by a long speech of Proteus (4. 492-569). In it, he replies to Menelaus' request for information about the fate of the other heroes on their return from Troy. Proteus' wisdom appears to encompass all three types of divine knowledge. First, he describes in great detail and vividness the deaths of Ajax and Agamemnon, both events in the recent past (4. 499-537). Turning briefly to the future, the Old Man of the Sea advises Menelaus to return home quickly, where he may find his brother's murderer Aegisthus *either* dead *or* alive. Then, making use of his power of vision (τόν ἴδον), he describes the present situation of Odysseus on Calypso's isle (4. 555-560). And, finally, Proteus prophesies without being asked:

σοὶ δ' οὐ θέσφατόν ἐστι, διοτρεφὲς ὦ Μενέλαε,
Ἄργει ἐν ἱπποβότῳ θανέειν καὶ πότμον ἐπισπεῖν,
ἀλλά σ' ἐς Ἠλύσιον πεδίον καὶ πείρατα γαίης
ἀθάνατοι πέμψουσιν. . . .

---

[37] Cf. Macrobius' commentary on the *Somnium Scipionis*, I. 7, where Macrobius cites Homer and Vergil for examples of "the sort of ambiguity that is purposely used in prophecies." For the characteristic ambiguity of oracles, see Stanford (1939), pp. 120ff.

For you, Zeus-nurtured Menelaus, it is not fated
to die and meet your fate in Argos, nurse of horses;
but to the plain of Elysium and the boundaries of the
   earth
the gods will send you. . . .
                  (4. 561-564)

Proteus seems to foretell Menelaus' bodily translation to Elysium and subsequent immortality, "because you are Helen's
consort and the son-in-law of Zeus" (4. 569).[38] But strictly
speaking, that is not what Proteus says. The negative form of
his first statement enhances the mystery of his words: "You
are not destined to die in Argos." We expect: "You will die
elsewhere." Menelaus' exemption from death is never explicitly stated, but is only indicated *ex silentio*. One may recall
Heraclitus' characterization of the Delphic oracle which "neither speaks, nor conceals, but indicates." Proteus' prophecy
retains a typical oracular obscurity, as Menelaus' thoughtful
reaction reveals: "And I pondered much in my heart as I went"
(4. 572).

The most important prophecy in the *Odyssey*, Teiresias' in
the Nekyia concerning Odysseus' homecoming, fairly bristles
with conditions, alternatives, and dark cryptic utterances.[39]
Odysseus' relation to Teiresias recalls that of Menelaus to
Proteus. The prophets' respective speeches convey much the
same kind of information, and the parallelism is emphasized
by the fact that goddesses—in one case, Circe, Eidothea, in
the other—instruct the heroes how to obtain it in the same
words:[40]

---

[38] Cf. E. Rohde, *Psyche*, 3rd ed. (Tübingen, 1903), pp. 68ff.

[39] For the cryptic tone of Teiresias' speech, see Reinhardt (1960a), pp. 101-
104. But Reinhardt's characterization of the speech as *religiös* (p. 102) seems
at once too imprecise and unhomeric. Page (1955), p. 49, n. 10, chidingly
remarks that "Teiresias ought to be able to do better than this."

[40] Proteus' tales of the Trojan heroes are replaced by Odysseus' encounters
with them in the Nekyia following Teiresias' oracle. A good discussion of
the parallels between Proteus and Teiresias can be found in Reinhardt (1960a),
pp. 94-104.

ὅς κέν τοι εἴπῃσιν ὁδὸν καὶ μέτρα κελεύθου
νόστον θ'. . . .

He will tell you the way and the lengths of the journey
and the return. . . .

                                        (4. 389-390 = 10. 539-540)

Yet neither Teiresias nor Proteus provides maps whereby the
heroes can navigate homeward.

Teiresias' speech can be summarized as follows: Odysseus'
return will be made bitter through Poseidon's anger at the
blinding of Polyphemus, but the difficulties of the journey
may yet be overcome if Odysseus leaves the cattle of the Sun
unharmed. Otherwise, his men will be destroyed, and he himself will return only late and in evil plight on a foreign ship.
On Ithaca, he will find arrogant suitors devouring his property
and courting his wife; and he must take his revenge. Thereafter, Odysseus must once again leave home and wander until
he comes upon men unacquainted with the sea, who do not
recognize the oar he carries on his shoulder. There, he is to
erect an oar, make due sacrifices to Poseidon, and return home,
where he will live to a ripe old age and die peacefully.

It is one of the *cruces* of Homeric scholarship that, despite
Circe's words and our reasonable expectations, Teiresias does
not give Odysseus instructions on how to get back to Ithaca.[41]
In the parallel case of Menelaus, one might argue that detailed
directions on the route between Sparta and Egypt are unnecessary. But Odysseus, in trackless regions beyond the confines
of the known world where all sense of orientation is lost,
needs help. Now, Teiresias' prophecy contains many things,
but it does not tell Odysseus how to get home; it only informs
him that his journey goes by way of Thrinacia. Yet, as soon
as Odysseus returns from the land of the dead, Circe asks him
what he had learned from the prophet (12. 34). Evidently, the
goddess had not known in what direction Odysseus' course
lay, but once informed that Thrinacia is to be one of the

---

[41] Cf. Reinhardt (1960a), p. 100: "Die Rede gehört zum Angefochtensten
der ganzen Odyssee. Was etwas heissen will." See also Page (1955), pp. 27-
43, and Bona (1966), 54ff. for a detailed doxography of the problem.

stations, she can direct Odysseus there with ease.[42] Circe imparts precise geographical information concerning the route to Thrinacia; she does not predict, and she is no more oracular than a map. The manner in which Circe and Teiresias describe Thrinacia crystallizes the differing character of their different speeches. Although she repeats Teiresias' prophecy verbatim (12. 137-141 = 11. 110-114), Circe adds many precise details concerning the number and nature of the cattle of the Sun as well as their guardians (12. 127-136). Circe's knowledge has no prophetic content but is purely visual knowledge, such as might suit a daughter of Helios. The two speeches do not duplicate each other; each one exemplifies a different kind of divine knowledge: Circe's, the clear and vivid account based on divine vision, and Teiresias', the mysterious ambiguity of prophecy.

Odysseus' reaction to the two speeches further underlines the difference between these two modes of knowing. Teiresias' dark oracle elicits only a resigned "so be it" (11. 139). It calls for no immediate action, and Odysseus quickly turns his attention to question the ghosts around him. Circe's indications, however, demand deliberation and choices. By the time Odysseus unfolds the instructions of the goddess to his men, he has silently made the decision to listen to the voice of the Sirens (12. 160), whereas Circe had only advised him *how* he might manage to hear them without injury "if you so wish" (12. 49). Moreover, as he exhorts his helmsman and companions, Odysseus has silently opted for his course between Scylla and Charybdis (12. 208ff). This decision is prefigured in the one question that interrupts Circe's disquisition (12. 111-114). If, he asks, they should escape total destruction at the hands of Charybdis, is there any hope of opposing Scylla and preventing her from snatching six of the crew as they sail by? Resignation to the impenetrable will of the gods is the appropriate response to the words of the prophet Teiresias, but

[42] Cf. O. Becker *Das Bild des Weges*, Hermes Einzel. 4. (Berlin, 1937), pp. 19-20. Becker defines δείξω ὁδόν (12. 25) as "den Weg zeigen (wie auf einer Landkarte)."

independent judgment, calculation, and finally action are demanded by the "objective" information provided by Circe. As the prophetic speech has its particular form, it also has a distinctive subject matter. As we have seen, the prophecy of Teiresias conforms closely to that of Proteus, although the former is considerably more complex because Odysseus' fate embraces greater complexities than does that of Menelaus. Nevertheless, both seers know which gods have been offended and have set up obstacles to the heroes' returns; they also know how those gods must be propitiated. "The immortal gods," we remember, "are not unknown to one another (5. 79-80)—nor to their prophets. In addition, the two prophets describe the great outlines of the heroes' fate, their destined returns, and their modes of death.

This individual fate, the overall shape of a man's life, the Greeks called *moira*.[43] The word itself is quite prosaic, meaning nothing more than 'portion' or 'share.' Thus, one can have one's due share of booty or property or meat at a feast. More abstractly, both gods and men expect their due share of honor; and one can speak or act *kata moiran*, that is, appropriately, or according to the demands of a given situation. In Book XV of the *Iliad*, Poseidon recalls the division of the cosmos among the sons of Cronus: Poseidon was allotted the sea as his sphere of influence; Hades, the nether world; while Zeus received the heavens. But earth and Olympus are common to them all. Let Zeus, says the indignant Poseidon, "even though mighty, remain in his third share" (τριτάτῃ ἐνὶ μοίρῃ XV. 195). In all these examples, *moira* retains its fundamental sense. In reference to the life of men, however, it takes on a special significance. While the *moira* of a god is his eternally allotted sphere of influence, the *moira* of a man is his allotted share of life defined temporally as the interval between birth and death. Since death is the inevitable lot of mortal men (*thnetoi*), *moira* frequently simply means death. A man's death, the

---

[43] For *moira*, in general, see E. Leitzke, *Moira und Gottheit im alten griechischen Epos* (Göttingen, 1930); W. C. Greene, *Moira* (Cambridge, 1944); and B. C. Dietrich, *Death, Fate and the Gods* (London, 1965).

"allotted day" (μόρσιμον ἦμαρ), or *moira* simply constitute the subject par excellence of prophecy. Everything else which may be fated is secondary and derivative from the essential fact of human mortality. Thus in the *Odyssey*, Teiresias foretells both the death of Odysseus and that of his companions; Theoclymenus (20. 365ff.) and others predict the violent end of the suitors, while Proteus alludes, as we have seen, to Menelaus' mysterious translation to Elysium.

But one's portion or *moira* may not be solely limited to death. Certain events in a man's life or the life of a people may be apportioned and subject to *moira* and, as a result, occur in an oracle. In the *Odyssey*, these appear to be certain crucial events or turning points, such as Odysseus' ultimate homecoming, the blinding of the Cyclops, and the termination of the Phaeacians' career as "escorters of men." The events themselves are fated, but exactly how and when is often left unclear. The episode at Thrinacia is such a pivotal moment in Odysseus' return; and here Teiresias' words are at their murkiest. Conditions and alternatives abound, but the vaguely threatening tone is at least partially belied by the event. Odysseus does indeed return home "having lost all his companions, late, and on a ship not his own," but the final homeward voyage is accomplished while Odysseus sleeps soundly, snugly wrapped in blankets—with more loot than he ever received at Troy.

The effect of *moira* on human life may, then, be intermittent, but it is always crucial. Adkins has aptly described the mechanism involved:

> The world under the influence of *moira*, in fact, is not so much like a piece of clockwork as it is like a game of celestial snakes and ladders. Most moves are free; but should one alight at the foot of one's own particular ladder, or at the head of one's own personal snake, the next move is determined.[44]

[44] A.W.H. Adkins, *Merit and Responsibility: A Study in Greek Values* (Oxford, 1960), p. 19.

The *moira* of an individual forms the particular shape of his life. Thus, the *moira* of an Achilles differs from that of an Odysseus. But no matter what a man's particular allotment may be, the *moira* of death is common to all.

If this is the way *moira* operates from the point of view of mortals, the question of the gods' relation to *moira* still remains. Whether the gods control *moira* or are subject to its workings is a venerable controversy in Homeric studies.[45] Yet the terms of the question are somewhat misconceived. The relation of *moira* and the gods in Homer must not be understood as simply hierarchical—which is superior to whom—but rather in epistemological terms. Zeus, we are told, "knows the luck and lack of mortal men" (μοῖράν τ᾽ ἀμμορίην τε καταθνητῶν ἀνθρώπων 20. 76). The gods, and Zeus in particular, know *moira*, and to that extent they are superior to mortals who do not. But in this case, knowledge is not power;[46] for the gods' knowledge of *moira* appears to limit their ability to intervene in the lives of men. Poseidon knows that his harassment of Odysseus must remain just that, since Odysseus is fated to make good his return. And Athena herself admits on another occasion:

ἀλλ᾽ ἦ τοι θάνατον μὲν ὁμοίιον οὐδὲ θεοί περ
καὶ φίλῳ ἀνδρὶ δύνανται ἀλαλκέμεν, ὁππότε κεν δὴ
μοῖρ᾽ ὀλοὴ καθέλῃσι τανηλεγέος θανάτοιο.

But from death, which is common to all, not even the
    gods
can rescue a man they hold dear, whenever it happens
that destructive *moira* of woeful death should seize him.
                                                    (3. 236-238)[47]

---

[45] For a survey of the question of the relative superiority of *moira* and the gods, see Dietrich (1965), pp. 179-93. For the possibility that the relation of the gods to *moira* may not be a matter of rank but cognitive, see Leitzke (1930), pp. 17-18 and Dietrich (1965), p. 221.

[46] Cf. *Prometheus* 248, where Prometheus claims as one of his great benefactions to mortals the fact that he has taken from them their foreknowledge of their fate.

[47] At 4. 753, Eurycleia incorrectly suggests that Athena can save Telemachus even from death. But there she is attempting to console Penelope.

The momentary vacillation of Zeus before he resigns himself to the fated death of his son, Sarpedon, at the hands of Patroclus (XVI. 431ff.) seems to contradict Athena's assertion. Yet Zeus' suggestion that he might save his son from death meets with an immediate rebuke from Hera. The other gods, she says, will not approve; and she intimates the possibility of a general rebellion in heaven. The other gods, too, after all, have sons fighting before Troy. Hera only hints at the consequences of Zeus' acting in opposition to what he knows to be fated: the collapse of all order both among the gods and in the relations between gods and men.

The natural order implies a hierarchy; and crucial to that hierarchy is the maintenance of the distinction between gods and men. The essence of that distinction is the opposition between divine immortality and human mortality. *Moira*, which is so often simply equivalent to death, forms a critical element in that dichotomy. Even those critical turning points which are *morsima* exist only in the lives of mortals, since, in the final analysis, there can be no pivotal movements in the eternal life of the gods.[48] *Moira* is, as we said, a principle of differentiation which both defines and differentiates the life of an Odysseus from that of an Achilles. But, first and foremost, it differentiates between men and gods.

For a moment, Zeus may raise the possibility of going against the natural order. Whether he has the ability to do so remains significantly moot. For even the briefest contemplation of the drastic consequences of such a move dissuades Zeus from such an undertaking. Tampering with *moira* means tampering with the natural hierarchy and jeopardizing the very position Zeus enjoys. "Take but degree away, untune that string, / and hark what discord follows."

DIVINE KNOWLEDGE: *Physis*

According to Homer, the gods not only excel men in their understanding of *moira*; they are also masters of another sphere

---

[48] At *Il.* XXII. 13, Apollo tells Achilles to stop chasing him, since "You will not kill me, since I am not destined (*morsimos*)."

of knowledge, one that cannot be defined in temporal terms, but which is ultimately not unrelated to their knowledge of "fate." It is the knowledge of the nature of things, a nature hidden from men. The Greek word for nature, *physis*, is first attested in Homer; and one can fairly claim that without the idea of nature there would be no Greek philosophy or science and ultimately no Western civilization as we know it. It is therefore all the more striking that *physis* occurs only once in the Homeric corpus—in a mysterious but important passage which demands to be taken as paradigmatic.

As Odysseus makes his way to the palace of Circe, searching for his men, the god Hermes suddenly appears and explains that Circe has transformed his companions into pigs. First advising Odysseus on how to deal with the goddess, Hermes proceeds to give him an herb which will act as an antidote to Circe's magic and render it impotent. At this point, Hermes reveals its *physis* to Odysseus:

> . . . μοι φύσιν αὐτοῦ ἔδειξε.
> ῥίζῃ μὲν μέλαν ἔσκε, γάλακτι δὲ εἴκελον ἄνθος·
> μῶλυ δέ μιν καλέουσι θεοί· χαλεπὸν δέ τ᾽ ὀρύσσειν
> ἀνδράσι γε θνητοῖσι· θεοὶ δέ τε πάντα δύνανται.

> . . . He showed me its *physis*;
> it had a black root, but a flower like milk;
> the gods call it moly, but it is difficult for mortal
> men to dig out; but the gods can do all.
> (10. 303-306)

Men can only see the visible part of the herb, the white flower. The gods, on the other hand, know also the hidden black root and hence the whole. As a result, the gods have a name for that whole, *moly*, whereas mortals do not.[49] In other words, to know the nature of a thing means to know both the visible and invisible components and to be able to name the whole with accuracy.

In Homer, the gods' knowledge of nature is infrequently

---

[49] Cf. J. S. Clay, "The Planktai and Moly: Divine Naming and Knowing in Homer," *Hermes* 100 (1972):130-31.

demonstrated by a mastery over nature. Theoretically, the gods may have the power to change the natural course of things, but they rarely exploit this ability.[50] Athena, to be sure, may lengthen the first night in which Penelope and Odysseus are reunited, and Poseidon petrifies the ship of the Phaeacians on its return.[51] But, characteristically for Homer, the most violent disruption of the course of nature is merely threatened rather than carried out. Enraged at the butchery of his cattle by Odysseus' companions, Helios threatens to shine among the dead—and we must assume that he has the power to do so (12. 377-383). Yet Zeus himself intervenes to prevent such a disruption of the natural order by allowing the sun-god to take revenge for his offended honor. Zeus' restraining function in this episode resembles that of Hera in the incident involving Sarpedon. Just as their knowledge of the *moira* of mortals restricts their hypothetical omnipotence, so also does the gods' knowledge of *physis* restrain their impulse to interfere with it.

The miraculous disruption of natural phenomena is, then, hardly a hallmark of the divine in Homer. Yet the interventions of the gods in the lives of men are founded on their knowledge of the *physis* of things as exemplified by the herb, *moly*. That *physis* unites two components, the one visible to all, the other hidden, the root of things. The gods' knowledge comprehends the whole and allows them to transform and manipulate the appearance of things. This ability, which one critic calls "*le pouvoir de la métamorphose*,"[52] is perhaps the

---

[50] Snell (1975), p. 34, draws a contrast to the story of Gideon (*Judges* 6:36-40) who tests God's support of Israel by asking God to make a fleece wet with dew while leaving the ground around it dry, and then reversing the process. God is expected to prove His godliness by disrupting the natural order of things. Snell adds: "dass . . . der Betende geradezu darauf besteht, dass das Natürliche sich umkehrt, wie Gideon es verlangt, und dass an dem Paradoxen sich der Glaube aufrichtet, gibt es nicht bei den Griechen."

[51] Cf. XVIII. 239-240, where Hera shortens the day; and XVI. 459, where Zeus sends down a rain of blood.

[52] A. Severyns, *Les dieux d'Homère* (Paris, 1966), p. 56. Severyns correctly observes the unity of the two aspects of this power: "Ils [les dieux] ont le pouvoir de la métamorphose. Ils en usent dans deux directions: tantôt, ils

most salient characteristic of the Homeric gods in their intercourse with men.

When they intervene in the lives of men, the gods generally
adopt some kind of disguise.[53] Their ability to disguise themselves is best exemplified by the figure of Proteus, who can
assume all manner of elemental and animal forms: a lion, a
snake, a leopard, a great boar, water, and a lofty tree (4. 456-
458). Zeus himself only communicates with men indirectly,
through signs, omens, or a messenger; but the other gods
usually appear in the guise of mortals. A master of such disguises, Athena shows up in the *Odyssey* as Mentes, Mentor,
Telemachus, a little girl, an anonymous Phaeacian at the contests, and a princely young shepherd. The divine presence,
while known to the poet and conveyed to his audience, often
masks itself as a friend or a stranger to the human actors. In
his critique of the immoral and lying gods of the poets—and
Homer in particular—Socrates singles out for special censure
those tales of divinities who, like wizards, manifest themselves
in various guises:

> Or do you think god is a wizard and able to appear at
> will in different forms at different times, sometimes
> changing his own *eidos* into may shapes, and at other
> times, deceiving us and making us think such things about
> him?
>
> (*Republic* 380d)

And yet, the "wizardry" of the Homeric gods of which Socrates complains must not simply be regarded in isolation or,
even worse, as an adjunct to the divine machinery which is
occasionally put into gear. Rather, it should be understood
as one facet of their more global power over external ap-

---

transforment comme bon leur semble un objet ou un être quelconque, tantôt,
ils se métamorphosent eux-mêmes en quelque chose d'autre." Cf. Snell (1975),
p. 34: "Die griechische Gottheit kann auch nicht aus dem Nichts etwas
erschaffen . . . sie kann nur erfinden oder verwandeln."

[53] For the mechanism involved, see J. S. Clay, "Demas and Audê: The
Nature of Divine Transformation in Homer," *Hermes* 102 (1974):129-36.

pearance. And that power, in turn, must be recognized as having its foundation in the gods' knowledge of *physis*.

It is striking that most divine interventions in Homer involve some sort of transformation of the look of a thing, whether it be of the gods themselves, or of men, or of inanimate objects. In the *Odyssey*, perhaps the most common act of divinity is the bestowal of *charis*, grace or beauty, on a mortal, rendering him momentarily more splendid or youthful and investing him in a special aura, which evokes wonder and admiration from all onlookers.[54] Yet the intervention of the god appears only to enhance what is already present; it effects no fundamental transformation. The verb generally used in these divinely caused beautifications is χεύειν or καταχεύειν, 'to pour' or 'to pour down over'; grace or comeliness is poured over a man like a liquid. On one occasion, when Athena beautifies Penelope for her first encounter with Odysseus, the goddess actually washes and anoints her with an ambrosial cosmetic:[55]

κάλλεϊ μέν οἱ πρῶτα προσώπατα καλὰ κάθηρεν
ἀμβροσίῳ, οἵῳ περ ἐϋστέφανος Κυθέρεια
χρίεται, εὖτ' ἂν ἴῃ Χαρίτων χορὸν ἱμερόεντα·
καί μιν μακροτέρην καὶ πάσσονα θῆκεν ἰδέσθαι,
λευκοτέρην δ' ἄρα μιν θῆκε πριστοῦ ἐλέφαντος.

First, for beauty, she washed her lovely features
with ambrosia, with which even the fair-crowned goddess
of Cythera
anoints herself, whenever she enters the lovely dance of
the Graces;
and she made her taller and more stately to look upon,
and whiter than freshly cut ivory.

(18. 192-196)

---

[54] Odysseus: 6. 229-235; 8. 18-20; 23. 156-158. Telemachus: 2. 12-13; 17. 63-64. Penelope: 18. 190-196. Laertes: 24. 367-369. Odysseus' companions: 10. 395-396. In almost all cases, the purely visual character of the change is emphasized by the use of a verb of perceiving or seeing. In the *Odyssey*, *charis* occurs five times and always in connection with divine beautifications. Cf. Treu (1968), pp. 55-59.

[55] Cf. Hera's preparations for the seduction of Zeus: XIV. 170-172.

The most explicit description of the mechanism involved occurs in a simile drawn from the art of metal-working, as Odysseus steps from his bath in the river and reappears among Nausicaa and her maids:

τὸν μὲν Ἀθηναίη θῆκεν, Διὸς ἐκγεγαυῖα,
μείζονά τ᾽ εἰσιδέειν καὶ πάσσονα, κὰδ δὲ κάρητος
οὔλας ἧκε κόμας, ὑακινθίνῳ ἄνθει ὁμοίας.
ὡς δ᾽ ὅτε τις χρυσὸν περιχεύεται ἀργύρῳ ἀνὴρ
ἴδρις, ὃν Ἥφαιστος δέδαεν καὶ Παλλὰς Ἀθήνη
τέχνην παντοίην, χαρίεντα δὲ ἔργα τελείει,
ὣς ἄρα τῷ κατέχευε χάριν κεφαλῇ τε καὶ ὤμοις.

Athena, offspring of Zeus, made him
bigger and more stately to look upon, and on his head
she arranged his curling locks, like to a hyacinth flower.
As when a skillful man pours gold over silver,
one whom Hephaestus and Pallas Athena have instructed
in every facet of his art, and he completes graceful
    works;
just so, she poured grace over his head and shoulders.
                                              (6. 229-235)[56]

In the gilding of silver, the silver is enhanced but not transformed. An already precious substance is rendered even more precious. The human, albeit divinely inspired, art of metallurgy can be said to be a master-art of civilization. To it corresponds the divine art of metamorphosis.

The apparently more radical transformation of Odysseus by Athena upon his arrival in Ithaca differs from the typical cosmetic transformations largely in degree and intention. The purpose of the latter has been to create admiration (*thauma*) for their objects.[57] But Odysseus' controversial metamorphosis[58]

---

[56] The simile is repeated at 23. 159-162.

[57] θηεῖτο δὲ κούρη (6. 237); πολλοὶ δ᾽ ἄρα θηήσαντο ἰδόντες (8. 17); τὸν δ᾽ ἄρα πάντες λαοὶ ἐπερχόμενον θηεῦντο (17. 64); ἵνα μιν θηήσαιατ᾽ Ἀχαιοί (18. 191); θαύμαζε δέ μιν φίλος υἱός (24. 370).

[58] For the traditional problems surrounding Odysseus' disguise, see Kirchhoff (1879), pp. 538ff. Kirchhoff's arguments are summarized by Page (1955), pp. 88-91.

is, on the contrary, intended to make him unrecognizable and contemptible in the eyes of all—until the moment and the means of revenge are at hand. As Athena tells Odysseus:

ἀλλ' ἄγε σ' ἄγνωστον τεύξω πάντεσσι βροτοῖσι·
κάρψω μὲν χρόα καλὸν ἐνὶ γναμπτοῖσι μέλεσσι,
ξανθὰς δ' ἐκ κεφαλῆς ὀλέσω τρίχας, ἀμφὶ δὲ λαῖφος
ἕσσω ὅ κε στυγέῃσιν ἰδὼν ἄνθρωπος ἔχοντα,
κνυζώσω δέ τοι ὄσσε πάρος περικαλλέ' ἐόντε,
ὡς ἂν ἀεικέλιος πᾶσι μνηστῆρσι φανήῃς
σῇ τ' ἀλόχῳ καὶ παιδί. . . .

But, come now, I shall make you unrecognizable to all men;
I will shrivel up the fair skin on your supple limbs,
and I will ruin the fair hair on your head; about you
I shall hang a rag, which will cause revulsion in the man who sees you;
then, I will dim your eyes which before were most beautiful,
so that you will seem a disgraceful sight to all the suitors,
and to your wife and child. . . .

(13. 397-403)

If one subtracts the props—the dirty rags, the worn deerskin, and the beggar's staff[59]—the physical changes involved in Odysseus' transformation consist of only three things: skin, hair, and eyes (cf. 13. 430-433). The same three items—what we may call surface phenomena—are generally singled out for description in the context of divine beautification, which suggests that the same mechanism is at work here. Rose appreciates the character of the change:

[Athena] does not alter anything below the surface, apparently, for when he [Odysseus] strips, the great muscles of shoulder and thigh are visible [18. 67-69]. . . . Even the skin is not so far altered that the old scar is not visible

---

[59] There is no reason to suppose that Odysseus' clothing and staff are not real objects rather than part of the transformation. This interpretation is supported by the verbs employed: ἀμφὶ . . . βάλεν, ἀμφὶ . . . ἕσσ', and δῶκε. See also 16. 173-174.

[19. 390ff.]. . . . The rest of the disguisement is indeed a simple change of clothes, his decent garments becoming rags. Hence it is that when those who know him well look closely at him, Penelope thinks at first that he has a certain resemblance to her husband, and later that it is indeed he, though this seems too good to be true, while old Eurykleia at once recognizes him by the scar on his thigh.[60]

Should, one might ask, the aging of Odysseus cause any more perplexity than the rejuvenation of Laertes (24. 367-369)? Upon his retransformation (16. 172-176), Odysseus himself explains to the wonder-struck Telemachus:

αὐτάρ τοι τόδε ἔργον Ἀθηναίης ἀγελείης,
ἥ τέ με τοῖον ἔθηκεν ὅπως ἐθέλει, δύναται γάρ,
ἄλλοτε μὲν πτωχῷ ἐναλίγκιον, ἄλλοτε δ' αὖτε
ἀνδρὶ νέῳ καὶ καλὰ περὶ χροΐ εἵματ' ἔχοντι.
ῥηΐδιον δὲ θεοῖσι, τοὶ οὐρανὸν εὐρὺν ἔχουσιν,
ἠμὲν κυδῆναι θνητὸν βροτὸν ἠδὲ κακῶσαι.

This is the work of Athena who grants plunder;
she turns me into whatever she wills, for she has the power—
sometimes like a beggar, at other times again,
like a young man wearing fine clothing.
Easy it is for the gods who inhabit broad heaven
either to glorify a mortal man or to debase him.
(16. 207-212)

As an expert at disguises, Odysseus of the many wiles can, to a certain extent, imitate the divine art of transformation. Thus, he affects a lack of oratorical skill when addressing the Trojans (III. 216-224); he calls himself Nobody in the cave of Polyphemus; he introduces himself as Eperitus to his father

---

[60] H. J. Rose, "Divine Disguisings," *Harvard Theological Review* 49 (1956): 64-65. Rose also clearly understands the connection between Odysseus' disguise and the disguises of the gods: "What I do think I see is a treatment of Odysseus' outward form much like the treatment the gods give their own bodies when they wish to appear to mankind. . . ."

(24. 304-308); and he manages to spy on the Trojans by disguising himself as a lowly creature very similar to the persona he adopts in Ithaca (4. 242-258). But duping the Trojans is easier than duping the Greeks, especially the members of his immediate household. Hence, on Ithaca, for Odysseus to be successful, the human art of deception must be supplemented by the divine art of transformation.

Circe performs the most complete physical transformation in the *Odyssey*, the one on Odysseus' companions. Yet even this occasion manifests the duality characteristic of such divine changes—between outward form and underlying substance. The men's appearance is totally transformed, but their minds and characters remain unaltered:

οἱ δὲ συῶν μὲν ἔχον κεφαλὰς φωνήν τε τρίχας τε
καὶ δέμας, αὐτὰρ νοῦς ἦν ἔμπεδος ὡς τὸ πάρος περ.

They had hands, voice, and bristles of pigs,
and also the build; but their minds were unimpaired,
   even as before.

(10. 239-40)

The typical rejuvenation and beautification accompanies their return to human form:

τῶν δ᾽ ἐκ μὲν μελέων τρίχες ἔρρεον, ἃς πρὶν ἔφυσε
φάρμακον οὐλόμενον, τό σφιν πόρε πότνια Κίρκη·
ἄνδρες δ᾽ ἂψ ἐγένοντο νεώτεροι ἢ πάρος ἦσαν
καὶ πολὺ καλλίονες καὶ μείζονες εἰσοράασθαι.

From their limbs the bristles melted away which
the baneful drug that Circe had given them had caused to
   grow before;
suddenly, they became men again, younger than before,
and far more beautiful and larger to behold.

(10. 393-396)

We can now better understand the need for Hermes' intervention in order to prepare Odysseus for his confrontation with Circe. Against Circe's divine art, the art of metamorphosis, the purely human arts, even the skills of an Odysseus, hold no sway. Hermes offers not only a talisman against Circe's superhuman power with the herb *moly*, but also an explanation of the connection between that mysterious art and nature.

The gods' ability to render men or things invisible through a dense air or mist, ἠέρ, constitutes a corollary to the divine art over external appearance. The same verb of pouring—ἀμφι- or περιχεύειν—used of divine transformations, describes the process of making objects invisible. Yet it must be emphasized that the gods cannot make things vanish "into thin air." Paris' sudden disappearance during the duel with Menelaus in the third book of the *Iliad* (381-382) requires two steps. Aphrodite first shrouds him in mist; only then does she physically translate him to his bedchamber. The mist merely conceals and acts as an optical illusion—as do many of the other aspects of the "wizardry" of the gods.

In the *Iliad*, the gods frequently exploit this device to rescue a warrior from imminent danger; but it also occurs in the *Odyssey*, when Odysseus approaches the city of the Phaeacians (7. 14-17), and again, after the slaying of the suitors, as he makes his way to Laertes' farm (23. 371-372). But surely the masterpiece of all such optical illusions occurs when, on Odysseus' return to Ithaca, Athena transforms the whole landscape of the island. The goddess intends to confuse Odysseus as to his whereabouts and to create an opportunity for the ensuing conversation:

> περὶ γὰρ θεὸς ἠέρα χεῦε
> Παλλὰς ᾿Αθηναίη, κούρη Διός, ὄφρα μιν αὐτὸν
> ἄγνωστον τεύξειεν ἕκαστά τε μυθήσαιτο. . . .
> τοὔνεκ᾿ ἄρ᾿ ἀλλοειδέα φαινέσκετο πάντα ἄνακτι,
> ἀτραπιτοί τε διηνεκέες λιμένες τε πάνορμοι
> πέτραι τ᾿ ἠλίβατοι καὶ δένδρεα τηλεθάοντα.

> The goddess poured a mist about it,
> Pallas Athena, the daughter of Zeus, so that she might
> make him unrecognizable and tell him all. . . .
> And that is why everything kept appearing differently to
>   their master,

the long paths and the harbors for mooring,
the steep cliffs and the flourishing trees.
(13. 189-191, 194-196)

Athena's purpose is not to conceal but to make all of Ithaca ἀλλοειδέα. This word, *alloeidea*, a Homeric *hapax*, sums up in a nutshell the peculiar power of the Homeric gods which we have been examining: the ability to render things *alloeidea*, to change the look of a thing or to make it invisible, and yet to leave its nature intact. Presented consistently by Homer, this ability represents the characteristic *techne* of the Homeric gods. The power to change form but not substance is the master-art of the gods. The human response, in turn, to manifestations of the divine, whether made visible directly through the revelation of a god or an omen or, indirectly, through the gods' effect on men or inanimate objects is, characteristically, wonder, θαῦμα or θάμβος.[61] Conversely, the experience of wonder or awe frequently raises the suspicion that a divinity is at work or somehow present. Thus, a work of art made by a god, or one akin to such a work in its perfection, produces wonder in the beholder. The products of divine craftsmanship in the *Iliad*, Hera's chariot (V. 725), the automatic tripods of Hephaestus (XVIII. 377), the armor which Hephaestus manufactures for Achilles (XVIII. 467), all are "wonders to behold." The superb golden armor of Rhesus, also a θαῦμα ἰδέσθαι, is more suited to the gods than to mortal men (X. 439ff.).[62] In the *Odyssey*, the accoutrements of the gods, the garments of Aphrodite (8. 366) and the purple cloaks the nymphs weave (13. 108), similarly provoke wonder in the spectator. Standing unseen at the threshold of the palace of

[61] For the meaning of θέομαι, θαῦμα, and θαυμάζω in Homer, see H. Mette, "Schauen und Staunen," *Glotta* 39 (1960):49-53. Also Bechert (1964), pp. 220-24; 362-65; 394-97.

[62] Bechert (1964), pp. 141-50, examines the formula θαῦμα ἰδέσθαι in Homer and concludes: "Die Dinge, von denen θαῦμα ἰδέσθαι in appositioneller Form ausgesagt wird, sind übermächtig, göttlich. Das Medium ἰδέσθαι drückt mit θαῦμα zusammen eine Beziehung des Menschen zum Göttlichen aus" (p. 148).

Alcinoos, resplendent with the golden dogs of Hephaestus and other divine gifts, Odysseus is awestruck (7. 133-134; cf. 90ff. and 132). Similarly, in Sparta, his son is amazed at the sight of Menelaus' splendid palace (4. 43f.). This amazement leads Telemachus to compare it to the dwelling of Zeus on Olympus (4. 74-75). Thus, even man-made objects can inspire wonder, for the source of the arts is divine. The gods, we are told, instruct mortals in weaving, metallurgy, and all other arts.[63]

The simile describing the beautification of Odysseus in terms of the gilding of silver (6. 232-235 = 23. 159-162) reveals the connection between the arts shared by the gods with mortals and the exclusively divine art of beautifying men. Like the artifacts that are the products of divine skill, human beings excite amazement in others when the gods suddenly transform or render them beautiful.[64] Often, especially when the transformed individual is a stranger, the wonder-filled onlooker mistakes him for a divinity. Odysseus, for example, marvels at the graceful Nausicaa and at first seems unsure whether she is a mortal woman or a goddess (6. 149ff.) She, in turn, likens the newly beautified Odysseus to "one of the gods who inhabit Olympus" (6. 243). Odysseus' sudden epiphany in the great hall of Alcinoos excites similar astonishment and uncertainty (7. 145; cf. 7. 199ff.) Finally, Telemachus at first refuses to believe that the transformed beggar can be anything but a god (16. 178ff.). In each of these examples, the sense of wonder calls forth a presentiment of the divine.

The epiphany or revelation of a divinity excites the same emotional reaction. A few instances from the *Odyssey* will suffice. Mentor's startling disappearance from Pylos arouses great astonishment among the Pylians and a sure, though belated, awareness of the divine presence (3. 372ff.). On Mentes' departure in Book 1, Telemachus' wonder results not so much from a vivid visual impression of the divine, as from his consideration of the whole import of his encounter and conver-

---

[63] Cf. V. 60-61 (building); XXIII. 306 (horsemanship); 7. 110 (weaving); 8. 481 (singing). For the works of Hephaestus as *thaumata*, see H. Schrade, "Der homerische Hephaestus," *Gymnasium* 57 (1950):49:50.

[64] Cf. note 57 above.

sation with the mysterious stranger. But, here again, wonder
precedes, and leads to, the recognition of a god hidden beneath
the mask (1. 323). Similarly, wonder and realization of divine
intervention coincide when Noemon discovers the real Mentor
still in Ithaca, while his double—who then must be a god—
accompanied Telemachus to Pylos (4. 653ff.)[65]
Thauma and *thambos* also accompany omens and other
signs of divine activity. An ominous flight of birds interrupts
the assembly on Ithaca; it is greeted with amazement (2. 155).[66]
On its return to Scheria, the ship that had carried Odysseus
to Ithaca is turned to stone by Poseidon, "so that all men may
marvel" (13. 157-158).[67] Alcinoos immediately recognizes the
divine origin of this sign (13. 172ff.) Finally, at the beginning
of Book 19, as Odysseus and Telemachus remove the arms
from the great hall of the palace, an invisible Athena holds a
golden lamp to light their way. Telemachus calls the eerie
glow emanating from Athena's lantern a *mega thauma* (19.
36).[68] Odysseus confirms the divine presence Telemachus only
suspects:

αὕτη τοι δίκη ἐστὶ θεῶν, οἳ Ὄλυμπον ἔχουσιν.

This is the way of the gods who inhabit Olympus
(19. 43)

Dike theôn, the natural or characteristic manner of the gods,
occurs only here in Homer,[69] and I take this scene to be at
least in part emblematic of the workings of the gods. It is their
nature invisibly to illuminate and gild our lives.

---

[65] This incident violates the rule enunciated by the b Scholium at V. 785
that the gods liken themselves to those not present. But here Athena intends
to reveal rather than conceal her interest in Telemachus.

[66] Cf. VIII. 75ff.

[67] Cf. II. 320.

[68] Cf. XV. 286ff. and XX. 344ff.

[69] Compare the expressions δίκη βροτῶν (not to have strength in their flesh
and bones after death, 11. 218); δίκη βασιλήων (to do or speak ἐξαίσιον,
4. 691); δμώων δίκη (to be able to make only small gifts out of fear of their
masters, 14. 59); μνηστήρων δίκη (to arrange feasts and give gifts, 18. 275);
δίκη γερόντων (to wash, eat, and sleep in comfort, 24. 255). These expressions do not occur in the *Iliad*, but consider similar phrases with θέμις.

From the human perspective, then, wonder unites the many
and diverse forms of divine activity in Homer. In general, the
relationship between men and gods expresses itself not in
terror, not in joy, and not in ecstasy, but in amazement. In
the first book of the *Metaphysics*, Aristotle asserts that the
first impulse toward philosophy arises from the sense of wonder and that the highest achievement of philosophy is the
science concerning matters divine. In a curious way, Aristotle's
argument has been anticipated by Homer who also recognized
that wonder is the origin of theology. Perhaps, however, we
ought not to find such anticipation all that surprising; for
Aristotle himself admits in this context: καὶ ὁ φιλόμυθος
φιλόσοφός πώς ἐστιν ("the lover of tales / myths is also in
some sense a philosopher" *Meta*. I. 2. 10).

BETWEEN GODS AND MEN I:
THE AGE OF THE HERO

Thus far, we have been concerned with the gods as they are
in themselves, and we have attempted in a preliminary fashion
to compare and contrast them with mortal men. We have yet
to consider, however cursorily, the *interaction* between gods
and men, its modes, scope, and limits. In the Homeric poems,
commerce between gods and men may assume various forms.
Divinities may be either visible or invisible; they may appear
in their true forms or, more commonly, in disguise; and if
disguised, they may choose to reveal or conceal themselves.
The gods may also indicate their will more indirectly, through
signs, dreams, and omens. All these possibilities can be doc-
umented in the Homeric poems, with further modifications
and refinements. It is not my intention to provide an extensive
catalogue of all such divine interventions.[70] Rather, I would
suggest that, taken as a whole, the character and scope of
divine involvement in the Homeric Epic represents a unique
world-historical moment situated somewhere between the
golden age and the age of men like us.

[70] See Kullman (1956) for the *Iliad*; for the *Odyssey*, see J. Mellitzer, "Das
Wirken der Götter in der Odyssee" (Ph.D. diss., University of Vienna, 1968).

The highest form of divine revelation is the epiphany of a god in his true form, which is, of course, anthropomorphic. The only description in Homer of the gods by a god occurs in the shield of Achilles, on which Hephaestus inscribes two cities, one at peace, the other at war. In the latter, two divinities, Ares and Athena, are depicted leading forth troops:

ἦρχε δ' ἄρα σφιν Ἄρης καὶ Παλλὰς Ἀθήνη,
ἄμφω χρυσείω, χρύσεια δὲ εἵματα ἕσθην,
καλὼ καὶ μεγάλω σὺν τεύχεσιν, ὥς τε θεώ περ
ἀμφὶς ἀριζήλω· λαοὶ δ' ὑπολίζονες ἦσαν.

Ares and Pallas Athena led them,
both of them golden, and wearing golden clothes,
beautiful and large, with their armor, even as gods,
both conspicuous; but the people were much smaller.
(XVIII. 516-519)

In comparison with mortals, the gods appear larger and more beautiful. In the presence of men, they are conspicuous and stand out. Their golden color signifies their imperishability.[71] In the palace of Alcinoos, after Odysseus materializes, apparently out of nowhere, Alcinoos suggests that the stranger may be some god from heaven. This, however, would be odd, since:

αἰεὶ γὰρ τὸ πάρος γε θεοὶ φαίνονται ἐναργεῖς
ἡμῖν, εὖτ' ἔρδωμεν ἀγακλειτὰς ἑκατόμβας,
δαίνυνταί τε παρ' ἄμμι καθήμενοι ἔνθα περ ἡμεῖς.
εἰ δ' ἄρα τις καὶ μοῦνος ἰὼν ξύμβληται ὁδίτης,
οὔ τι κατακρύπτουσιν, ἐπεί σφισιν ἐγγύθεν εἰμέν....

Always before, the gods appeared manifestly
to us, when we offered splendid hecatombs,
and they feasted in our company, sitting even as we.
And even if a traveler should meet them all alone,
they did not hide themselves, since we are near them....
(7. 201-205)

---

[71] Cf. Nagy (1979), p. 179.

Formerly, the Phaeacians always enjoyed the easy compan-
ionship of the gods, both in their public feasts and in their
private lives. The gods were accustomed to reveal themselves
undisguised, even as they appear on the shield of Hephaestus.
This special status is granted the Phaeacians because they are
"near the gods"—through their location, heredity, and manner of living. Another people who live at the ends of the world
share this privilege, the Aethiopians, whom the gods grace
with their presence at feasts. These peoples who inhabit the
remote edges of the Epic are the last residue of the golden
age.

On several occasions, Homer contrasts his heroes to men
of his own day—"such as men are now."[72] Men of the present
differ from the heroes not only in strength and martial accomplishment, but also in their relations with the gods. The
gods no longer join men in feasting nor do they beget children
on mortals. Their manifestations have become rarer in the
world of men "like us"; and intermediaries—seers, oracles,
and prophets—are required to interpret their increasingly obscure intentions toward mankind.

In the story of Prometheus, Hesiod offers an account of the
origins of the great schism separating gods and men (Theogony 535-616; Works and Days 42-105). Prometheus' attempt to deceive Zeus through the distribution of meat as men
and gods feasted together at Mekone, Zeus' hiding of livelihood (bios) from men, Prometheus' countertheft of fire in an
attempt to redress the balance in favor of mortals, and Zeus'
final revenge in the form of the first woman, Pandora—all
serve to define the condition of mankind. The successive acts
in the duel between Prometheus and Zeus, as well as the final
victory of the latter, stand, as it were, for the world's decline;
they explain the gulf that divides men from the gods, the

---

[72] οἷοι νῦν βϱοτοί εἰσ': V. 304; XII. 383, 449; XX. 287. A variant of
the formula occurs in the Odyssey (8. 222) when, characteristically, Odysseus
refuses to compare himself with the heroes of the past, but only with "such
men as are now, who eat grain upon the ground."

origins of scarcity, the consequent necessity of toil, procreation, and the inevitability of age and disease.[73]

In the *Works and Days*, Hesiod continues with a second account, a ἕτερος λόγος, as he calls it, which follows the great outlines of the Prometheus story (106-201). It likewise begins from the original closeness of gods and men (ὡς ὁμόθεν γεγάασι θεοὶ θνητοί τ᾽ ἄνθρωποι, 108) and ends with their permanent separation and the human condition as we know it. But in the Myth of the Ages, within the pattern of the steady decline from the golden age to our own, Hesiod inserts the Age of Heroes.[74] Men of the golden age died out; Zeus in anger destroyed the infantile race of silver. After the violent men of bronze annihilate themselves, Zeus makes a "juster and better" generation, "the divine race of hero-men, who are also called demigods." How these heroes are "made" is evident from the end of the *Theogony* (940ff.): they are the offspring of one divine and one mortal parent. A few of the products of such mixed unions are or become immortal— Dionysus, Heracles, and Ariadne—but the heroes are properly the mortal progeny of such unions.

The heroes are neither destroyed by the gods nor by each other, even though they engage in warlike deeds. They simply die out. The following age, the present Age of Iron, unlike the earlier generations, is not "made" but merely "established" (θῆκε, 173d) by Zeus. Hesiod suggests that the shift from the heroes to our time consists in the withdrawal of the gods from intercourse with mortals.[75] Men as they are now constitute the degenerate offspring of the heroes once the fresh infusion of divine blood has ceased.

[73] Cf. the interpretation of Vernant (1974), pp. 177-94; also Vernant (1979), pp. 37–132.

[74] Cf. the interpretation of S. Benardete, "Hesiod's *Works and Days*: A First Reading," ΑΓΩΝ 1 (1967):156-58.

[75] Benardete (1967), p. 158. Cf. the intriguing lines in Hesiod Frag. 204. 95ff. (Merkelbach-West), which suggest, despite their fragmentary condition, that Zeus' plan for separating gods and men coincided with the beginning of the Trojan war.

The scheme outlined by Hesiod is not contradicted by the contours of the Epic. The Homeric Epic takes for granted the separation of gods and men. Men, to be sure, are doomed to mortality. But the world of the Epic centers on the heroes who represent a stage in the relations between gods and men intermediate between the golden age and our own. The gods, who may still feast with the Aethiopians and the Phaeacians on the borders of the Epic, no longer appear openly to a group of men. Thus, at Pylos, Athena attends a feast in her honor unseen by the assembled Greeks (3. 435). The highest form of divine epiphany is granted only individually—usually at crucial moments—to the elect, the heroes, who are, after all, the children and grandchilden of the gods. In accordance with this "general rule of the Epic,"[76] Athena reveals herself to Achilles alone in the first book of the *Iliad* (I. 198). In Eumaeus' hut, she appears to Odysseus while remaining invisible to Telemachus:

στῆ δὲ κατ᾽ ἀντίθυρον κλισίης Ὀδυσῆϊ φανεῖσα·
οὐδ᾽ ἄρα Τηλέμαχος ἴδεν ἀντίον οὐδ᾽ ἐνόησεν,
οὐ γάρ πως πάντεσσι θεοὶ φαίνονται ἐναργεῖς. . . .

She stood in the vestibule of the hut, appearing to
    Odysseus;
nor did Telemachus see her before him or notice her;
for not to all do the gods appear manifest. . . .
                                        (16. 159-161)

Not only is divine epiphany limited to certain individuals; it is also not without its dangers. As Hera proclaims in the *Iliad*: "The gods are dangerous when they make themselves manifest" (XX. 131). We are reminded of Semele, who was literally incinerated by the splendor of Zeus' epiphany.

But there are indications in Homer that the heroic age is drawing to a close. The children of gods and men are now all mortal. Apotheosis seems to belong to the past or has become

---

[76] Kullman (1956), p. 105, calls it an "allgemeinen Regel;" F. Dirlmeier, *Die Vogelgestalt homerischer Götter* (Heidelberg, 1967), p. 30, elevates it to an "episches Gesetz."

problematic. Many of the heroes must trace back several generations to discover a divine ancestor. For those who are the direct offspring of the gods, the union of mortal and immortal is as productive of regret, pathos, and grief as of pride and glory. When, for example, Ares rages at the death of his son Ascalaphus and arms himself for revenge, Athena both reprimands him and consoles him: Zeus' anger, she says, will fall upon all the *gods* indiscriminately; moreover, it is impossible to save all the children of *men* (XV. 113-141). Zeus wavers for a moment whether to save his son Sarpedon, until Hera reminds him of the consequences (XVI. 431-449). Elsewhere, Zeus regrets his gift of immortal horses to the mortal Peleus. The conjunction can only lead to grief, since "of all things that breathe and walk upon the earth, there is nothing more miserable than man" (XVII. 446-447). Finally, the hero par excellence, Achilles himself, despairingly regrets the very ancestry on which his glory is founded, as he says to his mother:

αἴθ᾽ ὄφελες σὺ μέν αὖθι μετ᾽ ἀθανάτης ἁλίῃσι
ναίειν, Πηλεὺς δὲ θνητὴν ἀγαγέσθαι ἄκοιτιν.

Would that you had remained there, among the sea-goddesses,
living among them, and Peleus had married a mortal wife.

(XVIII. 86-87)

The conjunction of god and man in the *Iliad* finally leads to a tragic awareness of the unbridgeable gulf between them. But there are indications that this was not always the case as long as the apotheosis of men was a possibility, however rare. In the past, Zeus snatched Ganymede up to Olympus because of his beauty (XX. 234-235); he sired both Heracles and Dionysus on mortal women (XIV. 323-325); and the mortal Ino became the sea-goddess Leucothea and received divine honor (5. 333-335).

Calypso and Thetis, both goddesses attached to mortals, can be considered exemplars of the limitations imposed on the unions of gods and men in the Epic.[77] Calypso's affection for Odysseus harks back to an earlier era, when the gods cheerfully took their pleasure with mortals. In the Homeric Epic, however, genuine union is denied as much by the gods who thwart Calypso's offer to make Odysseus immortal as by Odysseus' own refusal. Thetis, on the other hand, is forced into a marriage of political convenience to a mortal.[78] For her, its fruit is only boundless grief. The goddess must suffer not only Peleus' old age but also the knowledge of Achilles' premature death.

The final book of the *Iliad* looks back to a time—perhaps the last time—when gods and men joined together in feasting at the marriage of Peleus and Thetis (XXIV. 62). At the beginning of the last book of the *Odyssey*, gods and men again come together, but this time they unite in mourning the death of Achilles (24. 64). These two passages stand as emblems to the heroic world and its passing.

BETWEEN GODS AND MEN II:
THE FUNERAL GAMES

The funeral games for Patroclus in Book XXIII of the *Iliad* constitute a paradigm of the interaction between gods and men in the heroic world. Such athletic competitions, *aethla*, are peaceful imitations of the far bloodier and more earnest contests the heroes engage in on the field of battle. Homer draws attention to the analogy by calling the labors of Heracles and those of Odysseus—especially the slaughter of the suitors—*aethla*.[79] In the games in honor of Patroclus, what

---

[77] H. Schrade, *Götter und Menschen Homers* (Stuttgart, 1952), p. 181, sees Thetis as the tragic counterpart to Eos and Calypso.

[78] In the *Iliad*, Thetis only alludes delicately to her unwilling acquiescence to her marriage to Peleus (XVIII. 432-434). But the story of her being married off to a mortal because she was destined to bear a child greater than his father is already mentioned in Pindar *Isthmian* 8. 27ff.). I believe this tradition was known and presupposed by Homer; it also explains Thetis' peculiar intimacy with Zeus in the *Iliad*.

[79] Labors of Heracles: VIII. 363; [XV. 639?]; XIX. 133; 11. 622, 624. Labors of Odysseus: 1. 18; 4. 241; 23. 248, 350. Archery contest: 21. 73, 106, 180, 268. Slaughter of the suitors: 22. 5, 27.

elsewhere ends in death and maiming leads only to a distribution of prizes. The playful microcosm of the games mirrors
the world where men suffer and die.

At the games, the onlookers behave like the gods when the
gods observe the deadly serious contests of men.[80] As Achilles
pursues Hector around the walls of Troy, the correspondence
is made explicit:

πρόσθε μὲν ἐσθλὸς ἔφευγε, δίωκε δέ μιν μέγ᾽ ἀμείνων
καρπαλίμως, ἐπεὶ οὐχ ἱερήιον οὐδὲ βοείην
ἀρνύσθην, ἅ τε ποσσὶν ἀέθλια γίγνεται ἀνδρῶν,
ἀλλὰ περὶ ψυχῆς θέον Ἕκτορος ἱπποδάμοιο.
ὡς δ᾽ ὅτ᾽ ἀεθλοφόροι περὶ τέρματα μώνυχες ἵπποι
ῥίμφα μάλα τρωχῶσι· τὸ δὲ μέγα κεῖται ἄεθλον,
ἢ τρίπος ἠὲ γυνή, ἀνδρὸς κατατεθνηῶτος·
ὡς τὼ τρὶς Πριάμοιο πόλιν πέρι δινηθήτην
καρπαλίμοισι πόδεσσι· θεοὶ δ᾽ ἐς πάντες ὁρῶντο.

Noble was the man who fled before, but the one who
    pursued swiftly was far better,
since not for an animal or an ox-hide
were they competing, such as are prizes in races for men;
but they raced for the life of Hector, tamer of horses.
As when prize-winning single-hooved horses run
with great speed around the laps; and a great prize waits,
either a tripod or a woman, in honor of a man who has
    died,
so did these two rush three times around the city of Priam
with their swift feet; and all the gods looked on.
                                        (XXII. 158-166)[81]

Like the gods, the mortal observers at the games for Patroclus
occasionally become passionately involved in the action, as

[80] More threatening than the analogy of sports fans is the image of Athena
and Apollo sitting in a tree and watching the battle in the likeness of vultures,
"rejoicing in men" (VII. 58-61). Consider also the *Hymn to Apollo* 189-193,
where the gods take their pleasure in listening to the sufferings of men, "as
many as they have at the hands of the immortal gods." On the gods as
observers of men, see Griffin (1980), pp. 179ff.

[81] Compare Pope's translation: "the gazing gods lean forward from the sky
. . . while eager on the chase they look. . . ."

when, for example, a quarrel breaks out between Idomeneus
and the lesser Ajax (XXIII. 448ff.). Twice, too, the onlookers
are moved to laughter: once, when, through the intervention
of Athena, Ajax ignominiously slips into a pile of dung and,
by default, gives the footrace victory to Odysseus (XXIII.
784).[82] They laugh again when the boaster Epeius, who had
won the boxing contest, is roundly defeated in the discus
throw (XXIII. 840).

Concerning the first and most important event, the chariot
race, Benardete and Vernant have made the essential points,
and I merely attempt to set forth a synthesis of their interpretations.[83] The contestants are presented in order of natural
excellence, in the order in which they should have won: Eumelus, who had the best horses, followed by Diomedes, Menelaus, Antilochus, and, finally, Meriones, whose horses were
the slowest. The lineup of the winners, however, is at odds
with this natural order: Diomedes comes first, followed by
Antilochus, Menelaus, and Meriones, with Eumelus coming
last. Two forces have upset the expected order: divine intervention and human *metis*.

With Diomedes on the verge of overtaking or tying Eumelus,
Apollo thrusts the whip out of Diomedes' hand. Athena takes
notice and not only restores Diomedes' whip, but breaks the
yoke of Eumelus' chariot. Divine intervention causes Eumelus,
who should have been first, to come last of all, while Diomedes,
who might have tied or come in second, emerges victorious.
Perhaps it is no accident that the gods, who can easily elevate
a hero or cast him down, exercise a greater negative than
positive influence.

The second disturbance in the anticipated order of winners

[82] Cf. Griffin (1980), pp. 183-84, who notes the similarity between the
carefree laughter of the gods and that of the Greeks at Ajax' discomfiture:
"This mirth proceeds from a delighted sense of one's own superiority; at ease
oneself, one enjoys the spectacle of others struggling or humiliated for one's
pleasure."

[83] Benardete (1968), pp. 10-11; Detienne-Vernant (1974), pp. 17-31. For
a more sociological interpretation, see J. Redfield, *Nature and Culture in the
Iliad* (Chicago, 1975), pp. 204-210.

arises from Antilochus' *dolos*, which throws the superior horses of Menelaus into disarray. Before the race, Nestor had advised his son how to maneuver his chariot in such a way as to compensate for his natural disadvantage. Nestor's speech culminates in a praise of *metis*:

ἀλλ' ἄγε δὴ σύ, φίλος, μῆτιν ἐμβάλλεο θυμῷ
παντοίην, ἵνα μή σε παρεκπροφύγῃσιν ἄεθλα.
μήτι τοι δρυτόμος μέγ' ἀμείνων ἠὲ βίηφι·
μήτι δ' αὖτε κυβερνήτης ἐνὶ οἴνοπι πόντῳ
νῆα θοὴν ἰθύνει ἐρεχθομένην ἀνέμοισι·
μήτι δ' ἡνίοχος περιγίγνεται ἡνιόχοιο.

But, come, my son, put in your heart *metis*
of every kind, so that the prizes may not escape you.
Through *metis* the woodcutter is far better than by force;
through *metis*, again, the helmsman on the wine-dark sea
steers his swift ship in the blustering winds;
through *metis* the charioteer surpasses charioteer.

(XXIII. 313-318)

Through the exercise of *metis*, then, Antilochus defeats Menelaus and attains second place instead of fourth. Menelaus, the man in the middle, remains in third place, as originally expected.

The parallel effect of *metis* and divine intervention is further emphasized by the response of the audience. Twice in the ensuing athletic events, the onlookers are wonder-struck, first when a *dolos* of Odysseus causes the wrestling match with the stronger Ajax to end in an unexpected draw (XXIII. 728).[84] Later, in the last contest, they again react with astonishment when the intervention of Apollo produces an upset victory in the archery contest between Teucer and Meriones (XXIII. 881). Wonder accompanies the disruption of the natural and predictable order, whether it be due to the intervention of the gods or the workings of human *metis*.

---

[84] A. Brelich, *Gli eroi greci* (Rome, 1958), p. 103, n. 94, points out that wrestling ". . . era il genere agonistico in cui la furberia aveva una riconosciuta importanza" and notes the special connection of Autolycus with the sport.

However, an epilogue to the chariot race follows which demands attention. To universal approbation, Achilles first suggests that Eumelus be awarded second prize, even though he came in last. Achilles tries to soften the blow caused by the interference of the gods. Antilochus, however, insists on keeping the rightful prize won by his *metis* and suggests that Achilles should console Eumelus with something else. Achilles assents with a smile. At that point, Menelaus, furious at Antilochus' trickery, addresses the assembled Greeks in the formal terms appropriate to a public meeting.[85] He proposes to let them act as judges and arbitrate Antilochus' offense to his *arete*. As an alternative, Menelaus suggests that Antilochus take an oath that the youth did not wittingly interfere with his chariot by a *dolos*. By quickly apologizing, Antilochus avoids perjuring himself. He offers his youthful inexperience as an excuse and the fact that his *metis* was "light," *lepte*. (Had it been *pukine*, 'dense,'[86] Antilochus' ruse would not have been discovered.) In a conciliatory gesture, Antilochus offers both his prize and additional gifts to Menelaus in order to remain in the latter's good graces. Graciously, Menelaus refuses them but warns Antilochus not to try to trick him again. As a sign of honor and respect, Achilles then gives the leftover prize to the aged Nestor, who no longer has the strength to compete. This little drama, the sequel to the contest itself, reveals a purely human sense of generosity, fairplay, and gentlemanliness which tends to soften the harsh realities of victory and defeat. Under certain circumstances, the heroes, when left to themselves, can act with nobility, humanity, and kindness.

BETWEEN GODS AND MEN III:
DIVINE FAVOR AND DIVINE HOSTILITY

. . . ὅστις ἀνθρώπου φύσιν
βλαστὼν ἔπειτα μὴ κατ' ἄνθρωπον φρονῇ.
(*Ajax* 760-761)

---

[85] Cf. Finley (1978), p. 109.

[86] Cf. Detienne-Vernant (1974), p. 22, who call attention to 9.445, where Odysseus describes himself under the ram as "thinking dense thoughts" πυκινὰ φρονέοντι.

Away from the sporting arena of the games, the gods intervene in bloody earnest, sometimes granting the heroes shining moments of glory, but also—and with equal ease—sometimes tripping them up cruelly, destroying them. The rest of
mankind, mere *anthropoi*, attract neither the signal favor nor
the terrible enmity of divinity.[87] The Epic hero, as we have
seen, inhabits a precarious and unstable zone between men
like us, *anthropoi*, and the immortals. Doomed on the one
hand to a mortality common to all men, the heroes—the de-
scendents of the gods—are all godlike as well. Their constant
epithets, by no means purely conventional, underline the
godlikeness of the heroes: δῖος, διίφιλος, διοτρεφής,
ἀντίθεος, ἰσόθεος, θεοείκελος, θεοειδές, θεῖος, θεοῖς
or ἀθανάτοισι ἐναλίγκιος or ἀτάλαντος.[88] To be godlike
demands divine assistance, yet the Epic *imitatio dei* is fraught
with danger; for there exists a line, invisible and shifting, but
nonetheless absolute, which separates gods from men. Only
the moment of transgression reveals its presence. By definition,
the Greek hero exists on the margins of this boundary.

The gods favor their mortal children for reasons of familial
solidarity and sometimes because of genuine affection. Frequently, too, close relations between gods and heroes are
founded on elective affinities—similarity of character or talents. The division of spheres of influence among the Olympians leads naturally enough to such special links: Zeus and
Athena support kings and warriors; Apollo favors singers and
seers; and golden Aphrodite looks after those of great physical
charm. Yet such divine favor is but half the story. Throughout
the Greek heroic tradition, precisely the god who has the
closest affinity to a given hero, and who may almost seem his
double, can finally become his deadliest antagonist.[89] The support of divinity—without which a hero can hardly be worthy
of the name—suddenly reverses itself into angry and destruc-

---

[87] On the Homeric distinction between *anthropoi* and *andres*, see Benardete
(1963), pp 1-5.
[88] Cf. Schrade (1952), p. 175.
[89] See Nagy (1979), pp. 142ff. for the antagonism of hero and god in Epic
and in cult.

tive hostility. The Epic alludes to numerous examples of this pattern: Orion and Artemis, Eurytus and Apollo, Thamyris and the Muses.[90] But perhaps the clearest statement of the abrupt and terrible reversal from divine protection to divine enmity comes in the threat of Aphrodite to a rebellious Helen:

μή μ' ἔρεθε, σχετλίη, μὴ χωσαμένη σε μεθείω,
τὼς δέ σ' ἀπεχθήρω ὡς νῦν ἔκπαγλα φίλησα,

Do not provoke me, wretched woman, lest in anger I
forsake you,
so that I come to hate you as much as I now terribly love
you.

(III. 414-415)

The alternations of Athena's support of Odysseus and her wrath against him likewise inform the *Odyssey* as a whole.

The hero who rises above the rest of mankind through divine providence constantly runs the risk of forgetting his mortal place in the scheme of things. The Greeks called such forgetfulness *hybris*.[91] The hero continually—no, necessarily—risks crossing the invisible line dividing men from the gods. Sooner or later, such transgression provokes divine wrath: *menis*. Pulling in contrary directions, divine favor and divine wrath oppose as well as mirror each other: the one elevating a mortal to heroic stature; the other, reducing him back to his mortality. A hero is a great man finally ensnared by his own greatness.

In early Greek thought, the friendship of the gods and their gifts are always double-edged and perilous. Paradigmatic in this respect is Hesiod's beautiful evil, the *kalon kakon*, whose name is Pandora. Endowed by the gods with all gifts, she

[90] Orion, the beautiful hunter, is killed by Artemis (5. 123-124); Eurytus, the bowman, by Apollo (8. 227-228); Thamyris is punished by the Muses (II. 594-600).

[91] Cf. Brelich (1958), p. 261, who says of *hybris* as follows: "in sostanza è sempre un disconoscimento dei limiti che la concezione religiosa greca pone all' essere umano—concezione ben più antica non solo della filosofia, ma di tutta la documentazione letteraria sulla grecità, dal momento che essa pervade anche la poesia omerica."

brings with her the gods' gifts to mankind: old age, disease, and scarcity. These "gifts" render final and eternal the break between mortal men who must labor for the grain they eat and the immortal gods who "live easy."[92] At the end of the *Iliad*, Achilles instructs Priam concerning the ambiguous character of the gifts of Zeus (XXIV. 527-533);[93] and to Hector's reproof, Paris responds:

οὔ τοι ἀπόβλητ' ἐστὶ θεῶν ἐρικυδέα δῶρα,
ὅσσα κεν αὐτοὶ δῶσιν, ἑκὼν δ' οὐκ ἄν τις ἕλοιτο·

Not to be rejected are the splendid gifts of the gods,
such as they may give; but no man would choose them
    willingly.

(III. 65-66)

Odysseus gives sage advice when he recommends that a man accept the gifts of the gods *in silence* (18. 142). Centuries later, Solon echoes the same ambivalence when he calls the gifts of the gods *aphukta*, "inescapable" (13. 64 West).

The constant exhortations throughout the Archaic and Classical periods to "think mortal thoughts" epitomized in the Delphic wisdom of "know thyself" conjoined with "nothing in excess" derive directly from the Homeric conception of the hero. This, in turn, is based on the hierarchical framework defining the disjunction between the nature of men and gods.

Odyssean Perspectives

The shield Hephaestus fashions for Achilles contains images of two cities: one at peace, the other at war. The gods appear conspicuously only in the city at war. It follows that the gods are far more conspicuous in the *Iliad* than in the *Odyssey*.

[92] Hesiod *Theogony* 570-617; *Works and Days* 53-105. Cf. the analysis of the Pandora story by Vernant (1979), pp. 98-132.
[93] Compare *Hymn to Demeter* 147 = 216: θεῶν μὲν δῶρα καὶ ἀχνύμενοί περ ἀνάγκῃ / τέτλαμεν ἄνθρωποι ("We human beings must endure the gifts of the gods by necessity, even if they bring us grief.").

Passionately involved in the struggles of the heroes—who are, after all, their children and grandchildren—the gods at Troy intervene incessantly on behalf of their favorites and grant them the opportunity to win glory. The primary contrast between mortality and immortality, and hence between gods and men, forms the focus of the action of the *Iliad*, in which violent death is constantly present. At the end of the poem, Achilles, who in his wrath has approached divinity, accepts the mortality that finally allies him more closely to old Priam and the corpse of Hector than to the gods.

On Achilles' shield, the city at peace contains two scenes: one the celebration of a marriage; the other a public assembly involving a judicial procedure. Marriage and justice, the continuity and legitimacy of the family, on the one hand, and the establishment of social order, on the other—both are essential to the city at peace, and both are central to the *Odyssey*. Marriage and justice are the affairs of *anthropoi*, men like us; and while the gods may legitimate both, neither demands constant divine intervention. The gods are not visible in the peaceful city; presumably, they have retired to the lofty isolation of Olympus and allow the world to run itself for the most part. The distance between gods and men appears to have grown in the *Odyssey*.

The *Odyssey* begins where the *Iliad* ends. The great heroes already belong to the past and have become the *genos hemitheon*,[94] the race of demigods, and the immaterial shades in Hades. Menelaus with his Helen lives on in embalmed splendor, no longer a *casus belli*, while the noble relic, Nestor, now recounts incidents from the Trojan War rather than his youthful exploits. Neither is capable of heroic enterprise. Even at Troy, Odysseus never quite fit in among the great heroes: his background left something to be desired; he referred with pride to his son rather than to his fathers (II. 260; IV. 354); and his greatest exploit was the Doloneia, a slightly distasteful nocturnal raid of questionable heroic stature.

---

[94] Cf. Nagy (1979), pp. 159-61, on the meaning of *hemitheoi* as "appropriate to a style of expression that looks beyond epic."

The issue of mortality has also been settled. It appears that Odysseus has heeded the warning of Apollo concerning the separation of gods and men. At the beginning of the *Odyssey*, he has rejected the blandishments of Calypso, offering him immortality. He will do so one more time. The generation of heroes through the sexual union of gods and men belongs to the past.[95] In her angry outburst at Hermes, Calypso knows this to be true (5. 118-144). She may offer Odysseus immortality, but for him it means death, as the many examples Calypso cites (5. 118-128) demonstrate.[96] The scope of the *Odyssey* is not as high as that of the *Iliad*—although it may be broader.[97] It concentrates neither on the sublime promise of immortality not on the oppressive weight of mortality, but rather on the nature and possibilities of human life within the set limits of birth and death. It follows that the challenge to the divine hierarchy no longer arises from the *bie* of an Achilles or Heracles, who would storm heaven itself. The last threat is different in kind and is posed by the last of the heroes, Odysseus, the hero of *metis*.

[95] This, in effect, is the theme of the *Hymn to Aphrodite*, which celebrates the last occasion of such a union, the birth Aeneas to Anchises and Aphrodite.

[96] Cf. Schrade (1952), p. 181. Cf. Scholia H.P.Q.T. at 5. 118 and P.Q.T. at 7. 257.

[97] The cosmic breadth of the *Odyssey* is indicated right from the outset by its reference to the *eschatoi andrôn*, the Aethiopians who live both where the sun rises and where it sets (1. 23-24), and to Atlas who "knows the depths of all the seas and holds up the tall columns which keep apart heaven and earth." (1. 52-54).

CHAPTER IV

THE ENCOUNTER OF ODYSSEUS AND ATHENA

Homer ist unter seinen Göttern so zu Hause und hat als
Dichter ein solches Behagen an ihnen, dass er jedenfalls
tief unreligiös gewesen sein muss. . . .

Homer feels so much at home among his gods and as
poet takes such pleasure in them that he must at any
rate have been profoundly irreligious. . . .
(Nietzsche, *Menschliches, Allzumenschliches* I. 125)

In the first chapter, our study of the beginning of the *Odyssey*
led to the conclusion that the wrath of Athena plays a crucial
role in the overall structure and shape of the poem. We must
now face the consequences of that view and answer the question it raises. Why was the goddess angered at Odysseus? As
a necessary preparation for that answer, we have examined
in the second chapter the multiple aspects of Odysseus from
various angles. Odysseus revealed himself to be the man whose
name means "divine wrath" and, above all, the hero of *metis*,
whose character embraces all the ambiguities of that term.
Moreover, some general observations concerning the Homeric
gods and their relations with men became necessary to set the
particular relationship of Odysseus and Athena in a larger
framework. The Homeric hero is distinguished both by the
signal favor he enjoys at the hands of the gods and by his
vulnerability to their wrath.

On the basis of these preliminaries, we can now return to
the question of Athena's wrath. The *Odyssey* itself speaks
only in the most general terms of its causes: "Not all the
Argives were conscientious or just," οὔ τι νοήμονες οὐδὲ
δίκαιοι / πάντες ἔσαν (3. 133-134). Some interesting, if allusive, external evidence does exist, however. A number of

epic poems, of which only fragments and late summaries have come down to us, filled in the gaps between the end of the *Iliad* and the beginning of the *Odyssey*. While these poems may be later in composition than the Homeric epics, the heroic traditions they incorporate must go back to the same sources as the *Iliad* and *Odyssey*. The *Odyssey* contains incidents that stem either from these poems themselves, or else from a common traditional source. It suffices to mention the story of Odysseus' spying expedition into Troy as recounted by Helen (4. 242-264); the tale of the wooden horse, sung by Demodocus (8. 499-520; cf. 4. 269-289); the funeral of Achilles (24. 36-92); and the death of Ajax (11. 543-560). In addition, the stories of the returns of the other Greek heroes—especially Agamemnon, Menelaus, and Nestor—serve as constant foils to the return of Odysseus.

Now, the wrath of Athena against the returning Greeks was a dominant motif in these traditions. It serves as the ending for one of the poems, the *Sack of Troy*, and it provides the opening for another, the *Returns* or *Nostoi*. On the basis of these poems from the Epic Cycle, we are able to compile a substantial dossier against Odysseus, one that would more than justify Athena's outrage. He murdered Palamedes, his rival in tricks and deception; he stole the Palladion, the sacred image of Athena that protected the city of Troy from capture: he brutally murdered Astyanax, Hector's young son. Odysseus is also implicated in a number of other questionable deeds.[1] Even the impoverished tradition which has come down to us provides us with an embarrassment of riches when it comes to Odysseus' *doloi*. This tradition in much greater fullness and detail must have been well known both to Homer and to his audience. Could Athena's anger have been aroused by any or all of these acts? Homer's silence is more than surprising; for the *Odyssey* does not mention or allude to even one of these crimes. We must remain open to the possibility that Homer was not interested in the traditional causes of the goddess' wrath—or at least not in their particulars. But we can fairly

---

[1] Cf. J. O. Schmidt (1885), pp. 7-27; and Bethe (1927), pp. 35ff.

assume that the audience of the *Odyssey* had some acquaintance with them, that they were in some sense prepared by these traditional stories to accept the notion of Athena's wrath. The tradition, then, within which Homer composed may well have laid the groundwork. Finally, however, it must be confessed that the external evidence of a fragmentary tradition cannot offer reliable answers to problems posed within the *Odyssey*. A different approach to the question of Athena's anger is necessary, one founded on the internal evidence of the poem. As we have seen, apparent within the confines of the *Odyssey* is the concealment, but not complete suppression, of the dark or Autolycan side of Odysseus. Likewise, I would suggest that the poem does not completely hide the cause of Athena's anger. Its discovery must begin with an analysis of the extraordinary dialogue between the hero and the goddess in Book 13, the first time in the poem they meet face to face.

The meeting of Athena and Odysseus on Ithaca, which one critic calls "the most spiritual of all Odysseus' adventures,"[2] forms the most extensive conversation between a god and a mortal in the Homeric Epic. The charm and humor of this encounter have often been praised, and the sophisticated wit of the repartee has been compared to the sparkling exchanges of Shakespeare.[3] At the same time, and notwithstanding its shimmering exterior, the encounter raises issues central to the *Odyssey*. In fact, the conversation fairly fits the definition of the Platonic dialogue given by Diogenes Laertius:

A dialogue is a discourse consisting of question and answer on some philosophical or political subject, with due

---

[2] "Das geistigste aller seiner Abenteuer"; W. Schadewaldt, *Heimkehr des Odysseus* (1946), p. 192, cited by H. Kleinknecht, "Platonisches im Homer," *Gymnasium* 65 (1958):75.

[3] For some appreciations, see W. M. Hart, "High Comedy in the Odyssey," *Calif. Pub. in Classical Philology* 12 (1943):276-78; Stanford (1963), pp. 30ff.; and Otto (1954), pp. 192-95. K. Reinhardt, "Homer und die Telemachie" in *Tradition und Geist* (Göttingen, 1960), p. 45, remarks: "Mir ist keine anmutvollere Verwandlung eines dichterischen Plans in ein gedichtetes Gespräch bekannt."

regard to the characters of the persons introduced and the choice of diction.[4]

The Platonic analogy is not otiose, for in our passage a matter of the highest importance—the nature of the relations between gods and men—is discussed with unsurpassed wit and irony. It is no exaggeration to say that a full interpretation of this scene demands the same critical acumen and awareness that a page of Plato requires of us.

Despite the admiration accorded to the exchange between Odysseus and his patron divinity, the uneven flow of the conversation has frequently aroused critical censure. For instance, Eduard Schwartz speaks of "the clumsy execution of the dialogue; the speeches which Odysseus and the goddess exchange often seem to refer back to words which one seeks in vain in what has preceded."[5] Both ancients and moderns have tried to repair what appear to be inconsequences and illogicalities by their usual method, the scissors, expunging a greater or lesser number of lines. Kleinknecht, who deals only with lines 187-354, notes that of these 168 verses, only 29 stand untainted by the suspicion of interpolation or contradiction by the last century of Homeric scholarship.[6] Similar figures could be adduced for the rest of the passage—all of which may be considered a final monument to the bankruptcy of the nineteenth-century tradition of Homeric philology. What such figures do, in fact, prove is that we have before us an extremely difficult text, and neither major nor minor surgery can remedy all the difficulties it presents.

---

[4] R. D. Hicks, trans., *Diogenes Laertius: Lives of the Philosophers:* Vol. 3: *Plato* (Cambridge, Mass., 1959), III. 48, p. 319.

[5] E. Schwartz, *Die Odyssee* (Munich, 1924), p. 56. For an interpretation along generally Unitarian lines, see Erbse, (1972), pp. 148-65. The dissertation of W. Krehmer, "Zur Begegnung zwischen Odysseus und Athene" (University of Erlangen-Nürnberg, 1973), contains the most recent and exhaustive doxography on the passage. Although it contains some useful observations, Krehmer's work lacks any particular focus, being largely a Unitarian defense of the scene against the strictures of the Analysts.

[6] Kleinknecht (1958), p. 59, n. 4.

To make sense of the passage as it stands means to trace the movement of this dialogue—or rather, duel of wits—between the cleverest of the gods and the wiliest of mortals. Such an attempt requires careful attention to the ploys, diversionary maneuvers, and gambits on both sides, to what is taken up and what is ignored, to what is said and what is left unspoken.[7] The conversation between the goddess and Odysseus occurs at the pivotal moment of the *Odyssey*, at the time the hero has finally reached home. The scene forms a bridge between the wandering adventures of the past and the reestablishment of Odysseus on Ithaca.[8] At the opening of Book 13, the end of the old and the beginning of the new is signaled by what sounds like a second proem. We are told that the ship of the Phaeacians:

ἄνδρα φέρουσα θεοῖς ἐναλίγκια μήδε᾽ ἔχοντα,
ὃς πρὶν μὲν μάλα πολλὰ πάθ᾽ ἄλγεα ὃν κατὰ θυμὸν
ἀνδρῶν τε πτολέμους ἀλεγεινά τε κύματα πείρων . . .

carried a man, who had wits like those of the gods,
who previously had suffered many woes in his heart,
experiencing the wars of men and the grievous waves . . .
(13. 89-91)

While the Phaeacians attempt to propitiate Poseidon, who begrudges them their role as "painless escorters of all men," Odysseus awakens on a deserted beach on Ithaca. Yet he does

---

[7] See S. Besslich, *Schweigen—Verschweigen—Übergehen* (Heidelberg, 1966), pp. 120-23. Besslich recognizes "die Darstellung des Unausgesprochenen" as a characteristic of dialogue in the *Odyssey*: "Wenn etwa eine Frage nicht beantwortet wird, muss man zuerst versuchen festzustellen, ob diese Nichtbeantwortung als solche nicht einen spezifischen Sinn hat. . . . Gerade die Inkongruenz von Erwartung und Erfüllung, von Anrede und Erwiderung kann wichtig sein für die Aussage einer Dichtung, besonders wenn in ihr—wie in der Odyssee—das Geheimnisvolle und Indirekte, die Andeutung und das Unausgesprochene so sehr sind und in so manningfaltigen Brechungen poetisch wirksam werden" (p. 10).

[8] W. Schadewaldt, "Der Prolog der Odyssee," *HSCP* 63 (1958):29, describes the structure of the *Odyssey* as consisting of "die äussere Heimkehr" followed by an "innere Heimkehr" which begins precisely here, with Odysseus' landing on Ithaca.

not recognize his surroundings, for Athena has obscured the landmarks of the island with a mist, ἀήρ. In his discussion of the first half of this scene (13. 187-354), Kleinknecht emphasized the thematic importance of knowledge and of Odysseus' progress from sleep to waking ignorance of his whereabouts— due to the goddess' mist—to the certain revelation of reality when he finally recognizes his native Ithaca.[9] The introductory lines (187-197), containing three forms of the word for knowing (ἔγνω, ἄγνωστον, γνοίη) and two of the word for seeing (ἀλλοειδέα, ἔσιδε), already indicate the centrality of the problem of knowledge. At the beginning, seeing is not the equivalent of knowing, for when Odysseus first sees his native land, he groans and makes a gesture of despair (13. 197-198), "nor did he recognize it" (13. 188). But later, "he saw his land; then truly did much-enduring Odysseus rejoice" (13. 352-353). Thus, the focus of this entire sequence centers on the issues of ignorance and knowledge, appearance and reality. However, by tracing these themes only up to Odysseus' recognition of Ithaca, Kleinknecht overlooks the manner in which these same issues extend well beyond the moment of recognition and inform the whole exchange between Athena and Odysseus. Kleinknecht also fails to understand the role of *metis*, and its companion, *dolos*, throughout the scene. *Metis* is precisely that quality of mind that seeks to grasp a fleeting reality. As Detienne and Vernant put it, *metis* "applies itself to realities which are fleeting, changing, disconcerting, and ambiguous, which do not permit either precise measurement, nor exact calculation, nor rigorous logic."[10] *Dolos*, in turn, is the means to a domination of a reality that will not stand still.

The landscape that opens before Odysseus' eyes is not only different from Ithaca; its features keep changing: τοὔνεκ᾽ ἄρ᾽ ἀλλοειδέα φαινέσκετο πάντα ἄνακτι (13. 194).[11] *Alloei-*

---

[9] Kleinknecht (1958), pp. 59-75.

[10] Detienne-Vernant (1974), p. 10.

[11] Wilamowitz, *Die Heimkehr des Odysseus* (Berlin, 1927), p. 7, n. 2, preferred to read φαίνετο, calling φαινέσκετο "schlechtes Iterativum." But Kleinknecht (1958), p. 62, correctly translates: "alles erschien . . . immer

dea, which occurs only here in Homer and whose significance we have already discussed in connection with the gods' mastery over appearances, is, as we shall see, a key word to the entire passage. The mist which the goddess pours over the island is a trick, a *dolos* with a purpose; Athena thereby creates an opportunity to make Odysseus unrecognizable, so that no one may know him before he has punished the suitors (13. 191-193), and to allow her to inform him about conditions at home. The introduction of Odysseus' disguise has seemed premature to many,[12] but its foreshadowing at the very outset of the scene points to its submerged relevance throughout the conversation. It is the ultimate purpose for Athena's coming.[13] Eumaeus can and does tell Odysseus about wife and child and the behavior of the suitors in the following book, but only Athena can effect Odysseus' transformation.

The ever-changing landscape which greets Odysseus offers a palpable challenge to the hero's *metis*. But his first reaction as he looks about him is a combination of disappointment, anger, and a despair whose very vehemence both touches and amuses us, since we know the man to be home at last. He repeats the lines that introduced the Cyclops adventure (9.

---

wieder anders aussehend." Erbse (1972), p. 151, misses the point by transferring the sense of φαινέσκετο from the shifting appearance of the landscape to Odysseus' repeated glancing at it.

[12] See the full discussion in Krehmer (1973), pp. 15-31. In adopting an ancient emendation of Aristophanes (reported in Scholium H at 13. 190), αὐτῷ, and taking μιν as a reference to Ithaca ("so that she might make it [Ithaca] unrecognizable to him"), Wilamowitz (1927), p. 6, n. 3, disposes of all mention of Odysseus' disguise here. But Heubeck (1954), p. 61, n. 93, defends the foreshadowing of the disguise motif: "Es ist ja gerade ein besonderes Kennzeichen des Odyssee-Dichters, um jeden Preis vorzubereiten und vorauszudeuten—selbst an Stellen, die für solche 'Vorbereitungen' nach unserem Empfinden . . . gar nicht geeignet sind. . . ." But more than mere preparation, the transformation of Odysseus and the transformation of Ithaca are closely related thematically and point to the crucial problem of appearance and reality throughout the scene.

[13] For a parallel, compare the juxtaposition of Athena's immediate purpose for going to Ithaca in Book 1—to send Telemachus after news of his father (1. 88-94)—with her ultimate purpose: "so that he may gain renown among men" (1. 95).

175-176) and the meeting with Nausicaa (6. 119-121), but this time in the form of a weary question:

ὤ μοι ἐγώ, τέων αὖτε βροτῶν ἐς γαῖαν ἱκάνω;
ἦ ῥ' οἵ γ' ὑβρισταί τε καὶ ἄγριοι οὐδὲ δίκαιοι,
ἦε φιλόξεινοι καί σφιν νόος ἐστὶ θεουδής;

Alas, to what land, to what kind of people have I come?
Are they violent and savage and unjust,
or are they hospitable and respecters of the gods?
(13. 200-202)

In the subsequent choppy monologue (13. 203-216), distracted questions, impossible wishes, expressions of helplessness, accusations, and curses all mirror the hero's agitated state of mind. For a moment, at least, the man of many wiles seems to lack all resources. Odysseus' overpowering sense of disappointment at what appear to be broken promises and deceptions of the Phaeacians has a parallel in only one other of his adventures. In Book 10, Odysseus describes how, within sight of Ithaca, his companions untied the bag of the winds while their master slept. Upon awakening, he recognized the damage they had done as the winds carried their ship away from home; for a moment, Odysseus tells us, he considered drowning himself (10. 49-51). In both instances, the Return had at long last seemed to be at hand, only to be suddenly snatched away.

Odysseus' present situation on the strand of Ithaca is both complicated and, in a sense, retrieved by the heap of gifts lying at his feet—gifts that he had charmed out of the Phaeacians by his enchanting storytelling. Odysseus first asks where he should hide the gifts (13. 203) and soon returns to the question (13. 207), since he realizes that their presence makes him especially vulnerable, "lest somehow they make me a prey to others" (13. 208). After cursing the Phaeacians roundly—but mistakenly—for deceiving him and abusing the laws of hospitality, Odysseus begins to regain his composure by turning his attention to what is at hand: the gifts, which he counts:

τῶν μὲν ἄρ' οὔ τι πόθει· ὁ δ' ὀδύρετο πατρίδα
γαῖαν
ἑρπύζων παρὰ θῖνα πολυφλοίσβοιο θαλάσσης,
πόλλ' ὀλοφυρόμενος.

And not one of them was missing. But he bemoaned his
    native land,
walking along the shore of the billowing sea,
shedding many a tear.

(13. 219-221)

Cast away on an unknown strand, Odysseus is the very picture
of despair. Yet, finally, the point of his initial anguish and
helplessness lies rather in how rapidly he manages to recapture
his self-possession, that same self-possession for which Athena
will soon praise him (ἐχέφρων, 13. 332).

Athena now approaches in the guise of a princely young
shepherd. The disguise is a double *dolos*. Not only does she
dissemble her own appearance, but she also resembles another
divinity, Hermes, who appeared to Odysseus on his way to
Circe's and gave him *moly* (10. 277-279), and who escorted
Priam to the tent of Achilles in the last book of the *Iliad* in
the guise of a young man of royal stock (XXIV. 347-348).[14]
The princely mien of the shepherd encourages Odysseus to
appeal to his sense of decency: "Save these things," he says,
pointing to the gifts, "and save me" (13. 230). Odysseus' first
speech to the would-be shepherd is unusually short and direct.
He comes as a suppliant and impatiently asks where he is.
But Odysseus' impatience at this moment is understandable.
The Phaeacians have turned out to be honest with respect to
the gifts. None was found missing. Perhaps they have kept
their promises after all. Athena responds with a description
of Ithaca (13. 238-247), which some scholars have found
simply false, while others have labeled it "idealized."[15] To the
extent that the goddess' description is not immediately rec-

[14] Cf. Scholium A at XXIV. 347, which cites the description of Athena at
13. 223 as a parallel to the description of Hermes as he appears to Priam.
[15] For a discussion, see Krehmer (1973), pp. 104-117.

ognizable as Ithaca and in fact contains some misleading elements, her words must be regarded as another *dolos*. This verbal *dolos* has an exact counterpart in the alternately revealing and concealing mist the goddess had shed over the island earlier.[16] But Athena's speech goes beyond mere playfulness and the pleasure of teasing. The whole epiphany of the shepherd and his speech is a trap, a trap with a purpose. The fame of Ithaca, the "shepherd" disingenuously remarks, has reached even as far as Troy. For only one reason: city-sacking Odysseus.[17] By joining the names of Ithaca and Troy at the very end of her description, the goddess creates an almost irresistible temptation—greater than that of the Sirens or the songs of Demodocus, which nearly cause Odysseus to reveal his identity prematurely. Athena's trap is calculated to make Odysseus give himself away.[18] But Odysseus, who only minutes before seemed totally despondent and without resources, not only resists the goddess' gambit, but outwits her. The rapid and complete recovery of his self-control, the superb mastery of the situation Odysseus demonstrates in his reply, thwarts Athena's expectation of an easy victory over the hero. Indeed, the first round goes to Odysseus.

Odysseus, to be sure, rejoices at the news that he is home, but on the point of answering, he restrains himself:

οὐδ᾽ ὅ γ᾽ ἀληθέα εἶπε, πάλιν δ᾽ ὅ γε λάζετο μῦθον,
αἰεὶ ἐνὶ στήθεσσι νόον πολυκερδέα νωμῶν.

[16] Cf. Krehmer (1973), p. 117: "Athene, die den Nebel über das Land ausgegossen hat, verhüllt es zusätzlich durch eine entstellende Beschreibung; zu der physischen Verhüllung durch den Nebel kommt die geistige durch das Wort."

[17] Cf. Eustathius 1740. 14.

[18] Krehmer (1973) has understood the point of Athena's teasing: "er soll sich spontan offenbaren, soll sich verraten" (p. 123). "Athene wolle ihren Schützling . . . auf die Probe stellen, ob er sich zu erkennen gäbe. Die Falle war geschickt gelegt, aber Odysseus ist nicht hineingegangen. In seiner raffiniert erfundenen Lügengeschichte verhüllt Odysseus seine Identität—so trifft Maske auf Maske, Inkognito auf Inkognito, und Athene wird mit ihren eigenen Waffen geschlagen" (p. 178).

Not for him to speak the truth, but he held back the
    word,
always guarding in his breast a mind full of trickery.[19]
                                            (13. 254-255)

This same self-restraint and suppression of immediate impulse
was, as we have seen, a crucial element in Odysseus' escape
from the cave of Polyphemus.

Odysseus' response to the shepherd, the first of his "Cretan
tales," can be compared to his other rhetorical masterpiece,
the speech to Nausicaa upon awakening in Scheria. There, the
situation demanded infinite tact and delicacy: to persuade the
shaken young princess that this briny, naked stranger before
her is decent, and can be trusted.[20] With Nausicaa, Odysseus'
main problem was his nakedness; here, it is the embarrassment
of the gifts lying around him on the shore. Much of what
Odysseus proceeds to tell the shepherd is calculated to explain
the presence of the gifts and to protect them. In fact, he manages to turn the encumbrance into a vehicle for improving his
vulnerable situation.[21]

Odysseus takes off from the shepherd's last words. Indeed,
he has heard of Ithaca even in Crete, from where he comes
with his possessions. He indicates that he is a man of family
and substance, now an exile for having murdered the son of
Idomeneus, Orsilochus. The latter had tried to strip him of
his spoils from Troy, because he refused to serve under Idomeneus, but instead led his own contingent. The murder of
Orsilochus was carried out under cover of darkness, by means

---

[19] These two lines intervene between the ἔπεα πτερόεντα προσηύδα and
the actual speech which normally follows immediately. This interruption of
normal formulaic sequence vividly illustrates Odysseus' suppression of his
immediate impulse. Cf. Krehmer (1973), p. 129.

[20] Cf. Stanford's (1965) commentary to the passage.

[21] The best commentary on the subtleties of Odysseus' speech remains
Eustathius' (1740. 54-1741. 49). C. R. Trahman, "Odysseus' Lies," *Phoenix*
6 (1952):35-36, gives little more than a summary of the same material. See
also R. Woolsey, "Repeated Narratives in the Odyssey," *CP* 36 (1941):173-
75. Woolsey examines each of the Cretan tales with a view to its immediate
purpose.

of an ambush. The murderer, now forced to flee, bribed some Phoenician sailors and asked them to take him to Pylos, but a storm drove them off course. Disembarking on Ithaca, the Cretan stranger fell asleep. The Phoenicians—contrary to their usual reputation as pirates—did not cheat him, but set his treasures down beside him as he slept, and went off.

Odysseus' tale, complicated enough to appear to be the truth, explains how he got to Ithaca, why he did not know where he was, and accounts for the treasures surrounding him—but it accomplishes much more. The Cretan indicates that he is a man to be reckoned with. He has been to Troy and refused to be subservient even to the King of Crete. He is quite capable of protecting himself and his possessions, as the story of Orsilochus warns, and would not hesitate to use guileful means, if the shepherd should have designs on them. On the other hand, as the allusion to the bribery of the Phoenicians suggests, the stranger might be willing to entertain the possibility of a hefty payment for help, if the shepherd so inclines. He implies that even the greedy Phoenicians were satisfied with their reward. Finally—and characteristically—Odysseus slips in the fact that he has not eaten the night before, angling for a meal, as he has so often before.

The speech is a tour de force whose every detail is geared to its effect on the would-be young shepherd. Odysseus presents himself as a man of *doloi* who will protect his possessions at all costs, one who might well be a grandson of Autolycus or a favorite of Hermes. The Cretan connection, as we have already seen, has many of the same implications.[22]

At this point, Athena smiles with amusement, strokes Odysseus, and reveals herself. Her dropping of disguise reminds us of the tale of Menelaus who, by means of a *dolos*, managed to force Proteus, the master of metamorphosis, to return to

[22] Whether the expression "All Cretans are liars," first attested in a fragment of Epimenides (6th cent. B.C.), is pre- or post-Odyssean cannot be determined with certainty. But Krehmer (1973), pp. 151-53, argues that the bad reputation of the Cretans was already proverbial in the period the *Odyssey* was composed. If so, Odysseus' adoption of Cretan origins would be a playful wink at the audience.

his true shape (4. 363-460).[23] In showing herself to Odysseus, Athena admits her admiration and appreciation for his *dolos*. Hers, on the other hand, had failed or, at the very least, had proved itself unnecessary. But the game is by no means over.[24] In fact, the major issues raised so far—knowledge and ignorance, reality and the fleeting character of appearances, trickery both verbal and physical (disguise)—continue to dominate the exchange between god and mortal to an even greater degree. Now recognizably herself, Athena first pretends to scold Odysseus. But we quickly realize that she is paying ironic compliments to the wily hero who will not even desist from trickery on his own ground:

κερδαλέος κ᾽ εἴη καὶ ἐπίκλοπος ὅς σε παρέλθοι
ἐν πάντεσσι δόλοισι, καὶ εἰ θεὸς ἀντιάσειε.
σχέτλιε, ποικιλομῆτα, δόλων ἆτ᾽, οὐκ ἄρ᾽ ἔμελλες,
οὐδ᾽ ἐν σῇ περ ἐὼν γαίῃ, λήξειν ἀπατάων
μύθων τε κλοπίων, οἵ τοι πεδόθεν φίλοι εἰσίν.[25]

A man would have to be cunning and thievish to surpass you
in all your tricks—even if he were a god.
Wretch, with the mind of a chameleon, master of tricks,
not even in your own land will you leave off your deceptive
and thievish tales—which you love from the bottom of your heart.

(13. 291-295)

Then the goddess quickly declares a mutual truce to trickery, since the two of them are both well-versed in the arts of deception:

[23] Eustathius 1742. 17 draws the parallel between Athena and Proteus.

[24] In reviewing the overall structure of the scene, Krehmer (1973), p. 286, incorrectly sees a significant break at 13. 286, "wo Athene das Spiel der Listen und Verstellungen beendet." Mutual dissimulation on the part of both Athena and Odysseus is, however, by no means at an end.

[25] For ποικίλος in relation to the vocabulary of *metis*, see Detienne-Vernant (1974), pp. 25-27. Eustathius 1742. 26, glosses πεδόθεν as ἐκ γενετῆς, 'from his origins' or 'ancestry.'

ἀλλ' ἄγε, μηκέτι ταῦτα λεγώμεθα, εἰδότες ἄμφω
κέρδε', ἐπεὶ σὺ μέν ἐσσι βροτῶν ὄχ' ἄριστος
ἁπάντων
βουλῇ καὶ μύθοισιν, ἐγὼ δ' ἐν πᾶσι θεοῖσι
μήτι τε κλέομαι καὶ κέρδεσιν.

But, come, let us talk no more of these things, for we
    both know
wiles, since you are by far the best of all mortals
in counsel and words, and I among all the gods
am renowned for my *metis* and wiles.
(13. 296-299)

Athena asserts that she is foremost among the gods for *metis*,
while Odysseus surpasses all mortals. Within their proper sphere,
then, each is supreme. But Athena emphasizes that Odysseus
cannot be her equal in one important respect:[26]

οὐδὲ σύ γ' ἔγνως
Παλλάδ' 'Αθηναίην, κούρην Διός, ἥ τέ τοι αἰεὶ
ἐν πάντεσσι πόνοισι παρίσταμαι ἠδὲ φυλάσσω,
καὶ δέ σε Φαιήκεσσι φίλον πάντεσσιν ἔθηκα.

Indeed, you did not recognize
Pallas Athena, daughter of Zeus, who always
stands by you in all your toils and guards you,
and who made you welcome among all the Phaeacians.
(13. 299-302)

Odysseus has, in fact, just proven himself incapable of seeing
through (the Greek uses a verb for knowing, ἔγνως) the shepherd's disguise. Admitting Odysseus' excellence at concocting
stories and *doloi*, the goddess lays claim to an essential superiority which Odysseus, as a mere mortal, can never attain.
    Suddenly, the goddess breaks off and explains her reasons
for coming. She wants to weave a *metis* (μῆτιν ὑφήνω) with
Odysseus. She will help him hide the gifts which he owes to
her benevolence, and she will explain what the hero must still
endure at home, stressing the need for further secrecy and

---

[26] Eustathius 1742. 33 cites 13. 299ff. as a σημεῖον, an 'example' or 'proof'
of Athena's excellence at wiles.

patience. Athena mentions the Phaeacians twice in her speech and claims credit both for Odysseus' cordial reception there and his gifts. One might want to refer back to the episode to check the validity of Athena's claims. The gifts, at least, are surely due more to Odysseus' charm in recounting his adventures—precisely his skill at telling *muthoi* for which the goddess has just praised him—than to any specific intervention by Athena.

Odysseus does not respond to the whole second half of Athena's speech. From the sketchiness of her remarks about his affairs on Ithaca, one might reasonably expect Odysseus to ask for further elucidation on the state of his household. But no such thing happens; Odysseus makes no inquiries and does not react to her warnings. Such an apparent inconsequence—and there are others in this scene—led older critics to suspect an intrusion in the text.[27] If Odysseus shows no awareness of what the goddess has just said, then her words could not have stood in an earlier version of the scene. A far simpler solution presents itself, however; Odysseus either overlooks or ignores the latter part of Athena's speech because his attention is focused elsewhere.[28] He returns the conversation to what she said earlier in her speech when she made a provocative point concerning Odysseus' ignorance of her disguise:

ἀργαλέον σε, θεά, γνῶναι βροτῷ ἀντιάσαντι,
καὶ μάλ᾽ ἐπισταμένῳ· σὲ γὰρ αὐτὴν παντὶ ἔϊκεις.

It is most difficult, goddess, for a mortal who approaches
    to recognize you,
even for a very knowledgeable one; for you liken yourself
    to everything.

(13. 312-313)

In other words, Odysseus refuses to be rushed into considering the business at hand, but instead goes back to Athena's implied

---

[27] For a review of opinions, see Krehmer (1973), pp. 182-85.

[28] Cf. Belzner (1912), p. 39: "Odysseus kann die Worte Athenes (306-310) gar nicht aufgreifen; denn diese sind für einen gläubigen Odysseus berechnet, unser Odysseus aber glaubt Athene nicht, muss also zuerst die Frage 324 ff. tun." Cf. Besslich (1966), pp. 121-22.

challenge. Echoing her own words (γνῶναι–ἔγνως), Odysseus appears to concede that as a mortal he cannot be expected to recognize a divinity, especially one with the Protean talents of Athena. He seems to assent to her claims to superiority; as a divinity, she necessarily surpasses the knowledge of mortals. But Odysseus continues; he knows (εὖ οἶδ᾽) full well that formerly the goddess was well-disposed toward him:

αὐτὰρ ἐπεὶ Πριάμοιο πόλιν διεπέρσαμεν αἰπήν,
βῆμεν δ᾽ ἐν νήεσσι, θεὸς δ᾽ ἐκέδασσεν Ἀχαιούς,
οὐ σέ γ᾽ ἔπειτα ἴδον, κούρη Διός, οὐδ᾽ ἐνόησα
νηὸς ἐμῆς ἐπιβᾶσαν, ὅπως τί μοι ἄλγος ἀλάλκοις.

But when we sacked the steep city of Priam,
and went on our ships, and a god scattered the Achaeans,
I did not see you, daughter of Zeus, thereafter, nor notice
you boarding my ship, so that you might save me from
    grief.

(13. 316-319)

Odysseus alludes unmistakably—though with some delicacy—to the wrath of Athena ("*a god* scattered the Greeks") and its immediate consequences for himself ("I never saw you thereafter"). Rather reproachfully, he adds that throughout his wanderings, he was completely on his own.

From seeming acquiescence, Odysseus has now moved to a second challenge, disputing Athena's claim that she stood by him constantly (13. 300-301). Then, withholding his trump card until the end, Odysseus declares that he did indeed recognize the goddess when she led him into the city of the Phaeacians (cf. 7. 18-77).[29] In short, Odysseus has rejected

---

[29] 13. 322-323 have met with almost universal condemnation since antiquity. Cf. the Scholia. Even Krehmer (1973), p. 204, who painstakingly defends every line of the whole encounter from Analyst attack, succumbs here; but his explanation for the interpolation is weak and ignores the movement of the dialogue up to this point. The awkward placement of the πρίν clause at 322 has been called "unmöglich" by Ameis-Henze, *Anhang*, and by Bethe (1922), p. 65. By withholding the πρίν clause, Odysseus saves the surprising reversal until the end of his speech, just as Athena had done moments earlier with the name of Ithaca. The idea, in both cases, is to catch one's opponent off guard.

Athena's assertion of her steadfast assistance as well as her contention concerning his inability to recognize her, thereby calling into question the goddess' self-proclaimed superiority. Athena has been lying, and Odysseus has found her out. Now thoroughly distrusting her, he suspects that Athena is merely trying to trick him.[30] Hence he implores her to tell him whether he has really arrived in Ithaca:

νῦν δέ σε πρὸς πατρὸς γουνάζομαι—οὐ γὰρ ὀίω
ἥκειν εἰς Ἰθάκην εὐδείελον, ἀλλά τιν' ἄλλην
γαῖαν ἀναστρέφομαι· σὲ δὲ κερτομέουσαν ὀίω
ταῦτ' ἀγορευέμεναι, ἵν' ἐμὰς φρένας
    ἠπεροπεύσης—
εἰπέ μοι εἰ ἐτεόν γε φίλην ἐς πατρίδ' ἱκάνω.

Now I beg you by your father—for I do not believe
I have come to sun-lit Ithaca, but rather that I wander
    through
some other land; I think you were taunting me
when you said that, in order to deceive me—
but tell me if truly I have come to my own homeland.
                                                (13. 324-328)

It may be surprising that Odysseus again raises the question of his whereabouts, for after the indications of the shepherd (13. 237-252), the issue appeared to be settled. But in the meantime, everything has been thrown into question. The shepherd was not what he seemed, but rather the goddess in disguise. Furthermore, Athena has not only boasted explicitly of her talents as a trickster, but Odysseus has also discovered her to be less than candid with him—even at the moment when she has called a halt to mutual deception.[31]

---

[30] Odysseus' distrust, even of—especially of?—divinities is characteristic. His very first speech in the *Odyssey* voices his suspicion of Calypso (5. 173-179), which is not altogether unjustified. In addition to the oaths he extracts from Calypso (5. 173-188) and Circe (10. 342-347), consider his disinclination to follow the well-meaning instructions of Leucothea (5. 356-364). Cf. Krehmer (1973), pp. 207-217.

[31] Cf. Besslich (1966), p. 122: "Der Jüngling stellt sich als unwirklich heraus und damit alles, was er gesagt hat."

As Odysseus had done before, Athena in her response does not immediately answer Odysseus' pressing question. Now it is her turn to be on the defensive. Instead of telling Odysseus what he wants so much to know, she charges him with always being distrustful and suspicious—which, she claims, is why she cannot abandon him, even in his misery. More compliments follow. Praising his presence of mind and self-control,[32] Athena notes that in his situation any other man would have rushed home to see his wife and children. But not Odysseus, who characteristically prefers to test his wife's loyalty before revealing himself. On the basis of Odysseus' Cretan tale, Athena has good evidence that he would not rush off to the palace without taking some precautions. But her remarks concerning Odysseus' desire to test Penelope appear out of the blue, and almost all commentators regard these lines as interpolations.[33] To be sure, the goddess' words here are premature, out of place, and involve something of a non sequitur; but they do demonstrate Athena's embarrassment. She flatters Odysseus and attempts to deflect his distrust of her to another object. In short, she employs a calculated diversionary tactic.[34] The goddess now turns to the reproach implied by Odys-

---

[32] For a discussion of the key terms, ἐπητής, ἀγχίνοος, and ἐχέφρων (13. 332), see Stanford (1963), pp. 30-34; Thornton (1970), pp. 83-84; and Krehmer (1973), pp. 216-17. The meaning of the first word is obscure. The Scholia, which Thornton follows, gloss it as λόγιος, 'eloquent,' while Stanford offers 'civilized,' and Krehmer suggests 'vernünftig.' None of these explanations are completely satisfactory.

[33] Cf. the H.Q. Scholia at 13.333. Even Belzner (1912), p. 35, who opposes other athetizations, remarks: "Die Verse sind unter keinen Umständen zu halten." But Wilamowitz' judgment (Homerische Untersuchungen, Philologische Untersuchungen 7 [Berlin, 1884], p. 106, n. 16) is telling: "das ist in Athenas munde, die Odysseus grade noch von hause fern halten muss, so verkehrt, dass man die absicht der interpolation . . . kaum begreift." Krehmer (1973), pp. 221-33, staunchly defends the lines, but does not understand them: "Was Athene hier sagt, ist uneinigeschränkt und ohne jeden Hintergedanken und Nebensinn lobend und anerkennend" (p. 228).

[34] Van der Valk (1949), p. 197, understands Athena's ploy: "By this adroit manoeuver she fixes the attention on another point so that her defense is now of secondary importance and can be settled by a few trifling remarks. Thus the lines 333-338 very aptly illustrate the embarrassment of Athena."

seus' earlier words concerning her absence during his years of wandering. She says she never doubted his ultimate return, after losing his companions. Cold comfort there. Her alibi for not helping Odysseus was the anger of Poseidon over the blinding of the Cyclops and her distaste for opposing her uncle. As we have already seen, this excuse is clearly unsatisfactory as it stands in that it does not fully cover Odysseus' accusation; he claims that Athena gave him no aid from the time he embarked from Troy until he landed in Scheria, and the account of the wanderings bears out his charge. Athena's alibi accounts for her absence only after the blinding of Polyphemus, whereas Odysseus accuses her of neglecting him *before* that time. Now, however, the whole subject is quickly dropped as the goddess returns to Odysseus' request for certainty concerning his whereabouts. Scattering the mist that had rendered the landscape unrecognizable, Athena points out the familiar landmarks of Ithaca. Ultimately, Odysseus is not so much convinced by what the goddess says as by the unimpeachable evidence of his own eyes.

In his gladness, Odysseus kisses the soil of his home and breaks into a prayer to the local nymphs, promising them gifts on the condition that Athena grant him his life and prosperity to his son. Responding with words of encouragement, the goddess urges him not to worry about the future, but first to attend to matters close at hand—the presents of the Phaeacians. The hero and his divine patroness now hide the gifts in the cave of the nymphs nearby and sit down together by an olive tree to take counsel for the future. Briefly describing the conduct of the suitors and the predicament of Penelope, Athena advises Odysseus to consider how to do away with his uninvited guests (13. 375-378).

The conversation has now returned to its starting point (13. 303; cf. 13. 190-193), when Athena first explained her purpose in coming.[35] The complex duel of wits between god and mortal has, in fact, come to a close. Odysseus no longer chal-

---

[35] Besslich (1966), p. 120, calls 13. 303-375 a "Zwischenspiel." Cf. p. 122, n. 52.

lenges the goddess and appears to overlook her transparent lie about Poseidon. The critical moment in this shift occurs when Odysseus assures himself that he has really returned home.[36] Rather than pursuing the question of the past and Athena's support—or lack of it—Odysseus now concerns himself only with ensuring that support in his future trials. Odysseus responds with a mixture of horror and gratitude to Athena's report about the suitors. Surely, he would have been trapped and met an end much like that of Agamemnon, if she had not revealed everything to him. Odysseus' tone has undergone a remarkable reversal: from challenging and provoking the goddess to slightly obsequious flattery. Odysseus, we know, was not the kind of man to run home impulsively without first ascertaining what kind of welcome he might expect. Athena has, after all, just finished complimenting him for this very quality! Moreover, Odysseus has already given ample proof of his sang-froid in the fabrication of his false identity as the stranger from Crete. Finally, even if Odysseus were a creature of impulse, Teiresias had clearly foretold to him the dangers waiting at home (11. 115-118), and Agamemnon himself had warned him to return in secret (κρύβδην, μηδ' ἀναφανδά, 11. 455). Given his innately suspicious and cautious nature and given the warnings he has received on his journey, it is well nigh impossible to imagine Odysseus' falling into a trap like the one that felled Agamemnon. This apparent inconsistency reflects the dramatic change in Odysseus' attitude toward Athena: from distrust and suspicion to gratitude and seemingly complete dependence. It is hard not to smile at this change.

Echoing Athena's words, (μῆτιν ὕφηνον, 13. 386; cf. μῆτιν ὑφήνω, 13. 303), Odysseus appeals to the goddess to help him in formulating a plan of revenge against the suitors. He ends with a request for her aid, alluding to her former assistance at Troy and his confidence in overcoming all obstacles with her support—even if 300 men were to stand against him. The

[36] Compare Besslich (1966), p. 122: "Zwischen den beiden Hinweisen der Athene auf die Zustände in Odysseus Haus liegt also die Wiederentdeckung der Heimat. . . . Auf das Kommende ist jetz alles ausgerichtet"(p. 123).

reestablishment of relations of familiarity and mutual trust is signaled by Odysseus' use of γλαυκῶπι, "bright" or "gray eyes," a common epithet of Athena, in the vocative.[37] Never again occurring in this form in the *Odyssey*, it is obviously a nickname suggesting intimacy. From the *Iliad*, we can gather that it is Zeus' favorite appellation for his favorite daughter.[38]

It appears, then, that the ever suspicious and distrustful Odysseus has been transformed into a model of gratitude and humility. Only once, at the very end of the conversation, does his old distrust flare up again. When Athena announces that she must go off to Sparta to bring back Telemachus, who has been seeking news of his father, Odysseus asks with barely controlled anger:

τίπτε τ᾽ ἄρ᾽ οὔ οἱ εἶπες, ἐνὶ φρεσὶ πάντα ἰδυῖα;
ἦ ἵνα που καὶ κεῖνος ἀλώμενος ἄλγεα πάσχῃ
πόντον ἐπ᾽ ἀτρύγετον, βίοτον δέ οἱ ἄλλοι ἔδουσι.

But why did you not tell him, you who know all in your heart?
Or did you somehow want him, too, to wander and suffer woes
on the barren sea, while others devour his livelihood?
(13. 417-419)

The recrimination burning in these words implicitly blames Athena for all Odysseus' former troubles and suggests that his old suspicions smolder just beneath the surface. Yet with Athena's renewed assurances (13. 421-428), the man of many wiles shows himself flexible enough to ignore the past in order to ensure the future.

In the meantime, a subject—foreshadowed at the very beginning of the scene (13. 191) and long submerged—has surfaced: Odysseus' disguise. To understand its connection with what has preceded, we must first look back at the issues of

---

[37] Ameis-Hentze at 13.389 speak of the "vertrauliches Ton."

[38] In *Iliad* VIII. 373, Athena predicts that the enmity between herself and Zeus, caused by his promise to Thetis, will someday subside: "There will come a day when he will again call me his dear *glaukopis*."

the prior duel of wits and, if possible, determine its outcome. The debate turned on the question of cleverness and knowledge. Athena first noted that, although Odysseus is the cleverest of mortals, he has only limited knowledge of the gods, given his inability to recognize her. In this important respect, he is necessarily inferior to her. While admitting his mortality, Odysseus rejects his supposed inferiority by citing an instance of his knowledge, his recognition of Athena on Scheria—thus challenging the goddess' contention. In turn, she responds to his challenge with the alibi of Poseidon; the entire matter is then dropped and appears to be settled. Thus, Athena seems to have the last word and to be the winner in the debate.[39] If it has taught us nothing else, however, this scene has proved that appearance is not necessarily reality, and that an apparent victory need not to be a real one. Further reflection shows the goddess' triumph to be largely apparent. By dropping the debate for a more useful end, Odysseus avoids antagonizing Athena in order to gain her support. In this complicated game of dissimulation, Odysseus plays the loser and gains an invaluable ally. In the duel between god and mortal, the mortal hero has won in an essential respect. Odysseus sacrifices an empty—and potentially dangerous[40]—victory for a substantial one.

The task before Odysseus now is his reinstatement to his former position in Ithaca, and its accomplishment requires secrecy, or, more precisely, a disguise. For this, divine aid remains essential.[41] In an earlier chapter, we saw that the ability to change the appearance of things, including themselves, constitutes an essential and characteristic component

[39] Cf. Erbse (1972), pp. 159-60: "dann bleibt die Göttin—*wie es sich gehört*—am Ende doch die Klügere" (italics mine).

[40] That danger is perfectly articulated in another context by Dione: "He who fights with the immortals is not long-lived, / nor do his children about his knees cry 'Papa,' when he returns from war and dreadful battle" (V. 407-409). Odysseus' fame depends precisely, as we have seen, on long life and return from battle.

[41] Otto (1954), who attempts a naturalistic or rationalistic explanation of the Homeric gods whenever possible, says of Odysseus' disguise: "Her [Athena's] transformation of him is the only miracle in the passage" (p. 195).

of Homeric divinity. The passage we have been analyzing has already given two dramatic examples of this power which Homer attributes to his gods: the mist that makes Ithaca look other than it is, and the shepherd disguise with which Athena first accosts Odysseus. The transformation of Odysseus into an old beggar will be the third example. The disguise will allow him to test the loyalties of the members of his household, to gather his needed allies, and to prepare for the battle with the suitors. But however cunning and clever Odysseus may be, he does not have the power to transform himself, a power that is specifically divine. The closest he can come to keeping his identity hidden is to suppress his name or give himself a false one, "for there is no man born who is completely nameless" (8. 552). During his wanderings among strangers such ploys could suffice. The Outis trick saved the day in the cave of the Cyclops, and in Phaeacia Odysseus holds back his name until he is certain of the kind of reception he will receive. In Ithaca, to be sure, he will lie about his identity, but it will not suffice merely to conceal his name. As Helen relates in Book 4 (244-258), at Troy, among strangers, Odysseus could get away with beggar's rags—but, even so, Helen herself recognized him. How, then, can Odysseus hope to hide his presence on Ithaca from his own family and close acquaintances—as well as his enemies? Athena's help is indispensable for Odysseus' reestablishment on Ithaca, since only a god has the power to alter Odysseus' appearance, to make him unrecognizable.

Odysseus needs Athena. At a certain point in the conversation, Odysseus ceased provoking the goddess and questioning her superiority. He pretended to be the loser in the contest of wits between them in order to use her and that power which is exclusively divine. In a certain sense, Odysseus has actually won the contest and successfully managed to outwit Athena. It may be considered the ultimate triumph of *metis* that it masks its greatest victory as apparent defeat.

We began from the question of the nature of Athena's wrath and hoped to find clues to its origin in this first and longest confrontation between the goddess and Odysseus. While Athena's anger is only hinted at (13. 317) and no particulars are given, its consequences, her abandonment of Odysseus during the major part of his wanderings, become a critical element in the conversation. Yet it is possible to discover the cause of Athena's wrath within the confines of this scene. In a sense, it reenacts the offense that originally provoked her anger. To put it simply, if not too crudely, *Odysseus is too clever; his intelligence calls into question the superiority of the gods themselves.*

Athena's reaction to this fundamental challenge, *menis*, differs from the anger of a Poseidon or a Helios. But, then, the issues between Athena and Odysseus are different. Odysseus has not merely offended one of her favorites, or wounded her honor, or trampled on one of her prerogatives. Nor has he challenged her in a particular sphere as Thamyris did with the Muses or Eurytus with Apollo.[42] Odysseus' challenge is far more radical. The final and permanent triumph of Zeus and the Olympian order, according to Hesiod, is assured by Zeus' swallowing or incorporation of the goddess Metis.[43] The offspring of this union is Athena, who, as she says of herself, "is famed for her *metis* among all the gods" (13. 298-299). Odysseus' intelligence, his *metis*, calls into question the fundamental hierarchy of gods and men and the boundaries separating them. To attempt to break through the limits that divide men and gods may lead to heroism and its reward, *kleos aphthiton*, 'imperishable fame,' but it surely exposes one to great peril. As long as the lines between gods and men remain blurred and unclear, the line between divine protection and divine wrath is necessarily imprecise.

By the nature of his offense, Odysseus, whose name, as we have seen, means 'divine wrath,' allies himself most closely with the so-called Great Sinners of the Nekyia (11. 576-600). These, whom Rohde calls, "the three who are hated by the gods,"[44] are punished not for a common class of crimes such

---

[42] II. 594-600; 8. 226-228.

[43] *Theogony* 886-900. Cf. Detienne-Vernant (1974), pp. 61ff.

[44] Cf. 10. 75 where Aeolus calls Odysseus "hated by the gods" (ἀθανάτοισιν ἀπεχθόμενος), when the latter returns to the island of Aeolia.

as oath-breaking, but for "offenses to the gods themselves."[45] Only in the case of Tityus is the offense explicitly mentioned: his attempted rape of Zeus' consort, Leto, a violation—presumably by force (note the emphasis on his great size)—of the divinely sanctioned relations between gods and men. In the cases of Sisyphus and Tantalus, no particular crimes are mentioned, but traditional accounts offer several explanations, all of which involve the attempt to out-trick the gods by means of *doloi*. Sisyphus, whom Homer calls "the wiliest of men," κέϱδιστος ἀνδϱῶν (VI. 153), managed to outwit death itself and to return to life from Hades.[46] Elsewhere, he is accused of "making public the secrets of the gods."[47] Similar charges of impiety are leveled against Tantalus, who is also said to have stolen nectar and ambrosia from the gods to give to mortals.[48] The tale of his serving up his son Pelops at a feast to which he had invited the gods is already recorded by Pindar, who rejects the impious implications of the story.[49] The common denominator in all these tales is the attempted transgression of the boundaries that separate gods from men, not by force, but by stealth and *metis*.

Rohde asserts that the tableaux of the Great Sinners in the Nekyia have no exemplary or warning function: they are singular and atypical.[50] True enough, if we consider them to be generalized exemplars for ourselves, who are unlikely to commit such extraordinary transgressions. But for Odysseus, the man of *metis* and *doloi*, the man whose very name signals his

---

[45] Rohde (1903), pp. 63-64. For the old controversy concerning this part of the Nekyia, see Page (1955), pp. 25-26.

[46] Eustathius 1701. 50-53. Cf. Scholium A at VI. 153 (= Pherecydes, *Fr. Gr. H.* 3. 119); Theognis 702-711; and Sophocles *Philoctetes* 624-625.

[47] Servius in his commentary to *Aeneid* 6. 616, describes Sisyphus as "qui deorum consilia hominibus publicavit." Cf. Plutarch *Plac. Phil.* I. 880 e-f; Sextus Emp. *Advers. Dog.* I. 54 = Kritias Fr. 2 *DK*.

[48] Cf. Eustathius 1700. 52-54; Euripides *Orestes* 10 and the Scholia *ad loc.* Ovid *Amores* 3, 7, 51, calls Tantalus *taciti vulgator*.

[49] Pindar *Olympian* I. 46-58. Cf. Euripides *Iph. Taur.* 386ff.

[50] Rohde (1903), p. 64: ". . . ihre Thaten so gut wie ihre Strafen [haben] nichts Vorbildliches und Typisches, beide stellen vielmehr völlig vereinzelte Ausnahmen dar. . . ."

peril, they provide an object lesson that he must not risk forgetting.

Compared with the relentless and eternal suffering of Sisyphus and Tantalus, Odysseus' punishment at the hands of Athena is light. But it lies not only in forcing Odysseus to cope with the Cyclops on his own, or to make his way through Scylla and Charybdis as well as to Hades and back without her help. If the offense of godlike Odysseus depends on his mental superiority and alertness, then the punishment the goddess devises fits the crime. It consists, after all, not only in the continual danger of physical destruction, but also in the constant threat of oblivion. It includes the fateful sleep which twice almost destroys the Return, once when the companions untie the bag of the winds within sight of Ithaca, and again on Thrinacia. It involves the gentler but no less dangerous temptation of forgetting—with Circe and Calypso, the Sirens, and even the charming Phaeacians—as well as the ever-present possibility of being forgotten on Ithaca itself. Or, to put it another way, Odysseus is constantly threatened by the prospect of being transformed from *metis* back into *outis*.

The dialogue we have traced shows that Odysseus has not forgotten the lessons of Sisyphus and Tantalus. At a certain moment, Odysseus resists the temptation to press his point, a point that would inevitably offend Athena and perhaps even reignite her wrath. To insist upon his advantage would imperil the final goal of all his adventures, all his sufferings, and all his *doloi*: his reestablishment as king in Ithaca.

The underlying issue in the conversation between Odysseus and Athena has been the difference between gods and men and the demarcation of their proper spheres. The setting of the dialogue in front of the cave of the nymphs provides an emblem for the entire discussion:

ἀγχόθι δ᾽ αὐτῆς ἄντρον ἐπήρατον ἠεροειδές,
ἱρὸν νυμφάων αἱ νηϊάδες καλέονται.
ἐν δὲ κρητῆρές τε καὶ ἀμφιφορῆες ἔασι
λάϊνοι· ἔνθα δ᾽ ἔπειτα τιθαιβώσσουσι μέλισσαι.

ἐν δ᾽ ἱστοὶ λίθεοι περιμήκεες, ἔνθα τε νύμφαι
φάρε᾽ ὑφαίνουσιν ἁλιπόρφυρα, θαῦμα ἰδέσθαι·
ἐν δ᾽ ὕδατ᾽ ἀενάοντα. δύω δέ τέ οἱ θύραι εἰσίν,
αἱ μὲν πρὸς Βορέαο καταιβαταὶ ἀνθρώποισιν,
αἱ δ᾽ αὖ πρὸς Νότου εἰσὶ θεώτεραι· οὐδέ τι κείνῃ
ἄνδρες ἐσέρχονται, ἀλλ᾽ ἀθανάτων ὁδός ἐστιν.

Nearby, there is a cave, lovely and dim,
sacred to the nymphs who are called Naids.
Inside, there are mixing bowls and jars
of stone; and there the bees store up their honey.
Within, there are stone looms of great size, and there the
    nymphs
weave sea-purple robes, a wonder to behold;
there, too, is water ever-flowing. Two are the entrances;
the one on the north can be entered by men,
but the one to the south is divine, nor do
men enter it, but it is the way of the gods.
(13. 103-112)

The contest between god and mortal has taken place in the
shadow of these two entrances. All along, the fundamental
question has been: who can rightfully enter where?

CHAPTER V

THE DOUBLE THEODICY OF
THE *ODYSSEY*

πάντες δὲ θεῶν χατέουσ᾽ ἄνθρωποι.
(3.48)

The apparent granting of one prayer out of a hundred
may well do more to make a man love his gods than the
apparent rejection of the other ninety-nine can do to
make him hate them. . . .
(K. J. Dover, *Greek Popular Morality*, p. 79)

The Epic encounter of god and mortal reveals both their similarities and their differences. If the *Iliad* exposes the tragic
aspects of this conjunction, the *Odyssey* dwells on its comic
dimensions. Precisely because they compare and contrast the
mortal with the immortal, both poems are able to celebrate
the human *as* human.

In the *Odyssey*, Homer rapidly narrows the question of the
relationship between gods and men by focusing on Athena
and Odysseus. The pattern of alternation between divine support and divine enmity is common to the Epic tradition as a
whole. However, the specific terms of this confrontation depend, as I have tried to show, on the particular character not
only of Odysseus but also on that of the divinity most closely
resembling him.

The challenge posed by Odysseus is an intellectual one, and
the contest between him and Athena is waged by diplomatic
means. As I have pointed out before, the *Odyssey* begins with
the end of the goddess' wrath. In Book 13, the dialogue between the hero and Athena reveals the nature and cause of
her wrath and leads to an apparent resolution of the conflict.
Yet any attentive reader of my argument will detect a number
of loose ends. If, as I have maintained, the wrath of Athena

serves as a crucial structuring principle of the poem, one must finally confront a simple question of paramount importance: why does Athena *stop* being angry?

One can, of course, argue, as many do, that in the course of his ten years of wandering and isolation, Odysseus has changed. One can, moreover, maintain that he has learned his lesson and has become a sadder and wiser man, a fit object of Athena's pity rather than of her wrath. And, indeed, the hero has learned many things in his journey through the cities and minds of men. He has learned in Hades that the heroism and glory of an Achilles constitute triumphs that are ultimately empty; that the exalted power of an Agamemnon can be brought low by a faithless woman; and that those who attempt to challenge the gods are punished. At his own expense, he has experienced the ruthless revenge of offended divinities. In addition, he has chosen toil and wakefulness over the ease of the Phaeacians and the sweet somnolence of the Lotus-Eaters. And, finally, he has learned to prefer home, family, old age, and death to the immortal enticements of Calypso. In other words, Odysseus has learned to think mortal thoughts.

I do not dispute or take issue with this view, for it obviously contains much truth. Yet such an interpretation betrays a fault common to much criticism of the *Odyssey*. The wanderings of Odysseus, and especially the so-called Great Wanderings the hero narrates in Books 9-12, take up only one-sixth of the poem. They do form the literally most wonderful—full of wonders—part of the poem; nevertheless, an interpretation of the *Odyssey* focusing exclusively on the Wanderings places too heavy a burden on these few books. Surely, if Homer had so desired, he could have spun out Odysseus' adventures to dominate the poem. There is no dearth of material, and I think we would all be pleased to have more details. It would delight us to know, for example, what songs the Sirens sang, what went on during the hero's year with Circe, and what it was about the Laestrygonian queen that made Odysseus' men despise her on sight. But Homer chose a different way to fashion his poem. A convincing interpretation of the *Odyssey* as a whole must at least attempt to take into account the proportions of the work as we have it.

Keeping that imperative in mind, I would like to articulate and develop some different considerations that influence Athena to make an end to her anger against Odysseus. These considerations will involve some further reflections on the role of the gods in relation to men in Homer. That subject has, in various guises, guided my exposition from the outset. It is now time to examine the political and social implications of Homeric theology as they emerge in the *Odyssey*. It seems best to begin our summation with some general remarks. According to a widely-held view, the *Odyssey* heralds a more advanced ethical conception of the gods and a more enlightened view of divine justice and human responsibility than is to be found in the *Iliad*.[1] The argument for the New Morality of the *Odyssey* centers on Zeus' opening speech to the divine assembly in Book 1. Placed at the beginning of the first scene of the poem, the speech is said to have a programmatic function, a theodicy that corrects, criticizes, and moves beyond the moral stance of the *Iliad*. The Iliadic attitude is best exemplified by Achilles' parable of the two jars at the threshold of Zeus. In Book XXIV, Achilles tries to console old Priam with a statement on the human condition:

οὐ γάρ τις πρῆξις πέλεται κρυεροῖο γόοιο·
ὡς γὰρ ἐπεκλώσαντο θεοὶ δειλοῖσι βροτοῖσι,
ζώειν ἀχνυμένοις· αὐτοὶ δέ τ' ἀκηδέες εἰσί.
δοιοὶ γάρ τε πίθοι κατακείαται ἐν Διὸς οὔδει
δώρων οἷα δίδωσι κακῶν, ἕτερος δὲ ἑάων·
ᾧ μέν κ' ἀμμείξας δώῃ Ζεὺς τερπικέραυνος,
ἄλλοτε μέν τε κακῷ ὅ γε κύρεται, ἄλλοτε δ' ἐσθλῷ·
ᾧ δέ κε τῶν λυγρῶν δώῃ, λωβητὸν ἔθηκε,

---

[1] Cf. Reinhardt (1960d), p. 6: "Verglichen mit de Ilias scheint die Odyssee von einer fortgeschrittenen Moral," Cf. Rüter (1969), p. 70, who finds in the *Odyssey* "ein empfindlicherer Sinn für Würde und Gerechtigkeit der Götter." Similarly, already Nitzsch (1826), p. 11: "Unverkennbar waltet in der Odyssee die Idee einer göttlichen Gerechtigkeit weit mehr vor, als in der Ilias. . . ."

καί ἓ κακὴ βούβρωστις ἐπὶ χθόνα δῖαν ἐλαύνει,
φοιτᾷ δ' οὔτε θεοῖσι τετιμένος οὔτε βροτοῖσιν.

There is no profit in icy lamentation.
For so the gods have ordained for wretched mortals
to live in misery, while they themselves live without care.
For two are the jars at the threshold of Zeus,
of the gifts, such as he gives—one of evils, the other of
    good;
and if Zeus who takes pleasure in thunder should mix
    them,
then a man sometimes has evil, and sometimes good.
But if he gives of the evils alone, Zeus makes him
    wretched,
and evil hunger drives him over the glorious earth,
and he wanders, honored neither by gods nor men.
                                        (XXIV. 524-533)

Achilles states that human happiness and misery are the gifts
of the gods, and man stands totally at the mercy of divine
whim. (His reference to wandering as an unmixed evil bears
noting, since the *Odyssey* is a poem about wandering.) One
can argue that, by contrast, the Odyssean Zeus responds to
Achilles' claim by charging mortals with their own unhap-
piness and rejecting divine responsibility for the human mis-
fortune men unfairly assign to the gods.[2]

[2] The first to put forth this view (in a rather sketchy fashion) seems to be
W. Jaeger in "Solons Eunomia," *Sitzungsberichte der Preussischen Akademie
der Wissensch.* (Berlin, 1926), pp. 73ff. For a clear and comprehensive statement, see F. Jacoby, "Die geistige Physiognomie der Odyssee," *Antike 9*
(1933):185-94. More recently, Rüter (1969), pp. 69ff. Voices have, to be
sure, been raised in opposition. Wilamowitz (1931), 2:118, in accordance
with his general view of the derivative character of Book 1, saw little new
in Zeus' speech. Heubeck (1954), pp. 81ff., emphasizes the similarities in the
moral tone of the two poems and finds that the *Iliad* already contains *in nuce*
the conceptions elaborated in the *Odyssey*. Nilsson (1955), 1:363, completely
rejects Jaeger's interpretation. Finally, H. Lloyd-Jones, *The Justice of Zeus*
(Berkeley, 1971), p. 31, maintains correctly that "It seems most unsafe to
conclude that the comparative moral simplicity of the *Odyssey* is due simply
to ethical progress made by the Greek world in the interval between the
composition of the two poems."

The precise words of Zeus in the *Odyssey* deserve attention. Zeus begins with a complaint:

Ὦ πόποι, οἷον δή νυ θεοὺς βροτοὶ αἰτιόωνται.
ἐξ ἡμέων γάρ φασι κάκ' ἔμμεναι. . . .

Alas, how men now blame the gods.
For they say that evils come from us. . . .
(1. 32-33)

He responds by defending the gods against this accusation: even on their own, men bring misery on themselves beyond what is fated. According to Zeus, evil may derive from sources other than the gods alone. Nowhere, however, does he deny that the gods can, in fact, be a source of human suffering, even though Zeus' assertion is often interpreted as containing such a denial. On the contrary, his speech suggests the existence of two sources of evil: one that is fated and comes from the gods, and another that is over and above what is fated, a kind of evil men bring upon themselves.[3]

An ancient commentator already recognized what we have observed: the apparent contradiction between Zeus' claims and the plot of the *Odyssey*. The Scholiast notes: "These things [what Zeus says] do not agree with the whole story which introduces the gods as the cause of many misfortunes."[4] The Scholiast goes on to propose two possible solutions to the problem: the one demands that we make a distinction between what the poet says and what one of the poet's characters may say; the second solution requires a precise inter-

---

[3] The clearest explication of this dualism comes not in later Greek literature but from Book VI of the *Iliad* (487-489), where Hector explains that no man can escape the fate, good or evil, which comes from the gods and over which he has no control. But whatever is above or beyond a man's destined portion (*hyper aisan* or *hyper moron*) is subject to human will and can be prevented or avoided by human action. In Aegisthus' case, he married Clytemnestra and murdered Agamemnon despite the warnings of Hermes. He thus acted *hyper moron* and, as a result, suffered *hyper moron* through the vengeance of Orestes. Aegisthus, like Hector, had the ability to avoid his premature death.

[4] Scholium Q *ad* 1. 33.

pretation of Zeus' words, οἱ δὲ καὶ αὐτοὶ σφῆσιν ἀτασθαλίῃσιν ("they even on their own by their own recklessness
. . ." 1. 33-34).[5] Both solutions, ἐκ προσώπου and ἐκ λέξεως,
in fact, coincide and go hand in hand. One must keep in mind
Zeus' defensive posture vis-à-vis the accusations of men. He
is responding to an accusation that he cannot completely deny.
He merely denies the claims of men that the gods are to blame
for *all* their troubles. In short, Zeus does what anyone in a
similar situation would do: he puts forth the best possible
argument for the defense.

Zeus continues his case for the defense with a timely example which proves not only that men get into trouble on
their own, but also that the gods do promote the cause of
justice and do not act only on the basis of whim. He refers
to Aegisthus' murder of Agamemnon and Aegisthus' punishment at the hands of Orestes. Throughout the whole *Odyssey*,
the story of Agamemnon, Aegisthus, Clytemnestra, and Orestes forms a constant foil and parallel to the tale of Odysseus.
In the first appearance of this exemplar, Zeus tries to relieve
the gods of blame for human misery. The paradigm of Aegisthus, while well chosen to bolster Zeus' argument, may not
be universally valid. In fact, upon reflection, it turns out that
only the fate of the suitors follows the pattern exemplified by
Aegisthus.[6] His wickedness and punishment serve as a model
for the suitors' bad end—and not necessarily for all human
life in general.

Interpretations that try to force the destruction of Odysseus'
companions and the sufferings of Odysseus himself at the
hands of Poseidon into the moral pattern of Aegisthus and
the suitors must be recognized for what they are: Procrustean
attempts to regularize and make uniform the morality of the
Odyssey. Schadewaldt finds Odysseus' men guilty of violating
their oath not to lay hands on the cattle of the Sun (12. 298-
303) and hence deserving of their punishment;[7] and Reinhardt

---

[5] For a discussion of this phrase, see pp. 35ff. above.

[6] Cf. Fenik (1974), pp. 210ff.

[7] W. Schadewaldt, "Der Helios-Zorn in der Odyssee," in *Studi in onore
di L. Castiglione* (Florence, 1960), pp. 861-76.

tries to justify the anger of Poseidon as a response to Odysseus' *hybris*.[8] But neither view will stand up before an objective examination of the respective episodes.[9] Moreover, the ethical consistency we desire eludes us from the very beginning.

As soon as Zeus has finished his speech, the view that the gods can and do load suffering on wretched mortals is vigorously stated in the very same opening scene—by a god— and admitted by Zeus himself. For Athena responds by applauding Zeus: Aegisthus, indeed, had a just end, such as all men deserve who commit similar crimes. Athena continues by inquiring about the fate of Odysseus, who suffers unjustly,[10] and she finally accuses Zeus himself of causing Odysseus' troubles. Zeus appears shocked at his daughter's charge. Indeed, he recognizes the superiority of Odysseus' intelligence and piety.[11] But he counters that Poseidon rather than he detains Odysseus. Thus does Zeus unequivocally acknowledge that the gods are, at least, *one* source of mortal ills.

The opening scene of the *Odyssey*, then, suggests not one but two conceptions of the role of the gods in human affairs. This, in turn, points to the fact the theodicy of the *Odyssey* is not single but double. Zeus' speech, to be sure, maintains that the gods are concerned with the workings of justice among men. But the ensuing exchange reveals that the gods may in fact hand out good and evil on the basis of caprice and whim rather than on the basis of justice.

We are thus faced with the fact that, from the very outset, the *Odyssey* presents what seems to be a massive internal contradiction—and no mere oversight, like the fact that a warrior who appears to die in one book returns to fight again

[8] Reinhardt (1960a), p. 69. Cf. E. Bradley, "The Hybris of Odysseus," *Soundings* 51 (1968):33-44.

[9] See the discussion of Fenik (1974), pp. 210ff. and pp. 229ff. below.

[10] Athena uses the word *dusmoros*, which can, of course, have the general sense of 'unlucky,' 'unfortunate.' See Leitzke (1930), p. 16. But not infrequently the word is closely linked to the action of the gods and means precisely 'having an evil or bad *moira*.' Compare XXII. 60; 7. 270-271; 20. 194ff.

[11] Zeus does not raise the possibility that there may be a tension betwen piety and intelligence.

several books later. This cannot be cited as an example of Homer's nodding, but can only be justified as a case of deep coma. The *Odyssey* appears from the beginning to be fundamentally flawed by a profound contradiction in its view of the nature of the gods and human life.

Students of the *Odyssey* have, to be sure, not remained insensitive to such a monumental discrepancy in the religious and moral perspective of the poem. For an earlier generation of scholars, the solution to all contradictions was the appeal to multiple authorship. Schadewaldt, a recent representative of the Analystic school, has in fact found it possible to detect the additions of his "B" poet to a preexisting *Odyssey* precisely on account of his moralizing outlook.[12] Unitarians do not deny the contradictions, but take refuge in appeals to newer tendencies not quite integrated into older materials.[13] Contemporary scholars, under the influence of Parryism, avoid all reference to theories involving several individual poets, but resort rather to views concerning the combination of various earlier and later strata of the "tradition." Their results are finally not dissimilar from those of the old Analysts. As Fenik admits:

> In the Odyssey the discrepancy [in the behavior of the gods] is patent and unmitigated. But the important point remains that both views are poetically serviceable and utilized for their own ends. Some such criterion as "one consistent picture of the gods" is useless because the unity of the Odyssey lies on a different level. These different views came into being at different times; in this respect the analysts have always been right. But these different times were probably anterior to the Homeric poems. . . .[14]

[12] See Schadewaldt (1958), pp. 15-32; and, above all, his list of passages ascribed to his "B" poet in "Der Helios-Zorn" (1960), p. 876.

[13] Cf. Rüter (1969), p. 82: "Die neuen Vorstellungen werden zur Geltung gebracht, wo es geht—an sichtbarster Stelle bereits im Proömium und Prolog—, daneben behalten die Geschichten unbekümmert um den Widerspruch ihre herkömmliche Motivation."

[14] Fenik (1974), pp. 220-221.

Plus ça change. . . . The harsh remedies of the Analysts are replaced by the diluted medicine of the neo-Analysts, but the outcome remains the same: the unity of the poem dies at the hands of the doctors.

I believe a resolution of these apparent contradictions is ultimately possible without recourse to evolutionary explanations. But such a resolution can only be achieved if we confront them forthrightly, and neither ignore them nor attempt to smoothe them over. The two views of the gods' influence on human life, while in a sense contradictory, appear continually side by side in the *Odyssey*, in what the characters say as well as the intricacies of the plot. They are so inextricably interwined as to render impossible any attempt to separate the strands into earlier, or Iliadic, and later Odyssean strata, or to ascribe one verse to poet "B" and the next to poet "A." The fabric of the poem simply disintegrates if we try to cut through these knots of contradiction. Such intricate intermeshings do not, however, preclude our following the threads to see where they lead. Perhaps, if we proceed patiently, we will find the red thread.

I will begin by looking at some of the general statements about the workings of the gods as expressed by the characters in the course of the narrative. In the first book, Telemachus scolds his mother for wanting to stop the singer Phemius from performing "the baneful homecoming of the Greeks:"

... οὔ νύ τ' ἀοιδοὶ
αἴτιοι, ἀλλά ποθι Ζεὺς αἴτιος, ὅς τε δίδωσιν
ἀνδράσιν ἀλφηστῆσιν ὅπως ἐθέλησιν ἑκάστῳ.

... Not the singers
are to blame, but rather Zeus, who gives
to each of grain-eating mortals whatever he wishes.
(1. 347-349)

Notwithstanding this weary resignation regarding the gods, a few lines later, this same Telemachus—after telling off the suitors—prays to Zeus for justice: "I pray to the gods who live forever, if ever Zeus should grant retribution" (1. 378-

379). One character adopts two very different attitudes toward the gods without, apparently, perceiving them to be contradictory.

In the third book, Nestor's son urges his guests, Telemachus and Mentor-Athena, to pour a libation and to pray to the gods, on the grounds that "all men have need of the gods" (3. 48). He does not explain what he means, but it is a question we can ultimately not avoid. Furthermore, Peisistratus' statement raises a corollary question: do the gods have need of men? Are there mutual dependencies which determine the relations between gods and men? If we are not yet ready to answer these questions, we must, at the very least, not lose sight of them in our investigation.

Shortly thereafter, Nestor attributes the bitter homecoming of the Greeks to Zeus and Athena as a punishment for their injustice (3. 132-135). After Nestor relates the revenge carried out by Orestes for the murder of his father, Agamemnon, Telemachus expresses the hope that the gods may grant him similar strength to repay the suitors' outrages. But then he breaks off:

ἀλλ᾽ οὔ μοι τοιοῦτον ἐπέκλωσαν θεοὶ ὄλβον,
πατρί τ᾽ ἐμῷ καὶ ἐμοί· νῦν δὲ χρὴ τετλάμεν ἔμπης.

But the gods have granted me no such good fortune,
not for my father or for me. Hence endurance is
necessary.

(3. 208-209)

Again, in one and the same speech, Telemachus asks the gods for justice and, on the other hand, implies the futility of such a prayer, since the gods apportion prosperity or misery to mortals without respect for deserts. The worldly-wise Helen consoles Menelaus and Telemachus as they grieve for the absent Odysseus, not only with the wonderful drug of forgetfulness, Nepenthe, but also with a bit of proverbial wisdom:

ἀτὰρ θεὸς ἄλλοτε ἄλλῳ
Ζεὺς ἀγαθόν τε κακόν τε διδοῖ· δύναται γὰρ
ἅπαντα.

But the god, Zeus, at different times to different men
sometimes gives good, sometimes evil, for he can do all
things.

(4. 236-237)

Although we have reason to doubt Zeus' omnipotence, his
ability to grant good and bad fortune is the clearest sign of
his great power. The virginal Nausicaa addresses a similar
view to the shabby and storm-battered Odysseus:

ξεῖν', ἐπεὶ οὔτε κακῷ οὔτ' ἄφρονι φωτὶ ἔοικας,
Ζεὺς δ' αὐτὸς νέμει ὄλβον Ὀλύμπιος ἀνθρώποισιν,
ἐσθλοῖς ἠδὲ κακοῖσιν, ὅπως ἐθέλῃσιν, ἑκάστῳ·
καί που σοὶ τάδ' ἔδωκε, σὲ δὲ χρὴ τετλάμεν ἔμπης.

Stranger—since you do not resemble a bad or witless
man—
Olympian Zeus himself apportions good fortune to men,
both to the noble and the base ones, just as he wishes.
And somehow to you he has given this fate, and you
must endure it.

(6. 187-190)

No statement could more clearly assert that the gods operate
without any attention to just deserts. A faith in divine justice,
on the other hand, is maintained just as strenuously in other
passages.

When he wrongly believes that the Phaeacians have deceived
him, Odysseus himself prays:

Ζεύς σφεας τίσαιτο ἱκετήσιος, ὅς τε καὶ ἄλλους
ἀνθρώπους ἐφορᾷ καὶ τίνυται ὅς τις ἁμάρτῃ.

May Zeus of suppliants punish them, he who
oversees other men too and punishes whoever errs.

(13. 213-214)

And in speaking of the suitors, Eumaeus vigorously proclaims
the gods' devotion to justice:

οὐ μὲν σχέτλια ἔργα θεοὶ μάκαρες φιλέουσιν,
ἀλλὰ δίκην τίουσι καὶ αἴσιμα ἔργ' ἀνθρώπων.

The blessed gods do not love foul deeds,
but they reward justice and the lawful acts of men.
(14. 83-84)

Perhaps the most striking assertion of the gods' direct and continual concern for the justice of men occurs when a nameless suitor warns Antinoos to stop bullying the beggar—who is, of course, Odysseus:

Ἀντίνο᾽, οὐ μὲν κάλ᾽ ἔβαλες δύστηνον ἀλήτην,
οὐλόμεν᾽, εἰ δή πού τις ἐπουράνιος θεός ἐστι.
καί τε θεοὶ ξείνοισιν ἐοικότες ἀλλοδαποῖσι,
παντοῖοι τελέθοντες, ἐπιστρωφῶσι πόληας,
ἀνθρώπων ὕβριν τε καὶ εὐνομίην ἐφορῶντες.

Antinoos, you did no fine thing in striking the poor
    beggar,
and you'll be cursed if somehow he is a god from heaven.
The gods in the likeness of strangers from foreign parts,
in all shapes and sizes visit cities,
watching over both the violence and justice of men.
(17. 483-487)

Quite different in tone are the bitter reflections of Eurycleia, just before the famous recognition scene, over the fate of her master:

ἦ σε περὶ Ζεὺς
ἀνθρώπων ἔχθαιρε θεουδέα θυμὸν ἔχοντα.
οὐ γάρ πώ τις τόσσα βροτῶν Διὶ τερπικεραύνῳ
πίονα μηρία κῆ᾽ οὐδ᾽ ἐξαίτους ἑκατόμβας,
ὅσσα σὺ τῷ ἐδίδους. . . .

Zeus hated you
beyond all men, even though you had a godly heart.
For no man ever burned so many fat thigh pieces
to Zeus the thunderer or chosen hecatombs
as you used to give to him. . . .
(19. 363-367)

Despite his piety, Eurycleia complains, Odysseus was paid back with misery by Zeus. The old nurse comes close to asserting the futility of sacrifice. The loyal cowherd contemplates the wretched old beggar and sees in him an exemplar of the gods' cruel indifference to man:

Ζεῦ πάτερ, οὔ τις σεῖο θεῶν ὀλοώτερος ἄλλος·
οὐκ ἐλεαίρεις ἄνδρας, ἐπὴν δὴ γείνεαι αὐτός,
μισγέμεναι κακότητι καὶ ἄλγεσι λευγαλέοισιν.

Father Zeus, no god is more dreadful than you.
You have no pity for men, once you bring them forth,
but wed them to evil and woeful sufferings.
(20. 201-203)

Amid such statements of the indifference or even the random cruelty of the gods, Odysseus can yet express the hope that the suitors may meet with justice:

αἲ γὰρ δή, Εὔμαιε, θεοὶ τισαίατο λώβην,
ἣν οἵδ᾿ ὑβρίζοντες ἀτάσθαλα μηχανόωνται
οἴκῳ ἐν ἀλλοτρίῳ, οὐδ᾿ αἰδοῦς μοῖραν ἔχουσιν.

Eumaeus, would that the gods might avenge the outrage
which these men in their violence so recklessly devise,
in another man's house, nor do they have a due measure
of shame.
(20. 169-171)

Finally, after all the suitors are slaughtered, Odysseus restrains Eurycleia's cry of joy with the following words:

οὐχ ὁσίη κταμένοισιν ἐπ᾿ ἀνδράσιν εὐχετάασθαι.
τούσδε δὲ μοῖρ᾿ ἐδάμασσε θεῶν καὶ σχέτλια ἔργα·
οὔ τινα γὰρ τίεσκον ἐπιχθονίων ἀνθρώπων,
οὐ κακὸν οὐδὲ μὲν ἐσθλόν, ὅτις σφέας εἰσαφίκοιτο·
τῷ καὶ ἀτασθαλίῃσιν ἀεικέα πότμον ἐπέσπον.

It is not pious to boast over slain men.
For destiny from the gods overtook these men and their
low deeds;

for they respected no man upon the earth—
whether good or bad—whoever might approach them;
therefore, by their own recklessness, they came to an
    unseemly end.

(22. 412-416)

These lines bring us full circle back to the beginning of our discussion. Odysseus urges restraint because he acknowledges in the suitors' end the workings of divine justice rather than purely human revenge. The example of Aegisthus enunciated by Zeus in the beginning of the *Odyssey* has been reenacted by the violent, shameless, and finally murderous suitors. Despite repeated warnings, they persisted in their wickedness and were finally punished by a more-than-human agency.

This review of passages has, I hope, not been overly tedious, but it does show that the characters in the *Odyssey* simultaneously entertain two quite different views of the gods without, however, considering them to be inherently contradictory. Perhaps the following observations may partially help to explain the problem. The notion of divine punishment for injustice is usually expressed in hopes and prayers, for which Greek has a separate verb form, the optative, whereas the idea that the gods randomly apportion good and evil—especially evil—is asserted as a matter of fact, in the indicative. It is significant that the former view generally appears in relation to the suitors, while the latter frequently occurs in connection with the fate of Odysseus.

Another point deserves attention. Odysseus' account of his adventures in Books 9-12 seems singularly free of general statements concerning the workings of the gods. Perhaps Odysseus does not care to speculate on the subject, or perhaps such speculation might be dangerous to a man pursued by hostile divinities. To boast of his ability to survive without the help of the gods might aggravate the gods' anger and lead to destruction, as the example of the Lesser Ajax proves (4. 502-511). Complaints of mistreatment at the hands of the gods might be fruitless or worse. Silence and endurance would appear to be the policy of prudence.

However that may be, one further passage demands examination; it contains side by side the two conceptions of divinity we have identified and allows us to understand the goals or ends of these two *Weltanschauungen*, if I may use the term. Still in his beggar's disguise, Odysseus urges the kindly suitor Amphinomus to get out while escape is still possible. He begins:

οὐδὲν ἀκιδνότερον γαῖα τρέφει ἀνθρώποιο
πάντων ὅσσα τε γαῖαν ἔπι πνείει τε καὶ ἕρπει.
οὐ μὲν γάρ ποτέ φησι κακὸν πείσεσθαι ὀπίσσω,
ὄφρ᾽ ἀρετὴν παρέχωσι θεοὶ καὶ γούνατ᾽ ὀρώρῃ·
ἀλλ᾽ ὅτε δὴ καὶ λυγρὰ θεοὶ μάκαρες τελέσωσι,
καὶ τὰ φέρει ἀεκαζόμενος τετληότι θυμῷ.
τοῖος γὰρ νόος ἐστὶν ἐπιχθονίων ἀνθρώπων
οἷον ἐπ᾽ ἦμαρ ἄγῃσι πατὴρ ἀνδρῶν τε θεῶν τε.

Of all things which breathe and walk upon the earth,
there is nothing more feeble than man.
For he says he will never suffer evil afterwards
while the gods grant him courage and strength;
but when, in fact, the blessed gods accomplish woes,
even these he must bear with an enduring heart.
For the mind of earthbound men
is such as the father of gods and men grants it, day by
day.

(18. 130-137)

Odysseus starts out from some general reflections on the nature of human life. His opening sentence calls to mind the words of Zeus in the *Iliad* when moved to pity the immortal horses of Achilles:

οὐ μὲν γάρ τί πού ἐστιν ὀϊζυρώτερον ἀνδρὸς
πάντων ὅσσα τε γαῖαν ἔπι πνείει τε καὶ ἕρπει.

Of all things that breathe and walk upon the earth,
there is nothing more wretched than man.
(XVII. 446-447)

Zeus dwells on the unbridgeable gulf between mortality and immortality. Odysseus' concern is more modest and characteristic of the *Odyssey*; it lies in the fragility of human happiness within the confines of mortality and the helplessness of man in the face of the random gifts of the gods. Not mortality, but the terrible instability of fortune trouble Odysseus. As he says, the only lesson to be learned from such a view is to bear with endurance what must be borne. One must, however, remember that in this speech Odysseus is trying to warn Amphinomus to leave, to avoid the coming destruction that awaits the suitors. Yet his lesson so far is endurance, not flight.

Now Odysseus continues: "For I once was on my way to being a man fortunate among men." On the basis of what has preceded, we expect Odysseus to give one of those accounts of his fall from prosperity, by the will of the gods, similar to his words to the nasty servant girl Melantho:

καὶ γὰρ ἐγώ ποτε οἶκον ἐν ἀνθρώποισιν ἔναιον
ὄλβιος ἀφνειόν. . . .
ἀλλὰ Ζεὺς ἀλάπαξε Κρονίων· ἤθελε γάρ που·

Even I once lived in a prosperous house,
fortunate among men. . . .
But Zeus, the son of Cronus, destroyed me, for somehow
he wished it.

(19. 75-76; 80)

Here, instead, a sudden shift shocks us:

πολλὰ δ' ἀτάσθαλ' ἔρεξα βίῃ καὶ κάρτεϊ εἴκων,
πατρί τ' ἐμῷ πίσυνος καὶ ἐμοῖσι κασιγνήτοισι.

I did many reckless things, yielding to force and violence,
and placing my trust in my father and brothers.

(18. 139-140)

We are unprepared for the novel idea of committing violent acts, even as we are strangers to the implication that the fall from prosperity is fit punishment for such violence. At the same time, we must realize that a statement of this kind is absolutely necessary to persuade Amphinomus to *do* something, instead of merely accepting whatever fate has in store for him.

Finally, Odysseus closes with an explicit message:

τῷ μή τίς ποτε πάμπαν ἀνὴρ ἀθεμίστιος εἴη,
ἀλλ' ὅ γε σιγῇ δῶρα θεῶν ἔχοι, ὅττι διδοῖεν.

Therefore, let no man be completely lawless,
but let him take in silence the gifts of the gods, whatever
they may give.

(18. 141-142)

The view of the gods as inscrutable donors of good and evil according to some unfathomable divine whim may lead to the *endurance* of misery and suffering; it cannot, however, encourage justice or piety. Only the hope or threat of divine reward or punishment can encourage the performance of just or pious acts. Hence to make Amphinomus *act*, Odysseus must shift from one conception to another.

Odysseus' words quietly suggest a possible tension between the truth of religion and its utility. It is a problem that Homer, who lays claim to superior knowledge of the gods, cannot and does not avoid. Suffice it to say for now that the contradictory views of divine activity expressed by the characters do not simply coalesce in some superficial manner, but run deep into the fabric of the poem. Furthermore, they cannot be understood as contradictory in a simple sense; the two conceptions of the gods teach different lessons and have different goals.

Turning now to what the characters *do*, to what happens in the poem, we can see that the working out of both views of the gods dominates the plot of the *Odyssey*. Leaving aside for a moment the wrath of Athena, we should look at the Polyphemus episode in these terms. The anger of Poseidon cannot by any means be viewed as an example of divine justice. Odysseus would be acquitted for the blinding of the Cyclops in any court of law on the grounds of self-defense and extenuating circumstances.[15] For his only alternative in Polyphe-

---

[15] Cf. Fenik (1974), pp. 210, 211: "the blinding was justified in terms of

mus' cave was to await his turn to be eaten. Yet no such considerations mitigate Poseidon's wrath. His motive is simply to avenge his son—brutal and impious though he may be. And to that end, he even enlists the support of Zeus (9. 553-555).

Similar but even more deadly is the fate of Odysseus' men on Thrinacia. Warned several times by Odysseus, they piously refrain from touching the cattle of the Sun.[16] But on the island a god becalms them. Starvation threatens. While the ever-vigilant Odysseus nods in a god-sent sleep, his men—with all due prayers and sacrifices and promises of restitution—slaughter the cattle for food. The cards are inexorably stacked against them. They are obliged to eat, and thereby to commit a crime, or to perish, just as with the Cyclops their choice had consisted either of maiming Polyphemus or of being eaten. But mortals, to remain mortals, must eat and avoid being eaten. Swift and complete punishment results; Helios demands the destruction of all of Odysseus' companions. Again, the extremity of their circumstances constitutes no defense. In both cases, Poseidon and Helios act with complete ruthlessness to protect their offended honor. The fundamental innocence of their victims receives no consideration whatsoever. One critic summarizes as follows:

> The relations between such gods and mankind are clearly not founded on justice, as may be seen from the reprisals they take against men in the poems. . . . The gods accept neither the plea of mistake, nor that of compulsion, nor that of self-defense, where their own interests are at stake.[17]

In the face of such gods who capriciously bestow good and evil, who ruthlessly protect their own prerogatives without any sense of justice or fairness, how does one live? The answer has already appeared on various occasions in the mouths of

---

Homeric or any other morality: Odysseus and his men would have perished if they had not acted. . . . This means, in turn, that it is impossible to justify Odysseus' sufferings at the hands of Poseidon in terms of Zeus' explanation of guilt and punishment in the prologue. . . ."

[16] Cf. Fenik (1974), pp. 212-13.

[17] Adkins (1960), pp. 62, 63.

several characters in the *Odyssey*: one must endure, try to survive as best one can by any means—by one's wits, if that is all one has. In addition, one is not compelled to practice justice, since the gods appear to have no interest in punishing crimes or rewarding virtuous actions. In other words, one is Odysseus, the much-enduring, much-suffering hero of many devices and many tricks. Odysseus' endurance and versatility, his amorality and his ability to live by his wits, to survive, make him the hero of a world without justice.

But that is not the whole story of the *Odyssey*. Throughout the poem, characters hope and pray to the gods for justice; and the final outcome answers their prayers. After all, Odysseus returns home, slaughters the suitors with the help of Athena, is reunited with his family, and reassumes the kingship of Ithaca. The suitors do pay for their crimes, just as Aegisthus paid for the murder of Agamemnon. So, on this occasion, justice is done, and a god, Athena, has actively promoted its cause.

In the last book, old Laertes, who has withdrawn from civil society and abdicated political responsibility in Odysseus' absence, learns of the slaughter of the suitors and cries out:

Ζεῦ πάτερ, ἦ ῥα ἔτ᾽ ἐστὲ θεοὶ κατὰ μακρὸν Ὄλυμπον,
εἰ ἐτεὸν μνηστῆρες ἀτάσθαλον ὕβριν ἔτισαν.

Father Zeus, you still are there, gods, on high Olympus,
if truly the suitors have paid for their reckless violence.

(24. 351-352)[18]

According to Laertes, the gods' existence is proved by their punishment of injustice. And to extrapolate from what he says, if the gods are never just, act only to protect their interests and according to whim, ultimately their very existence may be called into doubt. This raises a lurking question as to whether the gods can exist for any practical purpose without human belief in them. However that may be, Laertes' words suggest that men exert a kind of pressure on the gods to act justly,

[18] For the sentiment, compare Euripides *Suppliants* 731-733 and Fr. 577; also Aeschylus *Agamemnon* 1577ff.

at least once in a while. Otherwise, there is a danger that no one will attend to them.

Such, I believe, is the situation in Ithaca at the beginning of the poem. Things are stagnant, hopeless. Odysseus has been absent for twenty years; the suitors have been carousing in his palace for four; Penelope has run out of delaying tactics and spends her nights weeping, while Telemachus, on the verge of manhood, despairs over the fortunes of his house. Outside, political life has ceased; the assembly has not convened since Odysseus left for Troy. The suitors have succeeded in intimidating the citizens of Ithaca, who should be defending their king and his possessions.[19]

One is led to wonder whether the accusation with which the poem opens—that the gods are to blame for mortal ills—does not originate from Ithaca. It is the complaint of the good and innocent who feel oppressed and powerless. They cannot take comfort in the hope of rewards for virtue or punishment for wickedness in a life after death. The austere Homeric conception of the afterlife has the great advantage of relieving the living of fear of the dead; the shadowy ghosts in Hades, once buried, cannot haunt the living. A concomitant of this view is that it renders this life more poignantly precious and ultimately nobler precisely on account of its finitude. On the other hand, it has a signal disadvantage. The lack of any substantial existence after death renders impossible the deferral of individual justice. It therefore cannot be invoked to explain why the wicked sometimes prosper and the virtuous suffer. And we must remember that the suffering of the innocent is finally the greater cause of moral perplexity and outrage.

The answer to the problem of justice must, then, lie in the here and now. Two possibilities, both attested in early Greek thought, emerge. The iniquity of the one or the few is in fact

---

[19] This is the main point of the *agora* in Book 2 which demonstrates how the Ithacans have been reduced to silence and passivity by the bullying suitors. Telemachus' attempt to mobilize public opinion against them ends in failure and frustration.

punished, but such punishment also falls upon the innocent.[20] This explanation has no relevance to the situation at the beginning of the *Odyssey*; the suitors as yet still conduct themselves with impunity. The second solution proposes that the sins of the fathers are visited upon their innocent children.[21] In fact, several times in the *Odyssey*, the question is raised as to whether the behavior of the suitors toward the house of Odysseus can be explained as just revenge for wrongs suffered by them or their families at the hands of Odysseus.[22] But, on each occasion, Odysseus' goodness and fairness toward them is forcefully asserted,[23] and their crimes are compounded by their ingratitude.

If the mystery of evil abides, what remains but to blame the gods? In his passive despair, Telemachus has grown skeptical. He does not believe his father is alive; he even doubts he is his father's son. He doubts his own strength and questions the power or interest of the gods. To Nestor's well-intentioned remark that Telemachus would soon be rid of the suitors if Athena would stand by him, the young man responds resignedly:

οὐκ ἂν ἐμοί γε
ἐλπομένῳ τὰ γένοιτ᾽, οὐδ᾽ εἰ θεοὶ ὣς ἐθέλοιεν.

Not for me
may these things be, even if I should hope for them, nor
if the gods should wish it.

(3. 227-228)

But Athena, standing by his side at this very moment in the guise of Mentor, sharply rebukes Telemachus' skepticism.

Let us now recall that after the first Council of the Gods, Athena does not proceed to Ogygia, where Odysseus, whose misery she has just described, is held prisoner by the nymph

---

[20] For example, Hesiod, *Works and Days* 240ff.
[21] The *locus classicus* for this conception is, of course, Solon 13. 31-32 West.
[22] See, for instance, 2. 71-74.
[23] Cf. 16. 424-432.

Calypso. Instead, the goddess flies straight off to Ithaca. It is there that her help and intervention are most needed. It appears that Odysseus can wait, but the anomalous and anarchic situation in Ithaca requires Athena's immediate attention.

To return to the question from which we started, Athena stops being angry not primarily because Odysseus has changed or suffered enough during his ten years of wandering. It is not so much Odysseus himself, but the pressure of events on Ithaca that compels Athena to release Odysseus and to bring him home to set things right.

If this interpretation is correct, a better understanding emerges of the peculiar structure of the *Odyssey*. It is simple enough to enumerate some aspects of that peculiarity: the story takes up in Ithaca rather than on Calypso's isle; the first four books are devoted to Ithaca with even the prosperity and order of Sparta and Pylos seeming to describe Ithaca by contrast—all this we are told before we are permitted to focus on Odysseus. What is more, the whole second half of the poem concerns Ithaca. Lattimore remarks:

> Nearly nine books, more than twice the texts given to the Great Wanderings, are devoted to the time from Odysseus' arrival to his dropping of diguise and attack on the suitors, and for nearly nine books *very little happens*.[24]

But what does happen in these books is that the wickedness of the suitors and the virtue of those loyal to Odysseus are broadly developed in a leisurely fashion, so that the final outcome, the slaughter of the suitors, appears as the triumph of virtue over iniquity. Throughout, Athena goes so far as to egg on the suitors to act with increasing outrageousness, so that their punishment may seem even more exemplary.[25]

That final punishment is complete, and the *Odyssey* has a happy ending. Justice wins out, bad men meet a bad end, good men are rewarded, and Athena has benevolently and con-

[24] Lattimore (1965), p. 16 (italics mine).
[25] E.g., 18. 346-348; 20. 284-286, 345-346.

stantly labored to this end. Calling a halt to further reprisals, she inspires a truce in the last lines of the poem, inaugurating an era of peace and prosperity. The conclusion of the poem warns against wickedness and inculcates virtue and piety. The *Odyssey* ends as a moral tale with an edifying message.

But is such an interpretation sufficient? Can it be correct to view the poem simply as a poem of divine justice? One critic, whose work commands respect, Kitto, states the case for such a moral interpretation of the *Odyssey* with thoughtfulness and force, and he recognizes the manner in which the structure of the poem conveys the message that the gods "hate and punish, in the long run, human lawlessness."[26] Toward the end of his discussion, however, he poses the question of the relevance of Nausicaa, the Laestrygonians, and the rest to the moral earnestness of the poem, and responds that the question is "misconceived."[27] But the question is surely a valid one, and I must confess to being one of those who are unable to dismiss it so quickly. Just as I feel uneasy about an interpretation that focuses exclusively on Odysseus' adventures, I find myself equally dissatisfied with one that ignores them. Basically, the same kind of critical mistake is involved, placing the weight of interpretation on one part of the work, while playing down the rest. To view the *Odyssey* as a poem of divine justice ignores the darker moral contained in the wanderings of Odysseus, his experiences at the hands of the gods, and the very character and qualities of the hero of the poem.

Odysseus is somehow a misfit in the world of virtue and vice. Granted, many speak of him as a good and wise king and praise his gentleness and generosity.[28] Yet moral terms somehow fail to define him. His multiple qualities, his intelligence, his trickiness, his long-suffering endurance and courage, his ability to survive, are founded on, and bear witness to, a world not of justice, but of divine revenge and caprice. So we arrive once more at a curious paradox: the addressee

[26] Kitto (1966), p. 147.
[27] Kitto (1966), p. 140.
[28] For example, 2. 230-234; 4. 687-692.

of the poem is a man like the pious Eumaeus—the only character the poet calls "you"—but its hero is a man like Odysseus.

Beyond the piety of Eumaeus and the *metis* of Odysseus stands Homer, who encompasses and perhaps transcends both. His poem embraces both the Wanderings of Odysseus and the Revenge to form a unity. The Revenge insists upon a just world and benevolent gods; the Wanderings point to gods indifferent to men. Yet Homer does not simply assert the validity of one view over the other, nor does he proclaim one true and the other false. But does Homer try to mediate between these profoundly differing conceptions of the world, or does he, like Zeus at the beginning of the poem, merely imply their coexistence?

An answer to that question may lie in the exploration of what we earlier called the mutual dependencies of gods and men.[29] How and why do the gods need men, and for what reason, in turn, do men have need of the gods? Mutual interdependencies define, as we have seen, the nature of the Homeric hero; the heroes need the gods to be heroes. It is the marks of divine concern—be it divine favor or displeasure—that elevate men to the ranks of heroes. The gods, on the other hand, stand in need of the heroes for rather different reasons. Once the Olympian order has been permanently established and the power of Zeus made unassailable, there can be no substantial changes or revolutions in the eternal life of the gods. The Titanomachy is replaced by the mock theomachy (XXI. 385-513), a momentary diversion without serious issues or outcome, which provokes Zeus to Olympian laughter (XXI. 389-390). The gods need the heroes for entertainment, both for high tragedy and for low comedy.[30] But even the most tragic human drama enacted before the eyes of the gods reinforces their sense of their own superiority:

τῶν ἄλλων ἀπάνευθε καθέζετο κύδεϊ γαίων,
εἰσορόων Τρώων τε πόλιν καὶ νῆας Ἀχαιῶν
χαλκοῦ τε στεροπήν, ὀλλύντας τ᾽ ὀλλυμένους τε.

---

[29] Both the *Hymn to Demeter* and Aristophanes' *Birds* elaborate this theme.
[30] Cf. Griffin (1980), pp. 179ff.

Apart from the rest, [the son of Cronus] sat rejoicing in
  his glorious might,
observing the city of the Trojans and the ships of the
  Achaeans,
the flash of bronze, and both the killers and the killed.

(XI. 81-83)

The relations between the gods and mere *anthropoi* are, to
be sure far less intimate, as the gulf separating them becomes
wider. Yet even here the lack of self-sufficiency on the part
of the gods is apparent; the gods still require the attentions
of men in the form of prayers and sacrifices, which are at once
symbols of that separation and attempts to bridge it. The gods'
full enjoyment of their superiority remains incomplete without
the due homage of men.[31] Inattention to sacrifice or violations
of the honor due the gods meet with punishment as do attempts to usurp or challenge those honors. The germ of the
conception of divine envy, so prominent in Herodotus and
the Tragedians, can already be traced in the Homeric poems,
and not only in the exemplary cases of Thamyris and Eurytus.
Most touchingly, Penelope, finally reunited with her Odysseus, invokes it to explain their long separation:

θεοὶ δ᾽ ὤπαζον ὀϊζύν,
οἳ νῶϊν ἀγάσαντο παρ᾽ ἀλλήλοισι μένοντε
ἥβης ταρπῆναι καὶ γήραος οὐδὸν ἱκέσθαι.

The gods gave us misery,
they who begrudged us to remain together side by side,
to enjoy our prime and come together to the threshold of
  old age.

(23. 210-212)

The gods, Penelope suggests, were jealous of the happiness
she and Odysseus might have enjoyed, had their lives been
undisturbed.[32] While the gods care for the heroes, there is no

---

[31] Cf. 5. 100-102; 13. 128-130, 143-144.

[32] Similarly, 4. 181 and Schol. M.Q. *ad loc.* Cf. the discussion of *phthonos
theôn* in J. Opstelten, *Sophocles and Greek Pessimism* (Amsterdam, 1952),
pp. 232-39.

indication of their similar concern for mere *anthropoi*. But, nonetheless, the gods need men to reassure themselves of their blessedness, to maintain their position of superiority, and to preserve what they consider to be their prerogatives.

The corresponding need of men for the gods is based on an awareness of human powerlessness. That powerlessness is most acutely felt in the face of man's sense of his mortality. Yet here the uncompromising character of Homeric religion, which promises little in the afterlife and dwells insistently on the finitude of human existence, offers small solace. The heroes, to be sure, need the gods to win that glory and immortal fame which compensates at least in part for their mortality. But the promise of undying glory is neither proffered nor pursued by the common run of mankind, who must, willy-nilly, resign themselves to their mortality. Yet the *Odyssey*, which is far more concerned with men like us than with the heroes, and with the nature of common human experience rather than the great issue of mortality, tells us that "all men need the gods." That need arises not so much from man's sense of helplessness in the face of death, but from his awareness of his power-lessness in the face of injustice. Men harness the power of the gods to the cause of justice by invoking that power to punish evil-doers and to reward the virtuous. Both divine wrath and divine favor are brought down from the heavens to ensure the proper functioning of political and social communities. In the *Odyssey*, the wrath of Athena is finally deflected from Odysseus and transformed into righteous indignation against the suitors. Men need the gods to lend strength and majesty to justice.

To conclude, it is clear that neither men nor gods are self-sufficient but are bound together by mutual dependencies. We can now, I believe, answer the question whether Homer at-tempts to reconcile the double theodicy that informs his poem. Laertes' words—"You are still there, gods, on high Olympus, if truly the suitors have paid for their reckless violence"— point to the solution. The justice of the gods confirms their existence, while their indifference calls their meaning and, ultimately, their very existence into question. The prayers and expectations of men compel the gods to come down on the side of right at least once in a while. The occasional fulfillment of justice in an exemplary fashion by gods fundamentally indifferent to men but jealous of their prerogatives—perhaps that would be Homer's answer and the message of our *Odyssey*.

APPENDIX

DEMODOCUS AND HOMER

Readers will have noticed that I have refrained from taking a general stand on the question of Homeric composition, nor is an appendix the appropriate place to tackle so complex and controversial an issue. Moreover, as I stated at the beginning of this study, interpretation must remain primary; otherwise, all considerations of composition merely produce circular arguments. This is not to deny that specific points of interpretation may, in fact, have important implications for the problem of composition. What counts is the order of priorities.

The first song of Demodocus (8. 72-82) offers an example of the way the understanding of a particular passage can lead quite logically to a consideration of compositional questions. In this case, the compositional question is simultaneously an interpretive one concerning the relation between the *Iliad* and the *Odyssey*. I concluded my study of Demodocus' first song by suggesting that it both draws its inspiration from and looks back at the *Iliad*, and that it outlines a hypothetical alternative *Iliad*, modified and revised by the perspectives of the *Odyssey*.

Nagy's recent study of the hero in Epic[1] begins from an interpretation of this same passage; and although we are in close agreement concerning the substance and significance of the quarrel between Achilles and Odysseus, he comes to substantially different conclusions concerning the manner in which we ought to understand the relationship of the two Homeric Epics. To put it simply, Nagy argues that an epic tradition such as the one outlined by Demodocus did, in fact, exist, whereas I believe that Demodocus' first song alludes to a poem that never existed and was never composed. The silence of the post-Homeric tradition can, to be sure, be invoked to

[1] Nagy (1979), pp. 15-65.

strengthen my position, but I would concede that it need not be compelling. In the absence of positive evidence, the issues separating Nagy and myself must remain *sub judice*; yet because of their far-reaching implications, it seems appropriate to summarize his arguments and set out our differences.

Nagy, then, believes in the existence of the poem sketched by Demodocus in *Od*. 8. 72-82. But what appears to be echoes of the *Iliad* are not direct allusions to it at all. Since, Nagy claims, "our *Iliad* and *Odyssey* are parallel products of a parallel evolution,"[2] "it is not justifiable to claim that a passage in any text can refer to another passage in another text."[3] Apparent similarities are to be understood as references to the repertory of traditional material common to both the *Iliad* and the *Odyssey*. In this repertory, disputes involving rival heroes form a standard motif; and a traditional element in such rivalries is the opposition between *bie* and *metis*, which clearly underlies the quarrel adumbrated in Demodocus' song. On this basis, Nagy proceeds to characterize that song as follows:

> Demodokos, then, is alluding to an *Iliad*, but not to our *Iliad*. Like our *Iliad*, the *Iliad* that Demodokos could have sung would feature the *mênis* 'anger' of Achilles and Apollo. Unlike our *Iliad*, however, this Iliadic tradition would feature Odysseus, not Agamemnon, as the prime offender of Achilles. Unlike our *Iliad*, this *Iliad* would have the chief resentment of Achilles center on the slighting of his *biē* 'might'. An *Iliad* composed by Demodokos would have been a poem with a structure more simple and more broad, with an Achilles who is even perhaps more crude than the ultimately refined hero that we see emerging at the end of our *Iliad*. I have little doubt that such an *Iliad* was indeed in the process of evolving when it was heard in the *Odyssey* tradition which evolved into our *Odyssey*.[4]

[2] Nagy (1979), p. 41.
[3] Nagy (1979), p. 42.
[4] Nagy (1979), p. 65.

It is, of course, impossible to prove or disprove the existence of such poem. But Nagy's general approach solves—or at least circumvents—a very sticky problem in Homeric studies. It permits us to accept all the apparent allusions and cross-references between the Homeric Epics without, however, demanding our acceptance of literal cross-references between fixed texts. In other words, an apparent allusion in the *Odyssey* to an incident in the *Iliad* need not mean an allusion to the *Iliad* as we have it, but rather to that repertory of traditional motifs incorporated into our *Iliad*. In short, we can remain good Parryists and still allow ourselves to interpret the Homeric texts.

The first generation of Parryists had essentially removed the possibility of interpretation from the Homeric poems. What was allowed to every other ancient author was ruled impermissible for Homer. While I believe that a long oral tradition may stand behind Homer, I remain uncertain of the relation of the *Iliad* and the *Odyssey* to that tradition. But I, like other Homerists, am grateful to Nagy and others for restoring the possibility of interpretation to the Homeric texts—by whatever means. But that gratitude masks some genuine differences.

I am not convinced that the Tradition, with a capital 'T,' can bear the heavy burden Nagy assigns to it. In and of itself, the appeal to Tradition smacks a little of questionable Romantic notions. While it may be able to expand or compress, modify or recombine older material, and even introduce novel motifs and new conceptions, can the Tradition make cross-references where the precise context of the allusion carries the point? Or, finally, can the Tradition make jokes? Nagy himself speaks rather uncomfortably of the self-consciousness and self-reflectiveness of the Tradition.[5] But do such practices not require the existence of a closed tradition, one that has become fixed into a text?[6]

There remain some other objections which bear specifically

[5] Nagy (1979), pp. 20, 21.
[6] Cf. Pucci (1979), p. 125.

on Nagy's interpretation of Demodocus' song. The Achilles of Demodocus' alternative *Iliad* would, Nagy admits, have to be cruder than the "ultimately refined hero" of our *Iliad*, to be, in other words, a kind of Heracles, as the *Odyssey* presents him. Yet it is one of the great strokes of our *Odyssey* that the Achilles figure is in no wise coarsened, that he there remains the same noble and tormented hero we know from the *Iliad*. The strategy of the *Odyssey* is precisely to leave the greatness of Achilles intact because it ultimately serves to enhance the greatness of Odysseus.

The figure of Odysseus presents more complex problems. The outlines of his character suggest his origins in the realm of folktale and *Märchen*, in other words, in subepic genres. He is never quite at home in the heroic tradition, as his subsequent post-Homeric literary fortunes attest. He is more suited to Comedy; in Tragedy, he is either untragic (*Ajax*) or villainous, as in the *Philoctetes*. At any rate, the ambiguities of his character and origins deny him a stable heroic presence.

The fact remains that the elevation of Odysseus to heroic stature is a unique event in the Greek tradition. It is also a fragile and momentary accomplishment, the highly self-conscious culmination of a process gradually reversed in the post-Homeric age. To create a heroic Odysseus equal or superior to Achilles requires, as I have argued, a careful selection from traditional material—and even the self-conscious suppresion of parts of that tradition. I find it difficult to accept that the "Tradition" itself is capable of such profound self-reflection.

Nagy notes, as have others, the perfect complementarity of the *Iliad* and the *Odyssey*. "Between the two of them, the *Iliad* and the *Odyssey* manage to incorporate and orchestrate something of practically everything that was once thought worth preserving from the Heroic Age."[7] Yet within this totality, there appears to be "a deliberate avoidance"[8] of any overlapping. Nagy's explanation of what is known as Monro's Law seems peculiarly strained:

[7] Nagy (1979), p. 18.
[8] Nagy (1979), p. 21. Monro's Law already finds a formulation in the E Scholium at 3. 248: καλῶς ἀναπλήρωσις τῆς Ἰλιάδος ἡ Ὀδύσσεια λέγεται. ἃ γὰρ κατέλειψεν ἐκεῖ, ἐνταῦθα λέγει.

If the avoidance was indeed deliberate, it would mean
that the *Odyssey* displays an awareness of the *Iliad* by
steering clear of it. Or rather, it may be a matter of
evolution. Perhaps it was part of the Odyssean tradition
to veer away from the Iliadic. . . . there seems to be something traditionally self-conscious about all this. It is as if
there were a traditional suppression of anything overtly
Iliadic in the *Odyssey*.[9]

Now, traditional poetry is notoriously promiscuous. A good
story is readily adapted and incorporated into a different context. If it is a good story, no one will object that it really
"belongs" in the original narrative. The Odyssean poet would
have no reason to avoid references to incidents or episodes
drawn from the tradition of the *Iliad*; indeed, his audience
might well have applauded hearing the old stories in an un-
familiar setting. But a poet who consciously set out both to
rival and complement an existing *Iliad* might well suppress
Iliadic elements in his own poem. One could, indeed, argue
that such deliberate suppression suggests the identity of the
poet of the *Iliad* and the *Odyssey*. And another master storyteller will support such an argument. Odysseus himself refuses to repeat the tale of his years with Calypso, since he has
told it once before:

> τί τοι τάδε μυθολογεύω;
> ἤδη γάρ τοι χθιζὸς ἐμυθεόμην ἐνὶ οἴκῳ
> σοὶ καὶ ἰφθίμῃ ἀλόχῳ· ἐχθρὸν δέ μοί ἐστιν
> αὖτις ἀριζήλως εἰρημένα μυθολογεύειν.

> Why should I tell the story of these things?
> For already yesterday I told the story in your house
> to you and your great wife; it is hateful to me
> again to tell the story of things that have been said
> clearly.
>   (12. 450-453)

The *Odyssey* forms the perfect complement to the *Iliad*, by
no means only in its avoidance of overlapping incidents. On

---

[9] Nagy (1979), p. 21.

a subtler level, it corresponds and responds to the deepest concerns of the *Iliad*, some of which I have tried to elucidate in this study. Moreover, the *Odyssey* regards itself as emphatically post-Iliadic; it looks back at the *Iliad* and the world there represented as belonging to the past. I find it hard to believe that the poet whose shaping intelligence informs our *Odyssey* did not keep his eye constantly on the *Iliad*.

BIBLIOGRAPHIC REFERENCES

Adami, F. 1930. "Zu P. Linde, Homerische Selbsterläuterungen." *Glotta* 18: 111.

Adkins, A.W.H. 1960. *Merit and Responsibility: A Study in Greek Values.* Oxford.

―――. 1972. "Homeric Gods and the Values of Homeric Society." *Journal of Hellenic Studies* 92:1-19.

Ameis, K. F. and Hentze, C. 1879-1880. *Anhang zu Homers Odyssee.* 4 vols. Leipzig.

―――, eds. 1908-1920. *Homers Odyssee.* Revised by P. Cauer. 2 vols. in 4. Leipzig. Abbreviated as Ameis-Hentze.

Amory, A. 1957. "Omens and Dreams in the Odyssey." Ph.D. dissertation, Harvard University.

Athanassakis, A. N., trans. 1976. *The Homeric Hymns.* Baltimore.

Auerbach, E. 1953. "Odysseus' Scar." In *Mimesis: The Representation of Reality in Western Literature,* translated by W. R. Trask, pp. 3-23. Princeton.

Austin, N. 1966. "The Function of Digressions in the Iliad." *Greek, Roman and Byzantine Studies* 7:295-312.

―――. 1975. *Archery at the Dark of the Moon: Poetic Problems in Homer's Odyssey.* Berkeley.

Bakker, W. F. 1966. *The Greek Imperative.* Amsterdam.

Barmeyer, E. 1968. *Die Musen: Ein Beitrag zur Inspirationstheorie.* Munich.

Bassett, S. E. 1918. "Athena and the Adventures of Odysseus." *Classical Journal* 13:528-29.

―――. 1923. "The Proems of the Iliad and the Odyssey." *American Journal of Philology* 44:339-48.

Bechert, J. 1964. *Die Diathesen von ἰδεῖν und ὁρᾶν bei Homer.* Münchener Studien zur Sprachwissenschaft 6. Munich.

Bechtel, F. 1917. *Die historischen Personnenamen des Griechischen bis zur Kaiserzeit.* Halle.

Becker, O. 1937. *Das Bild des Weges*. Hermes Einzelschriften 4. Berlin.

Belzner, E. 1912. *Homerische Probleme*. Vol. 2. Leipzig.

Benardete, S. 1963. "Achilles and the Iliad." *Hermes* 91:1-16.

———. 1967. "Hesiod's *Works and Days*: A First Reading." ΑΓΩΝ 1:150-70.

———. 1968. "The *Aristeia* of Diomedes and the Plot of the Iliad." ΑΓΩΝ 2:10-38.

Benveniste, E. 1966. *Problèmes de linguistique générale*. 2 vols. Paris.

Besslich, S. 1966. *Schweigen—Verschweigen—Übergehen: Die Darstellung des Unausgeprochenen in der Odyssee*. Heidelberg.

Bethe, E. 1922. *Homer, Dichtung und Sage II: Odyssee, Kyklos, Zeitbestimmung*. Leipzig.

———. 1927. *Homer, Dichtung und Sage III: Die Sage vom Troischen Kriege*. Leipzig.

Bielohlavek, K. 1957. "Zu den ethischen Werten in Idealtypen der griechischen Heldensage (Herakles und Achilles)." *Wiener Studien* 70:22-43.

Bona, G. B. 1966. *Studi sull' Odissea*. Turin.

Borchardt, J. 1972. *Homerische Helme: Helmenformen der Ägäis in ihren Beziehungen zu orientalischen und europäischen Helmen in der Bronze- und frühen Eisenzeit*. Mainz.

Bowra, C. M. 1930. *Tradition and Design in the Iliad*. Oxford.

Bradley, E. 1968. "The Hybris of Odysseus." *Soundings* 51:33-44.

Brelich, A. 1958. *Gli eroi greci*. Rome.

Bremer, D. 1976. *Licht und Dunkel in der frühgriechischen Dichtung. Archiv für Begriffsgeschichte*. Suppl. 1. Bonn.

Burkert, W. 1960. "Das Lied von Ares und Aphrodite." *Rheinisches Museum* 103:130:44.

———. 1972. "Die Leistung eines Kreophylos: Kreophyleer, Homeriden und die archaische Heraklesepik." *Museum Helveticum* 29:74-85.

———. 1977. *Griechische Religion der archaischen und klassischen Epoche.* Stuttgart.

Calame, C. 1977a. "Le mythe des Cyclopes dans l'Odyssée." In *Il Mito Greco: Atti del Convegno Internazionale Urbino 1973,* edited by B. Gentili and G. Paioni, pp. 369-91. Rome.

———. 1977b. "L'univers cyclopéen de l'Odyssée." *Živa Antika* 27:315-22.

Calhoun, G. M. 1937a. "The Higher Criticism on Olympus." *American Journal of Philology* 58:257-74.

———. 1937b. "Homer's Gods: Prolegomena." *Transactions and Proceedings of the American Philological Association* 68:11-25.

———. 1939. "Homer's Gods—Myth and Märchen." *American Journal of Philogy* 60:1-28.

———. 1940. "The Divine Entourage in Homer." *American Journal of Philology* 61:257-77.

Carpenter, R. 1946. *Folk Tale, Fiction and Saga in the Homeric Epics.* Berkeley.

Cauer, P. 1923. *Grundfragen der Homerkritik.* 3rd ed. Leipzig.

Chantraine, P. 1954. "Le Divin et les dieux chez Homère." In *La Notion du divin depuis Homère jusqu'à Platon. Entretiens sur l'antiquité classique* 1:47-80. Vandoevres.

———. 1968-1980. *Dictionnaire étymologique de la langue grecque.* Paris. Abbreviated as Chantraine.

Clay, J. S. 1972. "The Planktai and Moly: Divine Naming and Knowing in Homer." *Hermes* 100:127-31.

———. 1974. "Demas and Audê: The Nature of Divine Transformation in Homer." *Hermes* 102-129-36.

———. 1976. "The Beginning of the Odyssey." *American Journal of Philology* 97:313-26.

———. 1980. "Goat Island: *Od.* 9.116-141." *Classical Quarterly* 30:261-64.

———. 1981-1982. "Immortal and Ageless Forever." *Classical Journal* 77:112-17.

Considine, P. 1966. "Some Homeric Terms for Anger." *Acta Classica* 9:15-25.

Detienne, M. 1967. *Les maîtres de vérité dans la Grèce archaïque*. Paris.

———. 1972. *Les jardins d'Adonis: La mythologie des aromates en Grèce*. Paris.

———. 1977. *Dionysos mis à mort*. Paris.

——— and Vernant, J.-P. 1974. *Les ruses de l'intelligence: la mètis des Grecs*. Paris.

Diehls, H. and Kranz, W., eds. 1954. *Die Fragmente der Vorsokratiker*. 7th ed. Berlin. Abbreviated as *DK*.

Dietrich, B. C. 1965. *Death, Fate and the Gods*. London.

Dimock, G. 1962. "The Name of Odysseus." In *Homer: A Collection of Critical Essays*, edited by G. Steiner and R. Fagles, pp. 106-121. Englewood Cliffs, N.J.

———. 1971. "Punishment in the Odyssey." *Yale Review* n.s. 60:199-214.

Dindorf, W., ed. 1855. *Scholia graeca in Homeri Odysseam*. 2 vols. Oxford. Cited as Scholia (*Odyssey*).

Dirlmeier, F. 1966. *Die Giftpfeile des Odysseus*. Heidelberg.

———. 1967. *Die Vogelgestalt homerischer Götter*. Heidelberg.

Dodds, E. R. 1951. *The Greeks and the Irrational*. Berkeley.

Dover, K. J. 1975. *Greek Popular Morality in the Time of Plato and Aristotle*. Oxford.

Ehmark, E. 1935. *The Idea of God in Homer*. Uppsala.

Else, G. F. 1949. "God and Gods in Early Greek Thought." *Transactions and Proceedings of the American Philological Association* 80:24-36.

Erbse, H. 1972. *Beiträge zum Verständnis der Odyssee*. Berlin.

———, ed. 1969-77. *Scholia graeca in Homeri Iliadem*. 5 vols. Berlin. Cited in Scholia (*Iliad*).

Eustathius. 1825-1829. *Eustathii Commentarii ad Homeri Iliadem et Odysseam pertinentes ad fidem exempli Romani editi*. Leipzig.

Fahr, W. 1969. ΘΕΟΥΣ ΝΟΜΙΖΕΙΝ. Spudasmata 26. Hildesheim.

Fenik, B. 1964. *Iliad X and the Rhesus: The Myth*. Collection Latomus 73. Brussels.

————. 1974. *Studies in the Odyssey*. Hermes Einzelschriften 30. Wiesbaden.

Finley, J. H. 1978. *Homer's Odyssey*. Cambridge, Mass.

Finley, M. I. 1978. *The World of Odysseus*. 3rd ed. New York.

Fitzgerald, R., trans. 1961. *Homer: The Odyssey*. New York.

Foley, H. 1978. "Reverse Similes and Sex Roles in the Odyssey." *Arethusa* 11:7-26.

Frame, D. 1978. *The Myth of Return in Early Greek Epic*. New Haven.

Frazer, J. G., ed. 1921. *Apollodorus*. 2 vols. Cambridge, Mass.

Friedländer, P. 1907. *Herakles*. Philologische Untersuchungen 19. Berlin.

Frisk, H. 1946. "ΜΗΝΙΣ: Zur Geschichte eines Begriffes." *Eranos* 44:28-40.

————. 1960-1972. *Griechisches etymologisches Wörterbuch*. Heidelberg. Abbreviated as Frisk.

Fritz, K. von. 1945-46. "Greek Prayer." *Review of Religion* 10:5-39.

Gaisser, J. H. 1969. "A Structural Analysis of the Digressions in the Iliad and the Odyssey." *Harvard Studies in Classical Philology* 73:1-43.

Galinsky, G. K. 1972. *The Herakles Theme*. Oxford.

Gernet, L. 1968. "Dolon le loup." In *Anthropologie de la Grèce antique*. Paris.

Glenn, J. 1971. "The Polyphemus Folktale and Homer's *Kyklopeia*." *Transactions and Proceedings of the American Philological Association* 102:133-81.

Greene, W. C. 1944. *Moira*. Cambridge.

Greindl, M. 1938. ΚΛΕΟΣ ΚΥΔΟΣ ΕΥΧΟΣ ΤΙΜΗ ΦΑΤΙΣ ΔΟΞΑ. Langerich.

Griffin, J. 1980. *Homer on Life and Death*. Oxford.

Groningen, B. A. van. 1946. "The Proems of the Iliad and Odyssey." *Mededeelingen der Koninklijke Nederlandsche Akademie van Wetenschappen, Afd. Letterkunde 9*, 8:279-93.

Güntert, H. 1919. *Kalypso: Bedeutungsgeschichtliche Unter-*

suchungen auf dem Gebiete der indogermanischen Sprachen. Halle.

Hart, W. M. 1943. "High Comedy in the Odyssey." *California Publications in Classical Philology* 12:263-78.

Hedèn, E. 1912. *Homerische Götterstudien.* Uppsala.

Heubeck, A. 1954. *Der Odyssee-Dichter und die Ilias.* Erlangen.

Hicks, R. D., trans. 1959. *Diogenes Laertius: Lives of the Philosophers.* Vol. 3: *Plato.* Cambridge, Mass.

Hirzel, R. 1902. *Der Eid.* Leipzig.

Hölscher, U. 1939. *Untersuchungen zur Form der Odyssee.* Hermes Einzelschriften 6. Berlin.

Hunger, G. 1962. "Die Odysseusgestalt in Odyssee und Ilias." Dissertation, University of Kiel.

Irmscher, J. 1950. *Götterzorn bei Homer.* Leipzig.

Jacoby, F. 1923-1958. *Die Fragmente der griechischen Historiker.* Berlin and Leiden. Abbreviated as *Fr. Gr. H.*

———. 1933. "Die geistige Physiognomie der Odyssee." *Antike* 9:159-94.

Jaeger, W. 1926. "Solons Eunomie." *Sitzungsberichte der Preussischen Akademie der Wissenschaften, Phil. hist. Kl,* pp. 69-85.

Jeanmaire, H. 1939. *Couroi et Courètes: Essai sur l'éducation spartiate et sur les rites d'adolescence dans l'antiquité hellénique.* Lille.

Jørgensen, O. 1904. "Das Auftreten der Götter in den Büchern ι-μ der Odyssee." *Hermes* 39:357-82.

Kahn, C. H. 1979. *The Art and Thought of Heraclitus.* Cambridge.

Kahn, L. 1978. *Hermès passe ou les ambiguïtés de la communication.* Paris.

Kakrides, T. 1921. "Die Bedeutung von πολύτροπος in der Odyssee." *Glotta* 11:288-91.

Keller, O. 1909. *Die Antike Tierwelt.* 2 vols. Leipzig.

Kirchhoff, A. 1879. *Die homerische Odyssee.* 2nd ed. Berlin.

Kirk, G. S. 1970. *Myth: Its Meaning and Functions in Ancient and Other Cultures.* Cambridge.

———— and Raven, D. S. 1957. *The Presocratic Philosophers.* Cambridge.

Kittel, G., ed. 1949-1978. *Theologisches Wörterbuch zum Neuen Testament.* Stuttgart.

Kitto, H.D.F. 1966. *Poiesis: Structure and Thought.* Berkeley.

Kleinknecht, H. 1958. "Platonisches im Homer." *Gymnasium* 65:59-75.

Klingner, F. 1964. "Über die Dolonie." In *Studien zur griechischen und römischen Literatur.* Zurich.

Köhnken, A. 1976. "Die Narbe des Odysseus." *Antike und Abendland* 22:101-114.

Krarup, P. 1948. "Verwendung von Abstracta in der direkten Rede bei Homer." *Classica et Mediaevalia* 10:1-17.

Krehmer, W. 1973. "Zur Begegnung zwichen Odysseus und Athene." Inaugural-Dissertation, University of Erlangen-Nürnberg.

Kretschmer, P. 1940. "Die vorgriechischen Sprach- und Volksschichten." *Glotta* 28:234-79.

————. 1947. "NEKTAP." *Anzeiger der Oesterreichische Akademie der Wissenschaft, Phil.-hist. kl.* 84:13-26.

Kuiper, K. 1919. "De Idomeneo ac Merione." *Mnemosyne* 47:35-54.

Kullmann, W. 1956. *Das Wirken der Götter in der Ilias: Untersuchungen zur Frage der Entstehung des homerischen Götterapparats.* Berlin.

Lactacz, J. 1975. "Zur Forschungsarbeit an den direkten Reden bei Homer." *Gräzer Beiträge* 3:395-422.

Lattimore, R., trans. 1965. *The Odyssey of Homer.* New York.

Lehrs, K. 1864. "Das Proömium der Odyssee." *Rheinisches Museum* 19:302-306.

————. 1882. *De Aristarchi studiis Homericis.* Leipzig.

Leitzke, E. 1930. *Moira und Gottheit im alten griechischen Epos.* Göttingen.

Lesky, A. 1967. "Homeros." *Sonderausgabe der Paulyschen Realencyclopädie der classischen Altertumswissenschaft.* Stuttgart. (= *RE* Suppl. 11:687-846).

Leumann, M. 1950. *Homerische Wörter.* Schweizerische Beiträge zur Altertumswissenschaft 3. Basel.

Levin, S. 1971. "The Etymology of νέκταρ: Exotic Scents in Early Greece." *Studi micenei ed egeo-anatolici* 13:31-50.

Lloyd-Jones, H. 1971. *The Justice of Zeus.* Berkeley.

Lobel, E. and Page, D. eds. 1955. *Poetarum Lesbiorum Fragmenta.* Oxford. Abbreviated as L.-P.

Lohmann, D. 1970. *Die Komposition der Reden in der Ilias.* Berlin.

Lowenstam, S. 1975. "The Typological Death of Patroklos." Ph.D. dissertation, Harvard University.

Luther, W. 1935. *Wahrheit und Lüge im ältesten Griechentum.* Leipzig.

Maehler, H. 1963. *Die Auffassung des Dichterberufs im Frühen Griechentum.* Hypomnemata 5. Göttingen.

Marg, W. 1956. "Das erste Lied des Demodocus." In *Navicula Chiloniensis: Festschrift für F. Jacoby,* pp. 16-29. Leiden.

———. 1957. *Homer über die Dichtung.* Orbis Antiquus 11. Münster.

Maronitis, D. N. 1973. Ἀναζήτηση καὶ Νόστος τοῦ Ὀδυσσέα: Ἡ Διαλεκτικὴ τῆς Ὀδύσσειας. Athens.

Mellitzer, J. 1968. "Das Wirken der Götter in der Odyssee." Ph.D. dissertation, University of Vienna.

Merry, W. W., ed. 1901. *Homer: Odyssey* 2 vols. Oxford.

Mette, H. 1960. "Schauen und Staunen." *Glotta* 39:49-71.

Muellner, L. 1976. *The Meaning of Homeric* EYXOMAI *through its Formulas.* Innsbruck.

Murray, G. 1934. *The Rise of the Greek Epic.* 4th ed. Oxford.

Nägelsbach, C. F. 1840. *Die homerische Theologie.* Nuremberg.

Nagy, G. 1974. *Comparative Studies in Greek and Indic Meter.* Cambridge, Mass.

———. 1976. "The Name of Achilles." In *Studies in Greek, Italic, and Indo-European Linguistics Offered to Leonard R. Palmer,* pp. 209-237. Innsbruck.

———. 1979. *The Best of the Achaeans: Concepts of the Hero in Archaic Greek Poetry.* Baltimore.

Nestle, W. 1940. *Vom Mythos zum Logos: Die Selbstentfaltung des griechischen Denkens von Homer bis auf die Sophistik und Sokrates.* Stuttgart.

Nilsson, M. 1924. "Götter und Psychologie bei Homer." *Archiv für Religionswissenschaft* 22:363-90.

———. 1955. *Geschichte der griechischen Religion*. Vol. 1. 3rd ed. Munich.

Nitzsch, G. W. 1840. *Erklärende Anmerkungen zu Homers Odyssee*. Hanover.

Opstelten, J. 1952. *Sophocles and Greek Pessimism*. Amsterdam.

Otterlo, W.A.A. van. 1944. "Untersuchungen über Begriff, Anwendung, und Entstehung der griechischen Ringkomposition." *Mededeelingen der Koninklijke Nederlandsche Akademie van Wetenschappen, Afd. Letterkunde* n.s. 7, 3:131-76.

———. 1948. *De Ringcompositie als Opbouwprincipe in de epische Gedichten van Homerus*. Verhandel. der Nederlandsche Akademie van Wetenschappen, Afd. Letterkunde 51, 1. Amsterdam.

Otto, R. 1922. *Das Heilige*. 9th ed. Breslau.

Otto, W. F. 1954. *The Homeric Gods*. Translated by M. Hadas. New York.

———. 1961. *Die Musen*. Darmstadt.

Page, D. 1955. *The Homeric Odyssey*. Oxford.

———. 1973. *Folktales in Homer's Odyssey*. Cambridge, Mass.

Pape, W. and Benseler, G. E. 1911. *Griechische Eigennamen*. 2 vols. Braunschweig.

Parke, H. and Wormell, D. 1956. *The Delphic Oracle*. 2 vols. Oxford.

Parry, A. 1971. Introduction to *The Making of Homeric Verse: The Collected Papers of Milman Parry*. Oxford.

Parry, M. 1971. *The Making of Homeric Verse: The Collected Papers of Milman Parry*. Edited by A. Parry. Oxford.

Pearson, A. C., ed. 1917. *The Fragments of Sophocles*. 3 vols. Cambridge.

Petegorsky, D. "The Cretan Tales, the Doloneia, and the Bow of Odysseus." Unpublished paper.

Pettazzoni, R. 1956. *The All-Knowing God*. Translated by H. J. Rose. London.

Philippson, P. 1947. "Die vorhomerische und die homeriche Gestalt des Odysseus." *Museum Helveticum* 4:8-22.

Podlecki, A. 1961. "Guest-gifts and Nobodies in Odyssey 9." *Phoenix* 15:125-33.

Pope, A. 1967. "Preface to the Iliad." In *The Poems of Alexander Pope*. Twickenham Edition, Vol. 7. London.

Prinz, F. 1974. "Herakles." In *Paulys Realencyclopädie des classischen Altertumswissenschaft*. Suppl. 14:137-96. Munich.

Privitera, G. A. 1970. *Dioniso in Omero*. Rome.

Pucci, P. 1971. "Lévi-Strauss and Classical Culture." *Arethusa* 4:103-117.

———. 1977. *Hesiod and the Language of Poetry*. Baltimore.

———. 1979. "The Song of the Sirens." *Arethusa* 12:121-32.

Radermacher, L. 1916. "Die Erzählungen der Odyssee." *Sitzungsberichte der Kais. Akademie der Wissenschaften in Wien. Phil.-hist. Kl.* 178:1-59.

———. 1943. *Mythos und Sage bei den Griechen*. Munich.

Rank, L. 1951. *Etymologiseering en verwandte Verschijneselen bij Homerus*. Assen.

Ranke, F. 1881. *Homerische Untersuchungen I: Doloneia*. Leipzig.

Redfield, J. 1975. *Nature and Culture in the Iliad: The Tragedy of Hector*. Chicago.

Reinhardt, K. 1960a. "Die Abenteuer der Odyssee." In *Tradition und Geist: Gesammelte Essays zur Dichtung*, pp. 47-124. Göttingen.

———. 1960b. "Homer und die Telemachie." In *Tradition und Geist: Gesammelte Essays zur Dichtung*, pp. 37-46.

———. 1960c. "Das Parisurteil." In *Tradition und Geist: Gesammelte Essays zur Dichtung*, pp. 16-36.

———. 1960d. "Traditions und Geist im homerischen Epos." In *Tradition und Geist: Gesammelte Essays zur Dichtung*, pp. 5-15.

———. 1960e. "Walter F. Otto." In *Vermächtnis der Antike: Gesammelte Essays zur Philosophie und Geschichtsschreibung*, pp. 377-79. Göttingen.

————. 1961. *Die Ilias und ihr Dichter.* Edited by U. Hölscher. Göttingen.

Risch, E. 1947. "Namensdeutungen und Worterklärungen bei den ältesten griechischen Dichtern." In *Eumusia: Festgabe für E. Howald,* pp. 72-91. Zurich.

Roeger, J. 1924. *ΑΙΔΟΣ ΚΥΝΕΗ.* Graz.

Rohde, E. 1895. "Nekyia." *Rheinisches Museum* 50:600-635.

————. 1903. *Psyche.* 3rd ed. Tübingen.

Roscher, W. H., ed. 1884-1937. *Ausführliches Lexikon der griechischen und römischen Mythologie.* Leipzig. Cited as Roscher.

Rose, H. J. 1956. "Divine Disguisings." *Harvard Theological Review* 49:63-72.

Rüter, K. 1969. *Odysseeinterpretationen: Untersuchungen zum ersten Buch und zur Phaiakis.* Edited by K. Matthiessen. Hypomnemata 19. Göttingen.

Russo, J. 1968. "Homer against his Tradition." *Arion* 7:275-95.

———— and Simon, B. 1968. "Homeric Psychology and the Oral Epic Tradition." *Journal of the History of Ideas* 29:483-98.

Schadewaldt, W. 1958. "Der Prolog der Odyssee." *Harvard Studies in Classical Philology* 63:15-32.

————. 1960. "Der Helios-Zorn in der Odyssee." In *Studi in onore di L. Castiglione,* pp. 861-76. Florence.

Schein, S. 1970. "Odysseus and Polyphemus in the Odyssey." *Greek, Roman and Byzantine Studies* 11:73-83.

Schmidt, J.H.H. 1879. *Synonymik der griechischen Sprache.* Vol. 3. Leipzig.

Schmidt, J. O. 1885. *Ulixes Posthomericus.* Berlin.

Schrade, H. 1950. "Der homerische Hephaestus." *Gymnasium* 57:38-55;94-122.

————. 1952. *Götter und Menschen Homers.* Stuttgart.

Schrader, H., ed. 1890. *Porphyrii Quaestionum Homericarum reliquiae ad Odysseam pertinentium.* Leipzig.

Schwartz, E. 1924. *Die Odyssee.* Munich.

Schwyzer, E. 1931. "Drei griechische Wörter." *Rheinisches Museum* 80:209-217.

Scott, J. A. 1936. "The First Book of the Odyssey." *Transactions and Proceedings of the American Philological Association* 67:1-6.

Sedlmayer, H. 1910. "Lexikalisches und Exegetisches zu Homer." *Zeitschrift für die Oesterreichischen Gymnasien* 61:294.

Segal, C. P. 1962. "The Phaeacians and the Symbolism of Odysseus' Return." *Arion* 1, 4:17-64.

Severus, E. von. 1969. "Gebet I." In *Reallexikon für Antike und Christentum*, edited by T. Klauser, Vol. 8:1134-258. Stuttgart.

Severyns, A. 1966. *Les dieux d'Homère*. Paris.

Shannon, R. 1975. *The Arms of Achilles and Homeric Compositional Technique*. Mnemosyne Suppl. 36. Leiden.

Shewan, A. 1911. *The Lay of Dolon*. London.

Snell, B. 1924. *Die Ausdrücke für den Begriff des Wissens in der vor-platonischen Philosophie*. Philologische Untersuchungen 29. Berlin.

———. 1975. *Die Entdeckung des Geistes: Studien zur Entstehung des europäischen Denkens bei den Griechen*. 4th ed. Göttingen.

Stanford, W. B. 1939. *Ambiguity in Greek Literature*. Oxford.

———. 1950. "Homer's Use of Personal πολυ- Compounds." *Classical Philology* 45:108-110.

———. 1952. "The Homeric Etymology of the Name Odysseus." *Classical Philology* 47:209-213.

———. 1963. *The Ulysses Theme: A Study in the Adaptability of a Traditional Hero*. 2nd ed. Oxford.

———, ed. 1965. *The Odyssey of Homer*. 2nd rev. ed. London.

Suerbaum, W. 1968. "Die Ich-Erzählungen des Odysseus." *Poetica* 2:150-77.

Sulzberger, M. 1926. "ONOMA ΕΠΩΝΥΜΟΝ: Les noms propres chez Homère." *Revue des Etudes Grecques* 39:381-447.

Thieme, P. 1968. "Nektar" and "Ambrosia." In *Indogermanische Dichtersprache*, edited by R. Schmitt, pp. 102-112 and 113-32. Darmstadt.

Thornton, A. 1970. *People and Themes in Homer's Odyssey.* Dunedin.

Trahman, C. R. 1952. "Odysseus' Lies." *Phoenix* 6:31-43.

Treu, M. 1968. *Von Homer zur Lyrik.* Zetemata 12. 2nd ed. Munich.

Valk, M. H. van der. 1949. *Textual Criticism of the Odyssey* Leiden.

——, ed. 1971-. *Eustathii Archiepiscopi Thessalonicensis Commentarii ad Homeri Iliadem pertinentes ad fidem codicis Laurentiani editi.* Leiden. Cited as Eustathius.

Vernant, J.-P. 1965. *Mythe et pensée chez les Grecs.* Paris.

—— 1979. "À la table des hommes." In *La cuisine du sacrifice en pays grec,* edited by M. Detienne and J.-P. Vernant, pp. 37-132. Paris.

Vidal-Naquet, P. 1981. "Valeurs religieuses et mythiques de la terre et du sacrifice dans l'*Odyssée.*" In *Le chasseur noir: Formes de pensée et formes de société dans le monde grec,* pp. 39-68. Paris.

Voigt, C. 1933. *Überlegung und Entscheidung bei Homer: Studien zur Selbstauffassung des Menschen bei Homer.* Berlin.

Von der Mühll, P. 1976. "Zur Frage, wie sich die Kyprien zur Odyssee verhalten." In *Ausgewählte kleine Schriften,* pp. 148-54. Basel.

Watkins, C. 1977. "À propos de ΜΗΝΙΣ." *Bulletin de la Société de Linguistique de Paris* 72:187-209.

Wender, D. 1978. *The Last Scenes of the Odyssey.* Mnemosyne Suppl. 52. Leiden.

Wilamowitz-Moellendorff, U. von. 1884. *Homerische Untersuchungen.* Philologische Untersuchungen 7. Berlin.

——. 1927. *Die Heimkehr des Odysseus.* Berlin.

——. 1931. *Der Glaube der Hellenen.* 2 vols. Berlin.

——. 1959. *Euripides Herakles.* 2nd ed. Vol. 2. Darmstadt.

Wissowa, G. et al., eds. 1894-. *Paulys Realencyclopädie der classischen Altertumswissenschaft.* Stuttgart. Abbreviated as *RE.*

Woodhouse, W. J. 1930. *The Composition of Homer's Odyssey.* Oxford.

Woolsey, R. 1941. "Repeated Narratives in the Odyssey." *Classical Philology* 36:167-81.

Wüst, E. 1937. "Odysseus." In *Paulys Realencylcopädie der classischen Altertumswissenschaft* 17, 2:1905-1996. Stuttgart.

INDEX OF SOURCES

INDEX OF NAMES AND SUBJECTS

LIBRARY OF CONGRESS CATALOGING IN PUBLICATION DATA

Clay, Jenny Strauss.
  The wrath of Athena.

  "Published for the Center for Hellenic Studies."
  Includes bibliographical references and index.
  1. Homer. Odyssea. I. Center for Hellenic Studies
(Washington, D.C.) II. Title.
PA4167.C54 1983   883'.01   83-2996
ISBN 0-691-06574-8

JENNY STRAUSS CLAY is Assistant Professor of Classics at the University of
Virginia. She is co-author of *Locke's Questions Concerning the Law of Nature* (forthcoming). Articles of hers have appeared in the *American Journal
of Philology*, *Philologus*, *Classical Journal*, and *Classical Quarterly*.

9198010